AF380837

Korean Newtro: *Where Youth Meets Tradition*

Korean Newtro: *Where Youth Meets Tradition*

Colin Marshall

Photographs by
Yoon Kwangjun

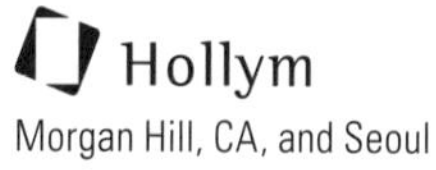

Morgan Hill, CA, and Seoul

Planned by Korea Heritage Service
Written by Colin Marshall
Photographs by Yoon Kwangjun

•

Published by Rhimm Sangbek
Directed by Lim Songhee
Edited by Hahm Minji
Copyedited by Richard Harris
Designed by nabi

•

First published in 2025
by Hollym International Corp., Morgan Hill, CA, USA
Phone 760 814 9880
Website www.hollym.com   Email contact@hollym.com

ꓚ Hollym

Published simultaneously in Korea
by Hollym Corp., Publishers, Seoul, Korea
Phone +82 2 734 5087   Fax +82 2 730 5149
Website www.hollym.net   Email hollym@hollym.co.kr

•

•

ISBN: 978-1-56591-533-6
Library of Congress Control Number: 2025947393

Printed in Korea

The content of this book represents the author's personal
perspective and may differ from the official stance of the
Korea Heritage Service.

Introduction
From *chonseureopda* to *meotjida*
006

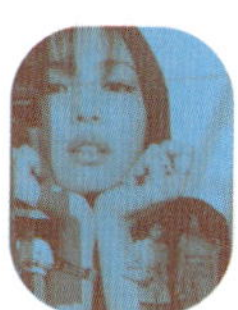

01
**The Emergence
of Newtro**
012

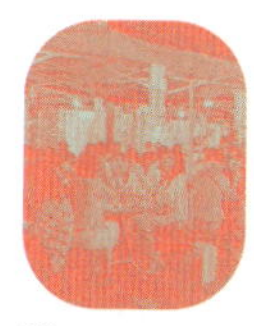

02
**Newtro
Neighborhoods**
020

03
**Visual
Art**
044

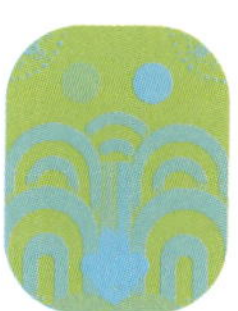

04
Design
060

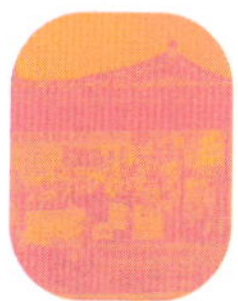

05
**Fashion and
Beauty**
076

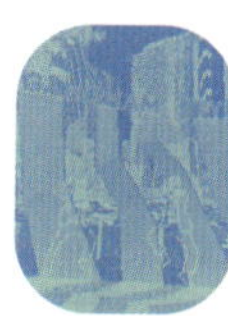

06
**Television, Film,
and Music**
092

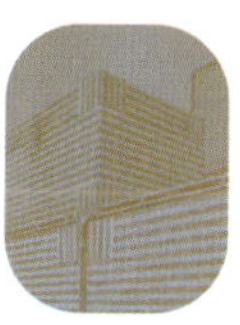

07
**Architecture and
Interior Design**
108

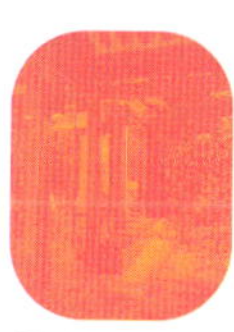

08
**Food and
Drink**
126

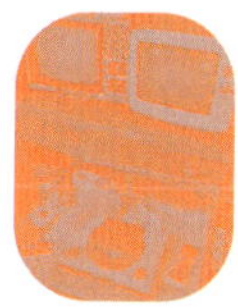

09
**The
Digital Age**
140

Epilogue
Can everything old in Korea stay new again?
154

From *chonseureopda* to *meotjida*

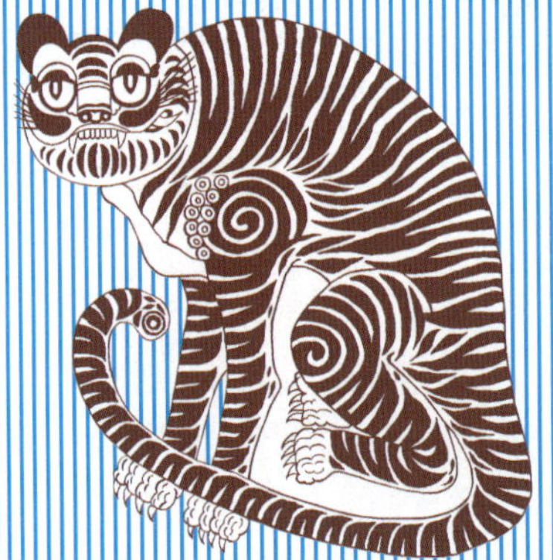

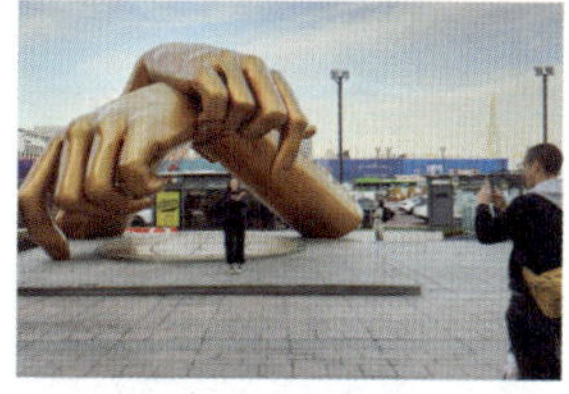

LARGER-THAN-LIFE GANGNAM STYLE
Psy's signature dance move has been immortalized as a selfie backdrop

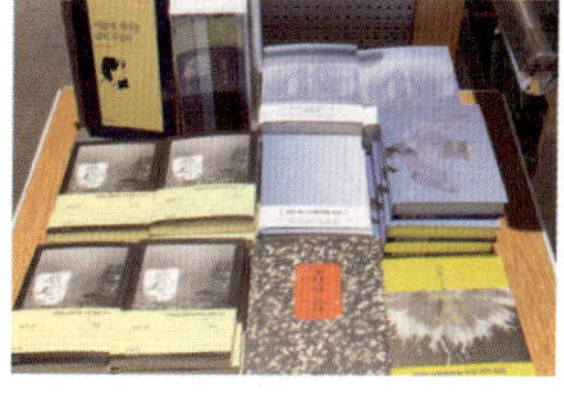

EVERYONE LOVES A LITERARY PRIZE WINNER
A niche novel when it was first published, Han Kang's The Vegetarian received bigger waves of attention in Korea when it won the Booker in 2016, and again when Han won the Nobel in 2024

South Korea has become cool. This is evidenced by the ever-increasing number of students from around the world who want to travel or even live here, having been first inspired, for the most part, by exposure to Korean pop culture. Music, television dramas, films, and even snack foods—all of these have offered gateways to a broader interest in many things Korean. Notably, the cultural phenomena that have most often captured the imagination of Westerners tend to be things they see as new. Although the beginning of the "Korean wave," or Hallyu, happened around the turn of the 21st century, the trends it set off remained confined mostly to Asia until the early 2010s. Then came the global phenomenon of Psy's satirical hit song and music video "Gangnam Style" (2012), the Man Booker International Prize-winning English translation of Nobel-laureate-to-be Han Kang's novel *The Vegetarian* (2016), the Billboard chart-topping boy band BTS, Bong Joon-ho's Academy Award-winning film *Parasite* (2020), and Hwang Dong-hyuk's acclaimed Netflix series *Squid Game*.

These works and others from the past decade or two have won Korea a larger and more diverse cohort of enthusiastic fans than ever before. But since at least the late 19th century, there have also been a relatively small—though passionately dedicated—number of foreigners drawn here by the charms of traditional Korean culture: the flavorful teas, the *hanok* courtyard houses, the musical storytelling of *pansori*, the *minhwa* folk painting style, the brilliant colors of formal *hanbok*, and all the other accoutrements of a Korea that historically really was a "Land of the Morning Calm," a saying that has become less apropos over time. Thanks to the unprecedentedly rapid economic development the country underwent in the second half of the 20th century, mornings in much of Korea are hardly so calm anymore, nor are all Koreans necessarily as familiar with the traditions of their forebears as once they were. In 21st-century South Korea, one at times feels a near-complete disconnect between present and past.

I certainly felt that disconnect, in any case, when I first arrived here in the summer of 2014. I'd been learning about Korea's language and culture in the United States for the better part of a decade by that point, so I'd already heard many expressions related to the notion that Koreans always, without exception, prefer the new to the old. It was around that same time, while making my first explorations through Korea, that I first heard the word *chonseureopda*. With the literal meaning of "village-like," it was applied dismissively to anything—a genre of music, a style of café, an article of clothing—that happened to be out of step with the trends of the moment, and was therefore not *meotjida*, or cool. What most astonished me was that I could witness those trends come and go before my eyes on the streets of Seoul in a matter of weeks.

Given that many of those same trends originated in other countries, especially Western countries, *chonseureopda* also seemed to

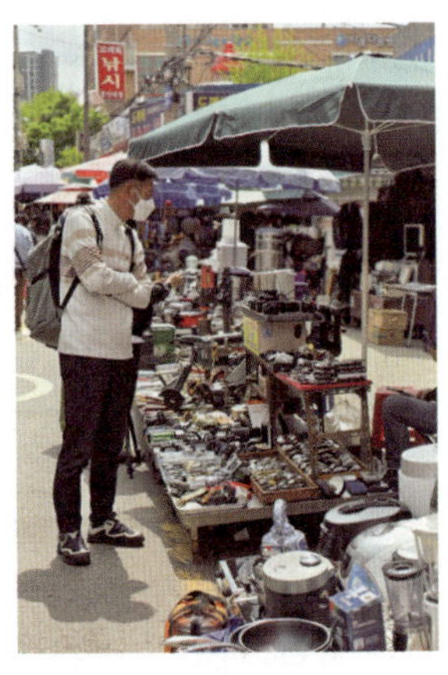

THE THRILL OF THE HUNT
Flea markets attract older bargain-hunters and younger cool-hunters alike

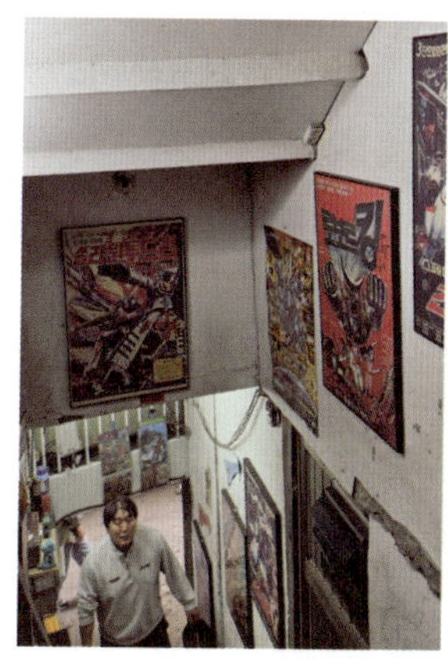

be a label for anything that looked or felt too identifiably Korean. Yet it was things identifiably Korean, especially those of decades past, that most fascinated me. Even in my early years here, I browsed the merchandise at the Dongmyo Flea Market, drank **ssanghwa-cha** (complete with egg yolk) at the **dabang** cafés of Eulji-ro, and dined with friends in the **pojangmacha** tents on the streets around Jongno, always in search of the distinctive Korean feel (or atmosphere)— **bunwigi**, to use the Korean term—not so often reflected in pop culture at the time. My taste for that sort of thing may have developed back when I was living in Los Angeles' Koreatown, whose businesses have preserved many qualities of Korea as it was 20, 30, or even 40 years ago.

Ten years ago, my inclination toward **chonseureoun** settings might have been taken as just another Westerner's eccentricity. But over time, I noticed that the aesthetics of Seoul's "hot places" were becoming steadily more appealing to me. It wasn't so much a matter of my having been Koreanized through living here as a matter of Korea's having discovered a new value in its recent past, especially the three or four decades that followed the Korean War (1950–53). This has been, in large part, the work of generations with little or no direct experience of those decades, and thus no reason to associate their styles with memories of poorer, more difficult times. All of a sudden, it seemed that young Koreans were creating spaces that drew inspiration from the forms, color schemes, and even fonts of times past, which, unsophisticated though they may look to some, nevertheless possess an elegance—and even, in some sense, an exoticism—all their own.

Since the end of the 2010s, this trend has been labeled *newtro*, a portmanteau of "new" and "retro" that refers to the reinterpretation of old Korean things for current Korean lifestyles. Nothing seems to be eligible for newtro revival unless it's at least 20 or 30 years old, but is there an upper age limit as well? For all my own interest in Korean life and pop culture in the postwar era, I would consider it a failure of imagination not to take note of the renewed appeal of eras deeper in the past as well. Walking through certain historic neighborhoods in Seoul and elsewhere, I've noticed many people wearing *hanbok*, both in relatively traditional forms as well as new designs created for everyday wear, or what we might call the "Gyeongseong style" of the 1920s and '30s (Gyeongseong being the name imposed upon Seoul by the Japanese during their occupation of the country between 1910 and 1945).

And of course, there remains much to be rediscovered in the cultural richness of the Joseon period (1392–1910). Joseon-set movies and TV shows have drawn large viewerships for practically as long as Korea has had movies and TV shows, and in recent years that form has been hybridized with different popular subgenres, up to and including the zombie apocalypse. By the same token, *pansori*, one of the period's most distinguished classical art forms, has also found new audiences through the dance-music adaptations of the group

Leenalchi, elements of whose disco sound also owe something to Western music from the 1970s and '80s. In Korea, the search for the next new thing has come to involve looking back to not just one chapter of the past but a variety of different chapters all at once, often presenting them in surprising combinations.

The phenomenon of Korean newtro, broadly defined, isn't playing out solely in hip neighborhoods and the mass media. Individual artists are also taking traditional forms like *hanji* papermaking and *minhwa* folk painting in their own directions while maintaining the continuity of those forms' essential qualities. The same holds true in the realms of architecture and interior design, where building and furniture types once assumed no longer to suit the lives of modern Koreans have, with the efforts of architects and designers who understand tradition without being overly bound by convention, found their way into sometimes unexpected contexts. In these and other areas, members of the so-called "MZ Generation," those born between 1980 and 2000, have proven as willing to be inspired by the Korea of centuries ago as the one they remember from their school days. They've also proven that, even if *chonseureopda* isn't the new *meotjida*, the two terms aren't mutually exclusive anymore.

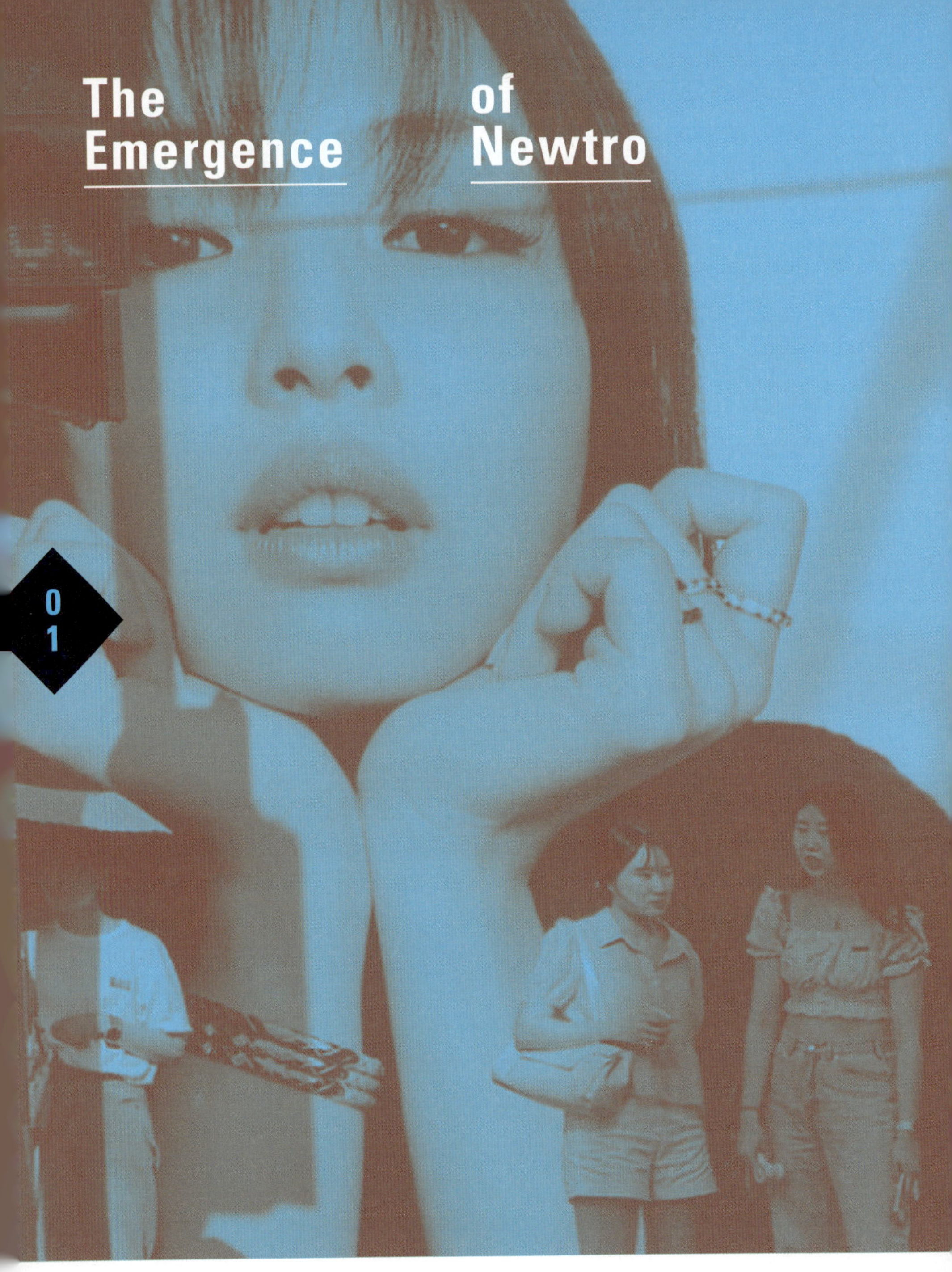

The
Emergence
of
Newtro
0
1

In combining "new" with "retro," two English words familiar not just in Korea but also many other countries the world over where English isn't natively spoken, "newtro" sounds like a contradiction in terms. This is, of course, part of its appeal, signaling a certain distance from both things new, with which Korea has been steadily inundated (and indeed infatuated) for decade upon decade, and things retro, engineered to cash in on the currently prosperous generation's nostalgia for the era of its youth. The argument that newtro is simply an updated version of retro overlooks a fundamental difference: as a trend or a marketing concept, retro primarily appeals to those old enough to remember the products, styles, and media it revives, while newtro targets those too young to have experienced them the first time around. Retro is based on the rediscovery of the past; newtro, on its discovery.

At this point, Korea's newtro phenomenon has proven just long-lived enough to evade the suspicion of being one of the countless youth culture fads that briefly sweeps this country before vanishing without a trace. It dates at least to the late 2010s, and for some was first legitimized by its inclusion in *Trend Korea*, a yearly publication spearheaded by Seoul National University consumer science professor Kim Nando. Since its launch in 2008, *Trend Korea* has documented—and, in some cases, perpetuated—a variety of the changes that have arisen in Koreans' ways of living, working,

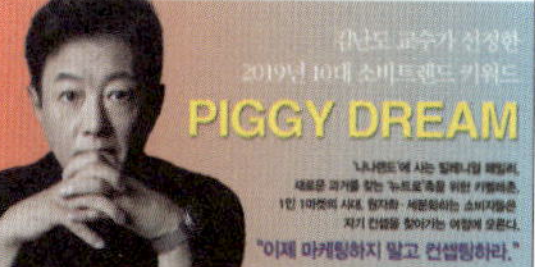

Each yearly volume attempts to predict— or conjure up—what will sweep the nation next

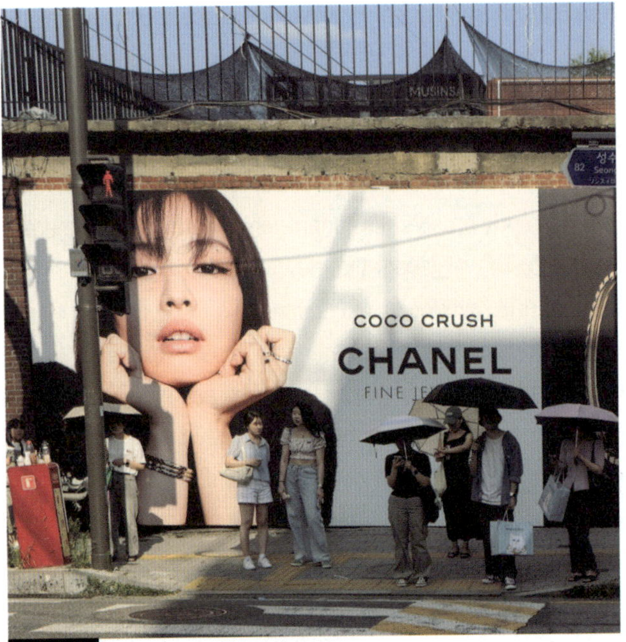

HIGH STYLE
Luxury advertising is liable to pop up anywhere in Seoul

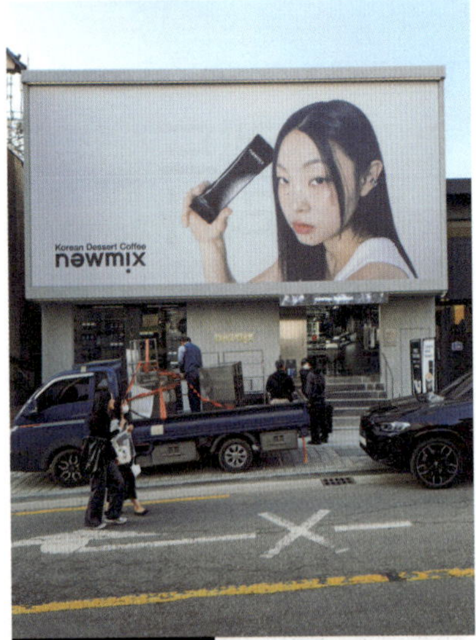

A MIX OF THE FINEST
In Korea, even instant coffee can be sold as a fashion item

and consuming. Although not all of the labels it applies to these phenomena end up sticking, those that do become mainstays of public discourse. Take, for example, *MZ sedae*, or "MZ Generation," which refers to the demographic born between 1980 and 2000, conflating the cohorts elsewhere separately defined as the Millennials and Generation Z.

In the United States, the sensibilities of the Millennials and Gen Zers, who now range from their mid-20s to their mid-40s, wouldn't seem to have much in common. But the argument for considering them together hinges on a commonality that also marks a major difference between them and the generations who came before: their having come of age with digital technology in general, and the internet in particular. The MZ Generation—also known as Gen MZ or simply MZers—was so defined in *Trend Korea 2019* (and I doubt a week has gone by since then without me hearing the term). Constituting a kind of human bridge between the cultures produced by analog and digital technology, they plausibly possess a distinctive capacity to appreciate both. It was thus suitable enough for the MZ Generation to appear in the same issue that contained a chapter on newtro, which reinterprets analog culture for a digital age.

Trend Korea 2019 also includes a table meant to clarify the differences between retro and newtro. Retro's meaning is rooted in the reproduction of the past; newtro's is rooted in unfamiliar things of the past. Retro's appeal is that of nostalgia and intimacy; newtro's, the novelty of new content with an analog feeling. Retro targets consumers in their 40s and 50s; newtro targets consumers in their teens and 20s—or, as they're known in Korea, the "1020" generation, who would have been born in the 2000s and 2010s, and who would thus be even younger than the MZ Generation. Not having been around to participate in the trends of the 1980s and '90s, they can experience everything from chunky athletic shoes and sportswear emblazoned with big, brightly colored logos to miniaturized 8- and 16-bit game consoles and instant cameras as not outdated but exotic.

For the novelty-seeking young members of the 1020 generation, newtro may be just another avenue of enjoyment, albeit one that holds a special fascination. But for many members of the MZ Generation, according to *Trend Korea*'s analysis, it could also provide a kind of psychological satisfaction made increasingly

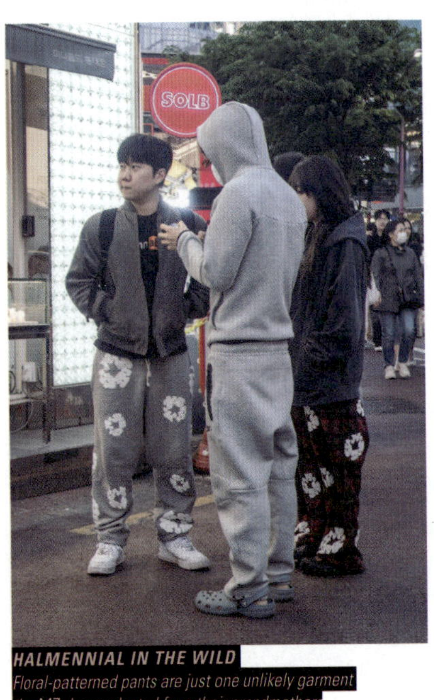

HALMENNIAL IN THE WILD
*Floral-patterned pants are just one unlikely garment
the MZs have adopted from their grandmothers*

difficult to come by amid the perpetual connection and digital distraction of the 21st century. A photo taken on film in a studio exists apart from the world of social media, just like a video game played at an old-school arcade exists apart from the world of globally networked competition. Those who take pleasure in this sort of thing may be tempted to keep looking further into the past, beyond what they dimly remember from early in their own lifetimes, all the way to the cultural artifacts they associate with their grandparents: whence emerged the curious subculture of the *halmennial*.

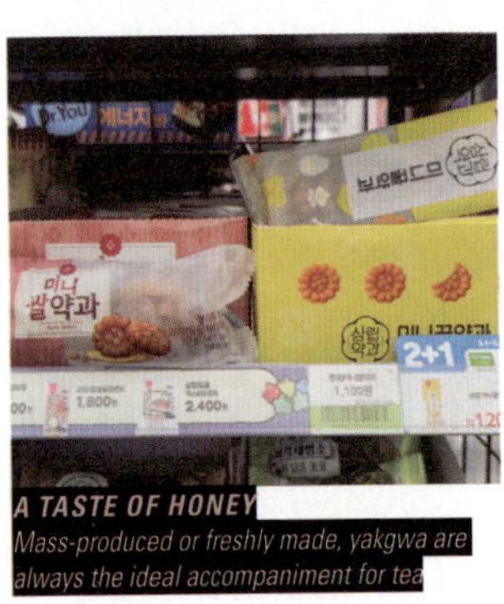

A TASTE OF HONEY
*Mass-produced or freshly made, yakgwa are
always the ideal accompaniment for tea*

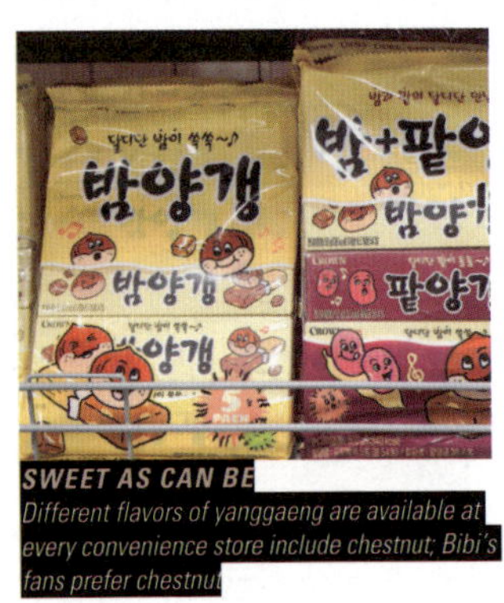

SWEET AS CAN BE
*Different flavors of yanggaeng are available at
every convenience store include chestnut; Bibi's
fans prefer chestnut*

A portmanteau of the Korean word *halmae*—short for *halmeoni*, grandmother—and "millennial," *halmennial* refers to certain backward-looking, generation-skipping tastes exhibited by members of the older half of the MZ Generation. The trend pieces that cover these tastes tend to focus on two areas in particular: clothing and desserts. The former manifests in the form of Millennials—belonging, numerically speaking, to what we might call the "2030" cohort—who seem to have raided their grandparents' closets for the often generously cut shirts, pants, sweaters, and vests with bold (some might say garish) patterns still worn by, for example, many older riders of the Seoul subway. Although *halmennial* may well combine these garments with other, more straightforwardly current fashions, they don't seem to wear them ironically, as I remember my high school and college peers doing in the United States of the early 2000s.

This enjoyment of things grandparental "as they are" extends to desserts as well. There have, of course, been new-wave sweets (and coffee drinks) incorporating the contrasting sweet and nutty powders known as *heukimja*, made of black sesame seeds, and *injeolmi*, made of soybeans. But for the most part, those traditional ingredients are being enjoyed by younger Koreans—and not just *halmennial*—as they've always been: on dishes like *tteok*, for example, glutinous rice flour pounded into a chewy texture and cut into different shapes. The same is true of such long-standing tea accompaniments as *yakgwa*, a deep-

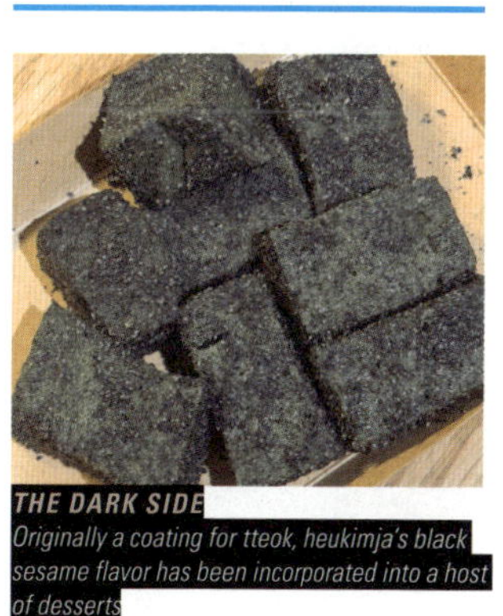

THE DARK SIDE
Originally a coating for tteok, heukimja's black sesame flavor has been incorporated into a host of desserts

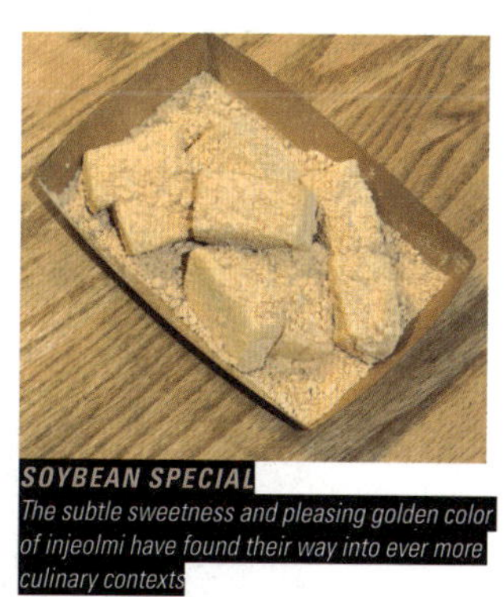

SOYBEAN SPECIAL
The subtle sweetness and pleasing golden color of injeolmi have found their way into ever more culinary contexts

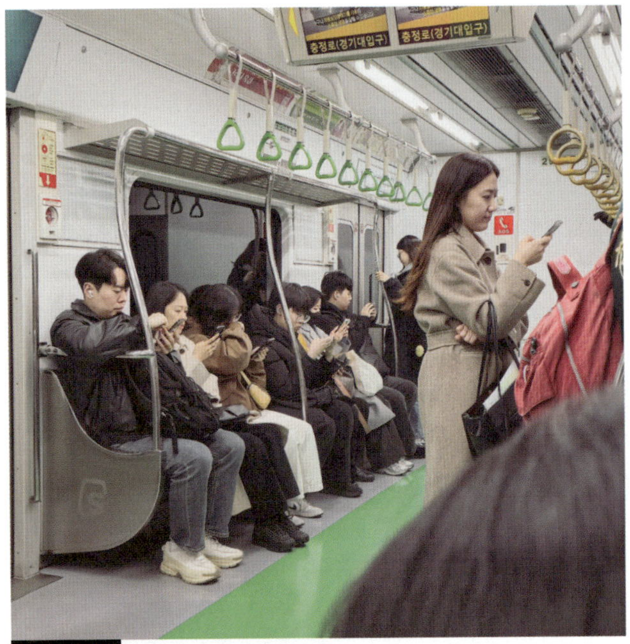

HEADS DOWN
Whether sitting or standing, Seoul metro riders pass their time one way above all: looking at their phones

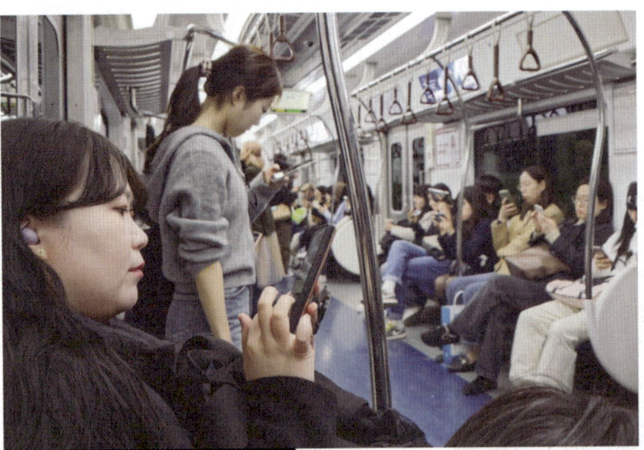

DIGITALLY ENHANCED COMMUTING
Watching videos, playing games, scrolling the news, and chatting with friends makes the ride pass a little faster

fried honey-flavored cookie, and *yanggaeng*, a traditional Korean jelly made of red beans, sugar, gelatin, and nuts or seeds. In recent years, convenience store chains have capitalized on *yakgwa*'s resurgence of popularity, bringing their own reinterpretations to market, and K-pop singer Bibi did her part for *yanggaeng* by name-checking it in a hit song.

It would only be natural for Bibi's fans to post videos of themselves having a bite of *yanggaeng*, or, after the prominent appearance of *dalgona* in the internationally popular Netflix series *Squid Game*, to do the same with that simple sugar candy and its various embedded shapes. Powerful trends may have been a part of Korean society well before the internet, but the emergence of social media, or, as it's referred to here, SNS (social networking service), greatly intensified them. It wouldn't be an exaggeration to say that the rise of *halmennial* style— sartorial, culinary, or otherwise—occurred in part due to how sharply it stands out from the other trends paraded on visually oriented social networking platforms. The same could be said of newtro as a whole, whose bold colors and charming forms inhabit a world apart from the muted, streamlined, internet-propagated global aesthetic of the early 21st century.

Halmennial and other newtro enthusiasts seek at once to escape the 21st century and to inhabit it. Wherever in the world we may be, we have no choice but to live in the present, and we can hardly ignore its particular stresses. Lacking direct access to the past, we reconstruct it through artifacts and memories, our own or others', and this encourages romanticization. It happens with not just other times but also other places: on Korean social media, I once saw a joke about how Koreans visit certain Western cities and marvel at the sight of people reading newspapers and books on the subway. Why, unlike the vast majority of Seoulites, do these foreigners not stare at their phones during the whole ride? One possible answer: they still value the kind of "analog life" that's been lost in Korea. The correct answer: their phones don't get an internet signal underground.

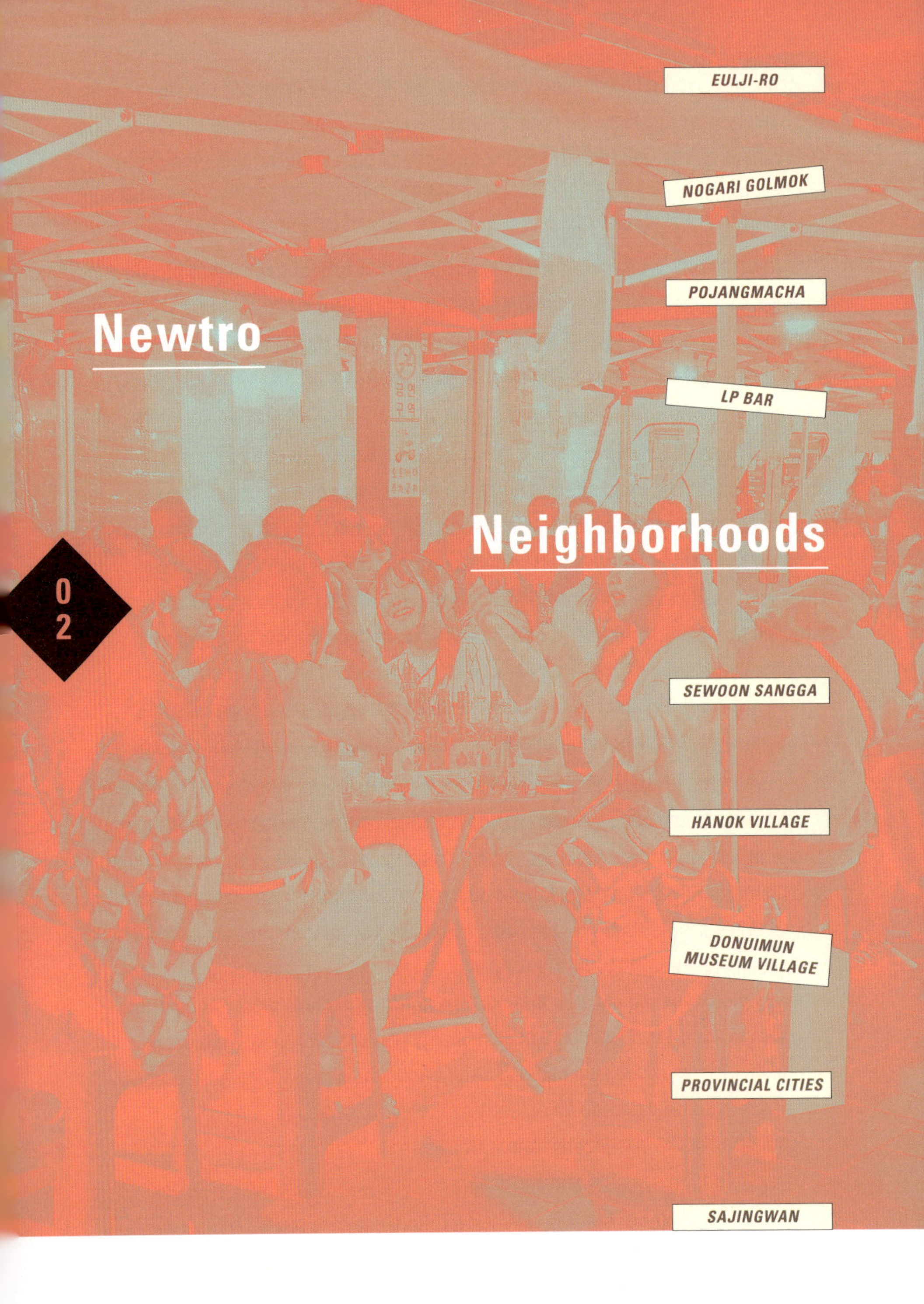

Newtro

0
2

Neighborhoods

That Korea has become world-renowned as a digitally advanced society makes the "analog life" left behind all the more an object of fantasy, especially to those young enough to have missed out on that life when it was the only option. Hence the appeal, to a certain segment of the 1020 generation, of vinyl records, photographs on film, and paper books. Ironically, these objects contribute to an aesthetic that translates quite well to social media. For some, part of the appeal of buying a piece of physical media lies in the potential to post yourself enjoying it. And those disinclined or unable to collect records, books, and other physical objects themselves can always choose to frequent one of the many cafés decorated with such things that—never mind the coffee itself—constitute ready-made retro backgrounds for social media shots. These spaces have become increasingly common in Seoul, and nowadays in practically every other region of the country as well.

In some areas, enough such cafés and other businesses that share their sensibility have opened to define entire "newtro neighborhoods," as we might now label them. No part of the capital makes quite as strong a claim to embody the spirit of newtro as Eulji-ro, the blocks surrounding the eponymous downtown street that, since the mid-2010s, have evolved into a delicate balance: on one end of the spectrum, there are small-scale hardware dealers and industrial workshops, as well as humble, long-beloved establishments where you can eat and drink; on the other, everything from third-wave coffee shops, design-forward cocktail bars, and inventive restaurants to art galleries and project spaces. What there isn't, at least for now, is much new building stock. The distinctive ambience of "Hipjiro," as Eulji-ro has lately been dubbed in the media, owes a good deal to the small scale (and often rough condition) of its built environment, which dates back to the 1960s.

In the decades after the Korean War, Eulji-ro took shape in the fast-reconstructing Seoul as a source of such practical items as lighting fixtures and sewing machines. More than half a century later, that aspect of the neighborhood remains in busy existence to an extent that surprises foreign tourists. (I've heard visiting fellow Americans liken it to a big-box hardware store broken into its component departments and spread across an urban landscape: one block for power tools, another block for plumbing fixtures, and so on.) Of course, the

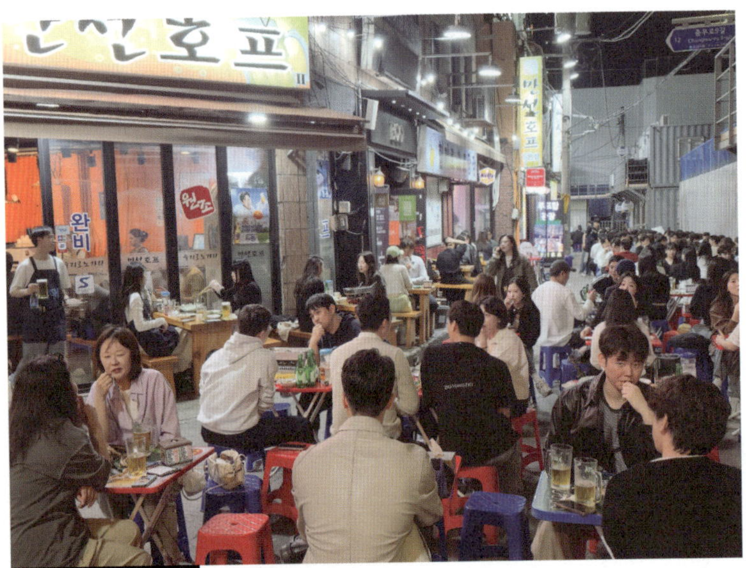

ONE NIGHT IN EULJI-RO
Pull up a plastic stool right there on the street and have a beer
— just don't forget the anju

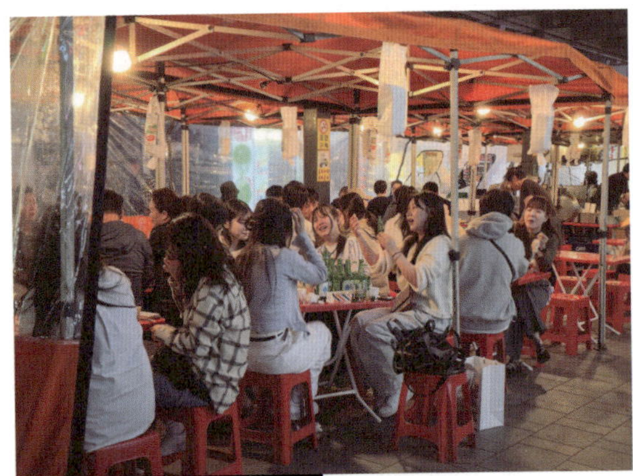

MEET ME AT THE POJANGMACHA
Some of these tent restaurants have just two or three tables;
others seat dozens, late into the night

foreigners who visit Eulji-ro aren't doing so to prepare for a home renovation project; they're looking to experience both Korea's past and its present, not least through food and drink. There could be few better places for that journey to lead in the evening than the pubs of Nogari Golmok, or "dried pollack alley," whose outdoor tables spill convivially out into the street.

Nogari Golmok's designation for preservation as a Seoul Future Heritage site in 2015 didn't prevent the closure, three years later, of its most widely known establishment, Eulji OB Bear, which since 1980 had been serving beer (OB standing for the beer brand Oriental Brewing) with a host of accompanying *anju*—side dishes without which no Korean drinking session feels complete—like dried fish, grilled sausages, and fried chicken. Much to the delight of its many regulars, young and old alike, Eulji OB Bear re-opened in 2024, not in Nogari Golmok but hardly far from it, on the other side of Eulji-ro itself. It is thus available once again as a nostalgic option for one *cha*, or "round," of a night out in Seoul.

Each of these rounds must take place at a different location, ensuring a maximum of variety. That, at any rate, is how I explain it to foreigners in Korea for the first time, as I seldom neglect to take them out to Eulji-ro at the first possible opportunity. No dining experience in the neighborhood seems to make as much of an impression on them as the one available at a *pojangmacha*, the tent restaurants that pop up in lines along certain streets every evening. "Restaurant" may be too grand a category for these operations, with their makeshift-looking dining areas assembled out of plastic chairs and tables and their kitchen staff consisting entirely of one *ajumma* or *halmeoni*, a woman of motherly or grandmotherly age, respectively. But she can always prepare a formidable range of dishes to go with your beer, *soju*, or *makgeolli* (or fermented rice wine, though it's also been compared to beer on occasion), from grilled mackerel and *sundae* (or blood sausage) to pork belly and chicken feet.

Enthusiasts of classic Korean film may well see *pojangmacha* onscreen many times before they get the chance to sit down at one in reality. Despite a great reduction of their numbers since the 1970s and '80s, when they commonly appeared in movies and television, more than a few survivors continue to hang on in Eulji-ro and certain other neighborhoods in cities across Korea. Thanks in part to the renewed interest in the recent past that has given rise to newtro and other related trends, *pojangmacha* are no longer seen as traces of a disorderly, impoverished past to be kept out of sight, if not swept away entirely. In fact, they've become attractions in their own right (albeit not especially cheap attractions, compared to what one might assume when looking at them), not least to the foreigners who exclaim, when I take them to one, "Now this is the real Korea!"

That line of thinking is understandable: in 21st-century Korea, where the old is in so many contexts totally overwhelmed by the new, anything that looks and feels plausibly unchanged for a few generations will stand out as "authentic." (In my experience, Western travelers in Asia tend to hold authenticity as paramount, whether or not they're prepared to identify it.) But to my mind, "the real Korea" could be just as plausibly represented by the new as the old, and perhaps most of all—notably in a country whose accelerated 20th-century modernization produced any number of surprising cultural and temporal juxtapositions—by a mixture of the two. That's what tends to be offered by the businesses most visibly aligned with Eulji-ro's newtro image, including boutiques, collectible shops, cafés, and bakeries that cultivate an atmosphere of the past, as well as "LP bars," where customers come to listen to the music as much as to drink.

The music at an LP bar isn't live. The owners put on selections from their often enormous collections of long-playing (hence "LP") vinyl records on sound systems assembled with carefully chosen vintage components like massive JBL speakers or McIntosh vacuum tube amplifiers. Such things can now be acquired in many places, the most fascinating being Sewoon Sangga, whose imposing megastructure cuts across Eulji-ro—and indeed, runs all the way from Toegye-ro at its south end to Jong-ro, more than a kilometer away, at its north end. Built in the mid-1960s at the behest of Seoul mayor Kim Hyeon-ok, whose development-mindedness earned him the nickname "the Bulldozer," and based on a design originally conceived by architect Kim Swoo-geun, whose work defined Korean modern architecture in the postwar decades, Sewoon Sangga opened as the country's first mixed-use complex, with electronics shops below and what were then considered luxurious offices and apartments above.

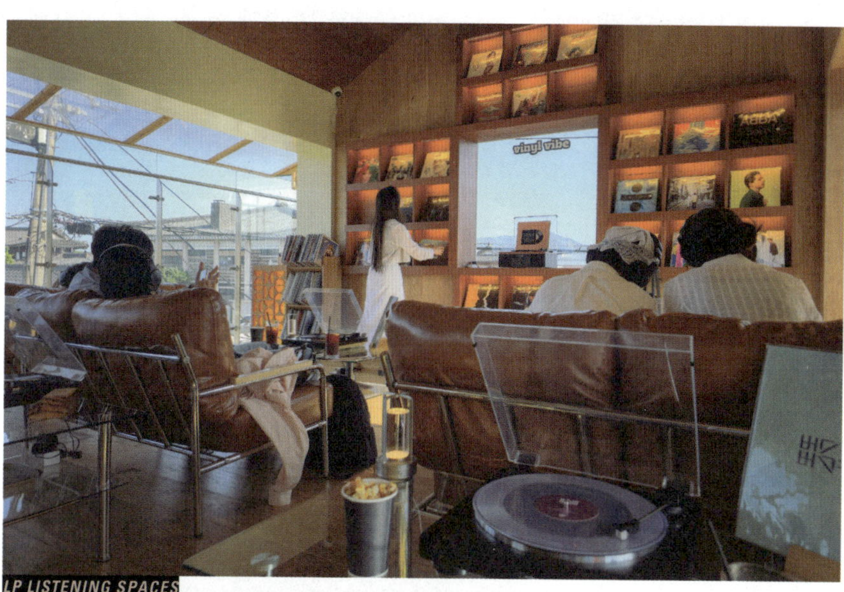

LP LISTENING SPACES
Vinyl record-stocked bars, cafés, and music libraries have become destinations for music-lovers and couples on dates alike

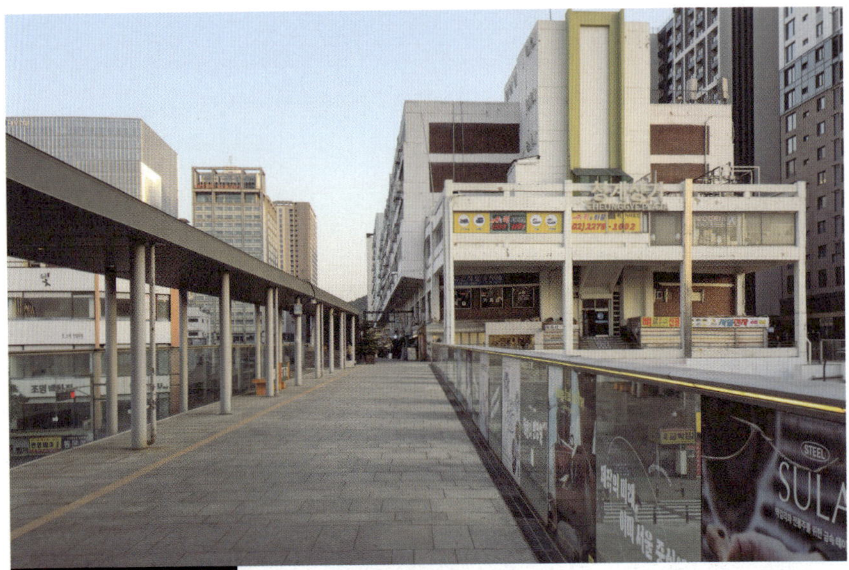

SEWOON SANGGA SURVIVES
Once slated for demolition, Kim Swoo-geun's 1960s mixed-use complex received
a series of revitalizing upgrades instead

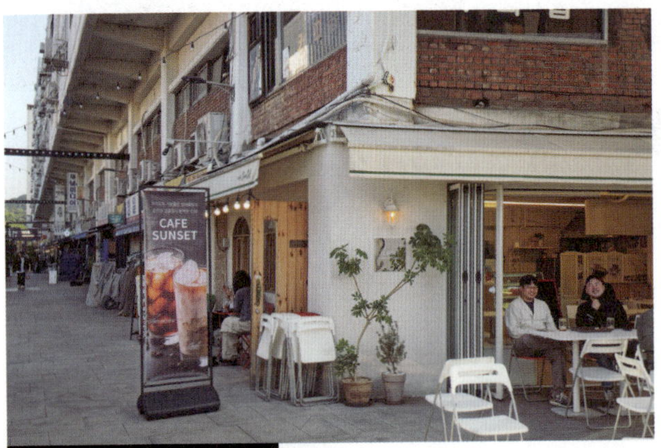

A PROMENADE ABOVE EULJI-RO
Trendy cafés, bars, and restaurants have filled up
Sewoon Sangga's public outer deck

Once a prestigious and unignorable symbol of modernity, Sewoon Sangga (the first word meaning "the energy of the world" and the second meaning "shopping center") later came to symbolize, in an equally unignorable fashion, the heavy-handed haphazardness of Korea's development under dictatorship. It fell into disrepute with age, becoming regarded by certain generations as primarily a source of pirated or otherwise illicit media. As its physical condition also deteriorated, the threat of demolition loomed ever larger. In any event, the wrecking ball was stayed, albeit after it had already brought down the complex's northernmost structure, by the 2008 financial crisis, which created the opportunity for the Seoul Metropolitan Government's Dashi Sewoon, or "Sewoon Again" project, to take flight. Since launching in 2015, that operation has aimed to re-integrate the ungracefully aging Sewoon Sangga into 21st-century Seoul, even outfitting it with new infrastructure.

An early phase of Dashi Sewoon restored the elevated bridges that once connected the upper decks of Sewoon Sangga's individual buildings. They'd been removed as part of an earlier urban revitalization project, the much-publicized 2005 conversion of Cheonggyecheon from an elevated freeway into a sunken linear park through which runs the eponymous stream. The bridges are thus in one sense new, and in another old, as is true of much within Sewoon Sangga today. The interiors of the buildings on its north end remain warrens of small-scale electronics dealers and workshops—some of them in continuous operation for most of the complex's history—though they now incorporate "maker spaces" geared toward connecting young DIY technology enthusiasts with the expertise concentrated there. But on the decks that wrap around the exteriors, one now encounters bars, galleries, and restaurants, as well as shops offering books, music, and film memorabilia. Above all else, however, one encounters cafés.

Longtime habitués of Sewoon Sangga have no doubt been regularly drinking coffee since the complex opened. Their brew of choice is usually *mikseu keopi* (literally "mix coffee"), instant coffee with generous quantities of sweetener and creamer included in the packet, which they can still purchase (or have delivered) from one of the hole-in-the wall shops that remain in some of the buildings. Yet *mikseu keopi* holds considerably less appeal for most Koreans under the age of 60, the demographic attracted by the coffee shops that have opened in Sewoon

Sangga in the post-Dashi Sewoon era. Among the earliest and most popular of those relatively new arrivals is a small place called Horangi, or "Tiger," notable for the line out its door that forms on weekends as well as during the weekday post-lunch coffee rush that besets even the less-hip cafés of the city—and perhaps even more notable for how old it looks.

With its detailed dark-wood paneling and sign whose Hangeul is surrounded by an elegantly hand-painted-looking border, Horangi's storefront resembles less a now-standard newtro tribute to the '80s, the '90s or even the '60s when Sewoon Sangga arose, and more a callback to the 1930s. Despite its unfortunate artistic ties to a decade in which Korea was a Japanese colony, that same decade, the 1930s, has also come to offer no small degree of inspiration to newtro lovers, and indeed to the entrepreneurs who would cater to them. In some cases, that legacy extends to the built environment. Take, for example, Ikseon-dong Hanok Village, about a ten-minute walk from Sewoon Sangga. The oldest *hanok* (or traditional courtyard house) village in Seoul, its residences were adapted for small lots and urban living conditions, though few remain residences today, most having been converted over the past decade into shops, restaurants, and, of course, cafés.

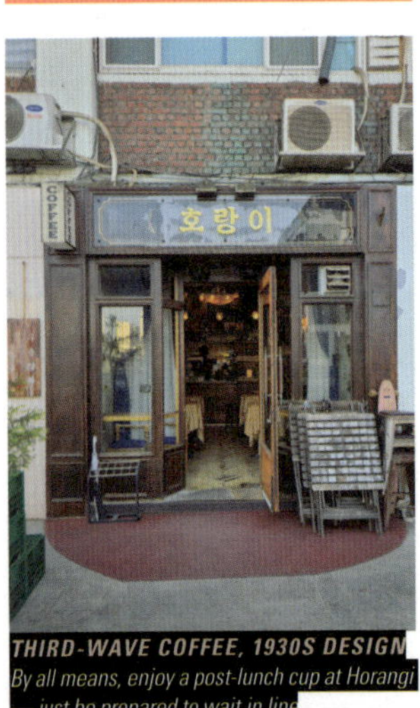

THIRD-WAVE COFFEE, 1930S DESIGN
By all means, enjoy a post-lunch cup at Horangi —just be prepared to wait in line

Much like Sewoon Sangga, Ikseon-dong Hanok Village was for some time not maintained as well as it could have been. Around the turn of the millennium, it seemed to be going the way of many an old Seoul neighborhood, deliberately left to its desuetude until its increasingly inevitable-seeming demolition and subsequent replacement by an *apateu danji*, or high-rise apartment complex. (Ironically, Ikseon-dong Hanok Village could be considered a forerunner of those very same complexes, being an experiment in Korean mass housing using the forms and materials of an earlier era.) Although a redevelopment plan was proposed in 2004, resistance proved sufficient to get it withdrawn 10 years later. Around that same time, the city of Seoul became more publicly revitalization-minded, encouraging the adaptive re-use of existing structures, of which the *hanok* of Ikseon-dong offered prime examples. Thus began the tired neighborhood's conversion into a perennial *hat peulleiseu* (literally "hot place").

In well under a century, Ikseon-dong Hanok Village turned from an "affordable housing" development avant la lettre into a popular destination where a *deiteu koseu* (literally "date course," or the sequence of stops when out on a date with romantic intentions) might include hand-drip coffee, a French meal not entirely dissimilar to the fare at a real Paris bistro, and shopping at a boutique like Teterot Salon (whose modernized *hanbok* feature prominently in *Trend Korea 2019*'s newtro chapter). In the West, such a transformation would be cited as a textbook case of gentrification, which has only in recent years found its way into the Korean language as a loanword. Predictably, Ikseon-dong's rents have risen dramatically, becoming unaffordable not just to what tenants remained from the time when the area was wholly residential, but also to the first wave of businesses that make it attractive to outsiders. The interior renovations of its buildings have also grown more and more radical, to the point of offending *hanok* purists.

Yet a *hanok* village it remains, in that most of its structures have kept to a single story built around a central courtyard space (whether or not that space, which could be more useful as a showroom or a dining area, any longer fulfills the function of a courtyard is still up for debate) and topped with a tiled roof curved at the edges. Rather than having been built in the style of the 1930s, which would make them examples of retro architecture, so to speak, they were genuinely built in the 1930s, and the style they've embodied since then has now become a cultural advantage. The newtro spirit is evident in Ikseon-dong in that, though what's inside its *hanok* may change—and, in some cases, change dramatically—their built form as a whole has been used more or less as found, much to the delight of young, selfie-taking visitors, Korean or otherwise.

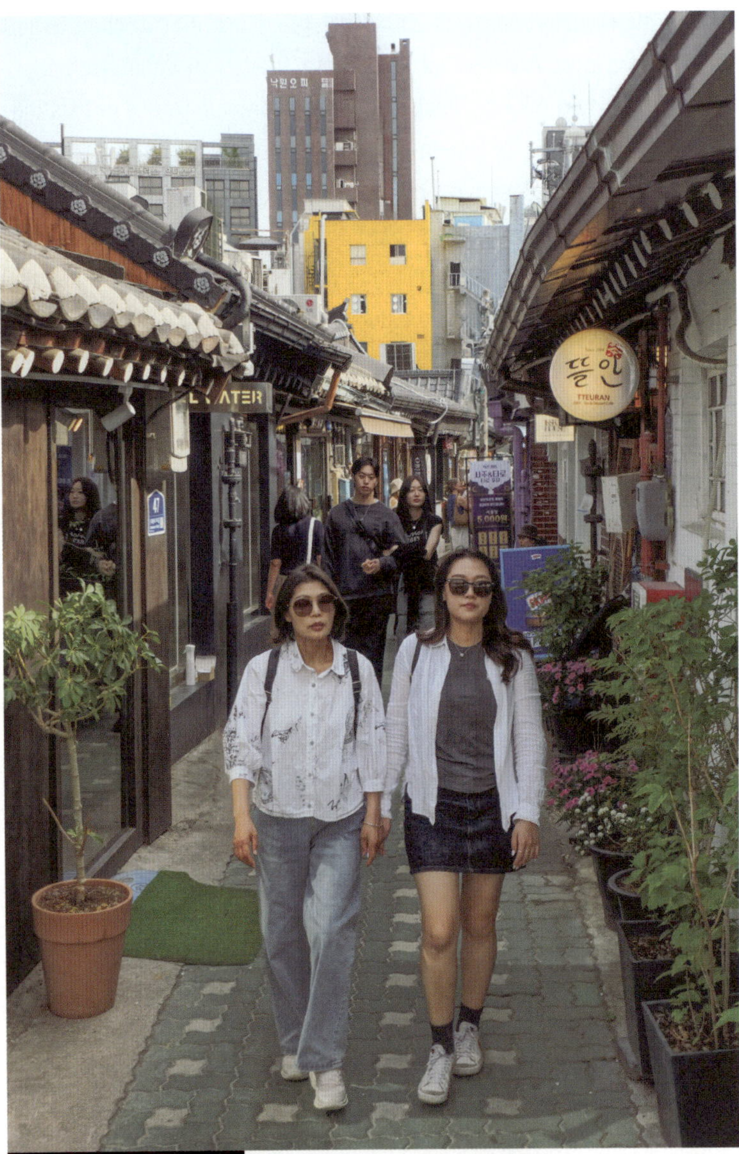

BEING SEEN IN IKSEON-DONG

Composed almost entirely of hanok, this former 1930s residential development feels like no other shop-and-restaurant quarter in Korea

If Ikseon-dong Hanok Village hadn't already existed, it would have been impossible to build in the same location today. Originally geared toward a humble stratum of Korean society, its low but densely packed urban *hanok* fit together in a scale more satisfying than that of, say, Bukchon Hanok Village to the north, which was laid out later as a district for the well-off and has long been a major tourist attraction in its own right. Ikseon-dong Hanok Village illustrates the principle endorsed by architect Jan Gehl in his influential textbook *Cities for People*: "Make sure there's never quite enough room." He goes on to explain that "in narrow streets and small spaces, we can see buildings, details and the people around us at close range. There is much to assimilate, buildings and activities abound and we experience them with great intensity. We perceive the scene as warm, personal, and welcoming."

The same could hardly be said about many of the more recently developed parts of Seoul, especially down on the broad streets and amid the high-rises of Gangnam. Hence, in part, the preservation efforts that have taken various forms over the past decade or so and which have given rise to not just hot places such as Ikseon-dong Hanok

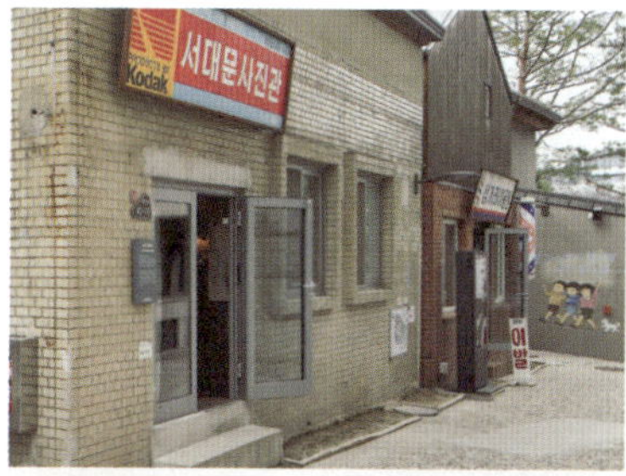

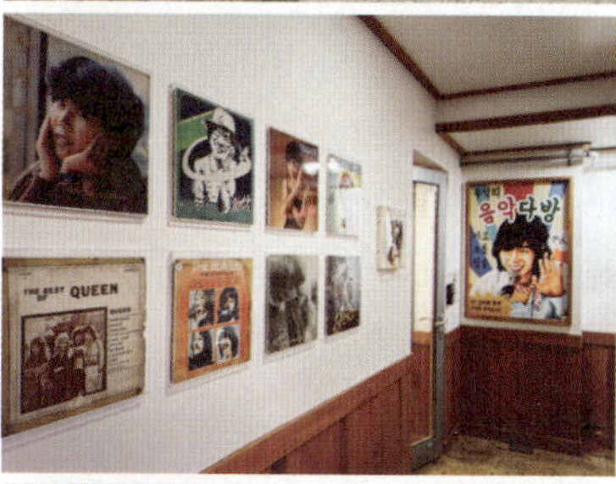

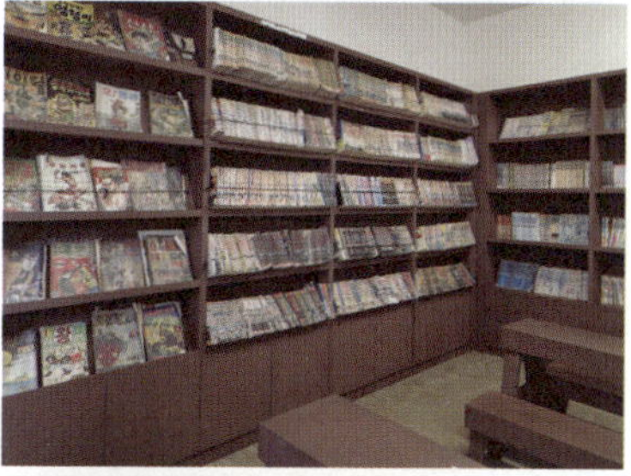

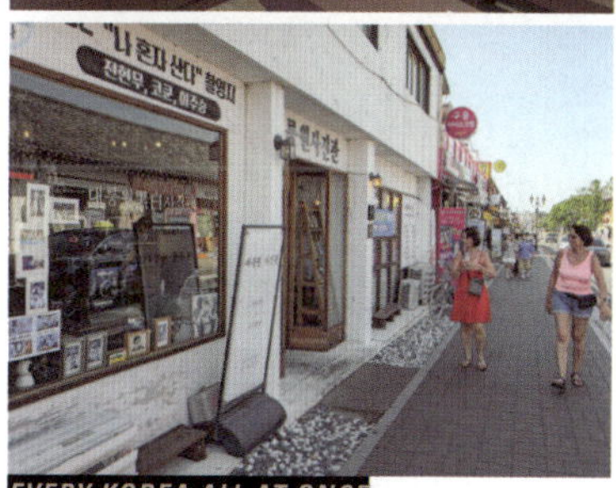

EVERY KOREA ALL AT ONCE
Decades of the past coexist in Donuimun Museum Village, inspiring nostalgia in adults and curiosity in children

Village, but also public cultural institutions like Donuimun Museum Village near Gyeonghuigung Palace, a palace on the west end of the old central portion of the city. (Donuimun itself is now usually called Seodaemun, literally the "west gate" of the wall that once enclosed Seoul.) Built around the carefully preserved remains of Saemuan, another neighborhood once slated for demolition, it contains urban *hanok* as well as examples of Korean building types from the turn of the 20th century through the 1980s, all renovated to host free exhibitions and experiences meant to bring the past back to life.

Since opening to the public in 2018, Donuimun Museum Village has incorporated more than a century of history, the earliest chapters of which have passed well out of living memory. But certain generations will find the world of their youth exhibited to them, and sometimes in a manner that turns out to be surprisingly attractive to their own children: perhaps in its replica of a mid-century cinema, complete with large-scale hand-painted posters; its 1960s *eumakdabang*, or "music café"; its *manhwabang*, or "comics room," reminiscent of the places

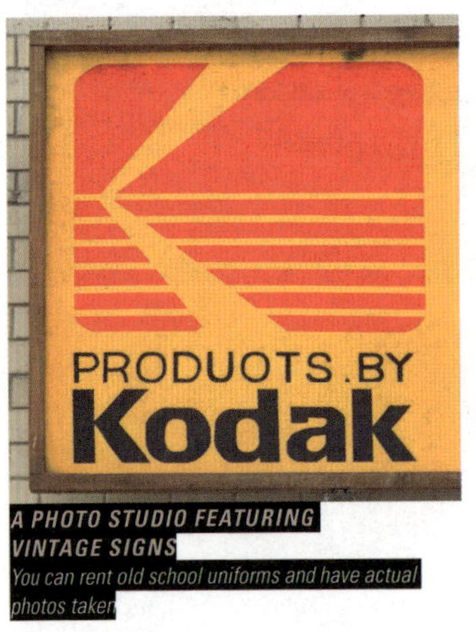

A PHOTO STUDIO FEATURING VINTAGE SIGNS
You can rent old school uniforms and have actual photos taken.

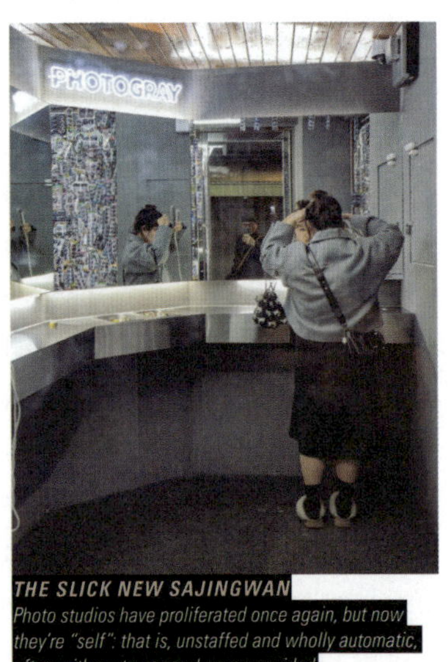

THE SLICK NEW SAJINGWAN
Photo studios have proliferated once again, but now they're "self": that is, unstaffed and wholly automatic, often with costumes and props provided

where generations of students have gone to avoid studying; or its arcade lined with machines offering unlimited free play of the video games of the 1980s. And there's a particular cross-generational appeal in its *sajingwan*, or photo studio, identified by a vintage sign with characteristically bright colors and misspelled English ("PRODUOTS BY KODAK").

Although few once-prominent categories of business could have been less expected to survive our digital age than the *sajingwan*, it has lately undergone a renaissance in several different forms. Most visible are the numerous selfie studios, often apparently unstaffed, that offer couples and groups of friends private booths in which to take their own pictures after decking themselves out with the accessories and props provided. (Sometimes those accessories and props are curated in accordance with a pop culture theme; a slant toward the retro is hardly unknown.) But other establishments offer fuller professional service, operating on the same basic model of the old-style family portraitists still hanging on here and there, but aiming to attract a much younger

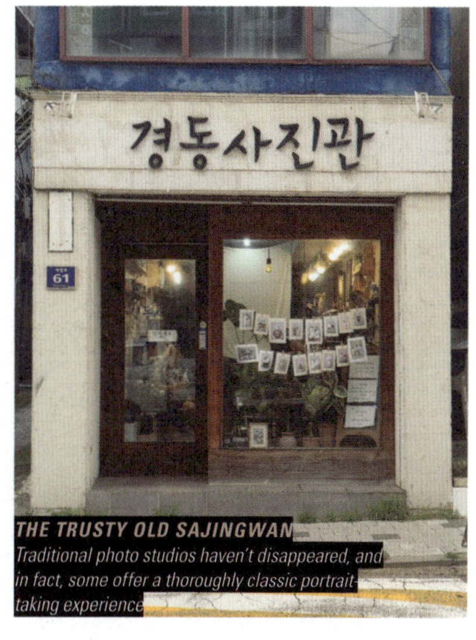

THE TRUSTY OLD SAJINGWAN
Traditional photo studios haven't disappeared, and in fact, some offer a thoroughly classic portrait-taking experience

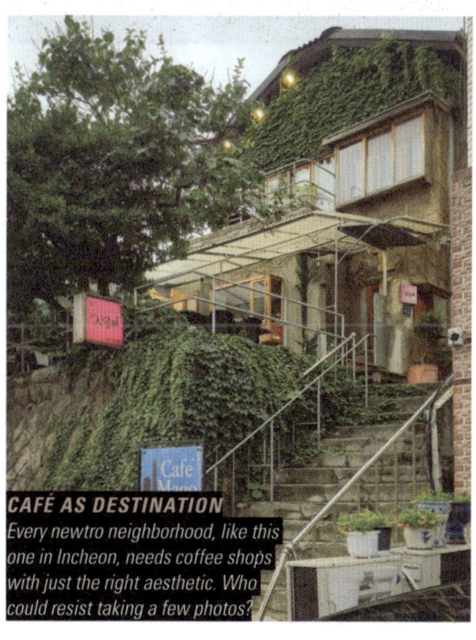

CAFÉ AS DESTINATION
Every newtro neighborhood, like this one in Incheon, needs coffee shops with just the right aesthetic. Who could resist taking a few photos?

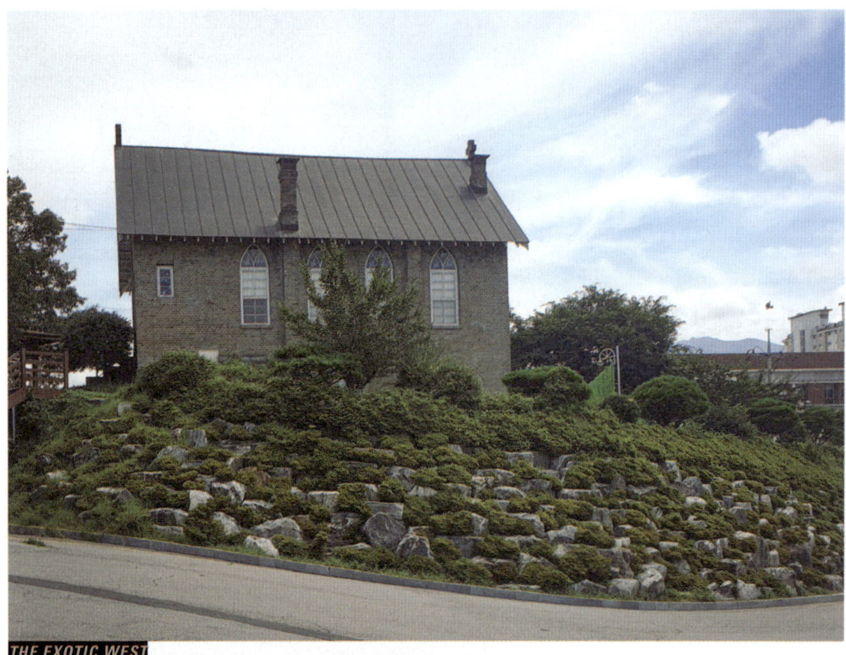

THE EXOTIC WEST
When missionaries settled in Gwangju's Yangnim-dong in the early 20th century, they built their own urban environment in the only style they knew

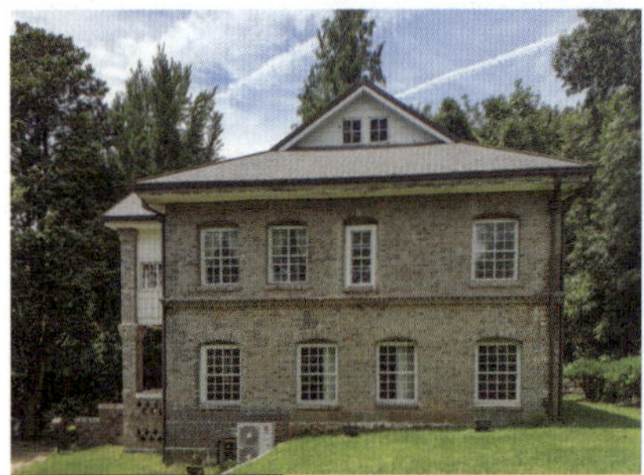

LUNCH ON THE LAWN
The former home of American missionary Dr. R. M. Wilson is the oldest Western-style building in Gwangju—and a decent picnic spot to boot

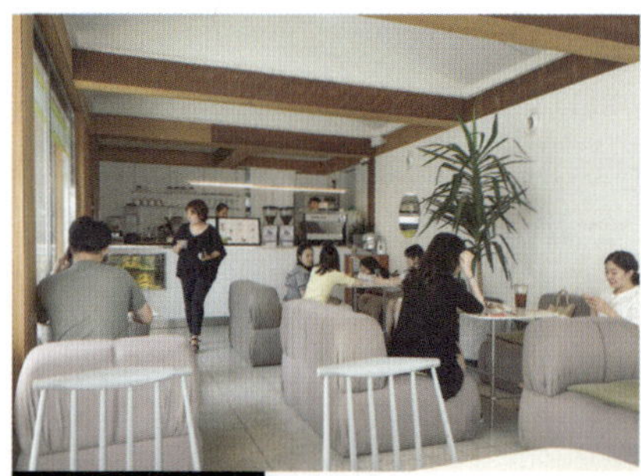

AMERICANO BREAK
Even in a "Western village," there's a wholly Korean coffee shop around the corner

clientele with settings and outfits drawn from the past. They do so not just in Seoul but increasingly in newtro-inflected areas of other Korean cities.

At this point, a tourist keen on getting out of the capital and into the far corners of Korea—something tourists still often neglect to do—could plan a wholly newtro-oriented cross-country itinerary. It could even start right in Incheon, the city west of Seoul with the international airport at which most foreigners arrive. While most people wouldn't know it today, Incheon was actually

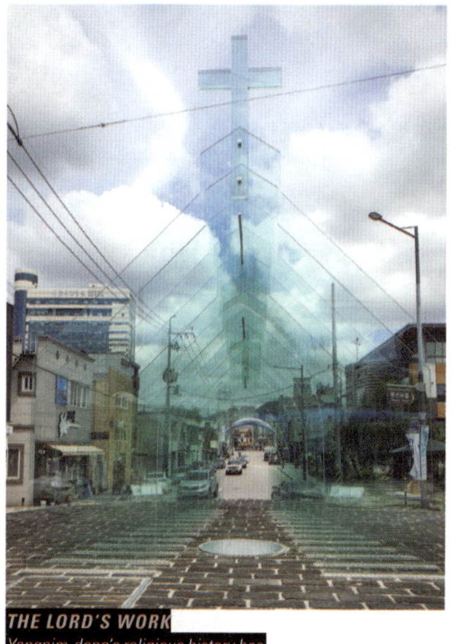

first developed as a result of its seaport, not far from which lies the neighborhood of Gaehang-ro, or "Open Port Culture Road." Once the home of Incheon City Hall, Gaehang-ro entered a prolonged period of decline after it was relocated to another part of town. Its fortunes only turned around in the late 2010s, with the launch of a small-scale urban revitalization effort called the Gaehang-ro Project that promoted the conversion of its disused hospital and salt warehouse buildings into cafés and culture spaces, among other establishments attractive to a younger demographic, as well as the creation of Gaehang-ro beer. Brewed in the neighborhood, it comes in bottles with a calligraphic design created by a local former movie signboard painter, which in Korea was a viable craft through the turn of the 21st century. His handmade advertisements would surely have hung at the Ae Kwan Theater, a cinema just east of Gaehang-ro that originally opened in 1895 (but which now looks like more of a throwback to 1985).

Although Incheon was long Korea's main port of entry, other regions of the country also had their own centers of foreign culture. In Gwangju, the largest city in the southwestern Jeolla provinces, that was Yangnim-dong, where Western missionaries settled at the beginning of the 20th century. There they had buildings constructed in imported architectural styles, which now stand as historic attractions that evoke the time when the area was known as a "Western Village." More recently, visitors also come to see Yangnim-dong's mostly *hanok*-filled Penguin Village, a stroll through whose mural-lined alleyways is tantamount to a ride in a time machine. Badly damaged by a fire in 2013, the neighborhood was reconstructed by its citizens as a kind of open-air museum of daily life as it was lived *yetnal*, a word that can mean a few centuries ago, a few decades ago, or even a few years ago. In the case of Penguin Village (a name, according to the conflicting stories available, which refers to the appearance or gait of one of the elderly residents who assisted in the repair effort), *yetnal* means the 1960s, '70s, and '80s. In the open-air museum of everyday life it has become, once-ordinary objects, from clocks and radios to kitchen tools and musical instruments, have been transformed into works of art, giving new meaning to the common Korean expression *yeppeun sseuregi* (literally "pretty trash").

Most of Korea's cities have also been shaped, in one way or another, by the darker chapters of the country's history: the Korean War, to name only the best-known example, whose fratricidal conflict that saw more than two million casualties on both sides of the border and created a mass refugee crisis. During the war, those refugees tended to head all the way across the country to Busan, on the peninsula's southeastern end, one of the few cities not overtaken by the North Korean invasion. One of the main areas in which they settled was Choryang-dong, near Busan Station, which has lately gained recognition as a newtro hot spot. As in Gwangju's Yangnim-dong, the landmark of a Christian church remains a testament to its history of Western influence. Nearby stand Busan's first modern building and Japanese-style house, both of which have been converted into cafés.

In much of the West, living high on a hill has long been synonymous with living high on the hog. But it's precisely the opposite in Korea, where the very term for a slum, *daldongne*, translates to "moon village," a reference to their relative proximity to that heavenly body. Thus, refugees looking for a place to live in Choryang-dong went upward, walking what's now known as Ibagu-gil, or "Story Road" (*ibagu* being the local dialect for the word "story" in Busan and its two surrounding Gyeongsang provinces, the equivalent of *iyagi* in standard Korean, and *gil* meaning "road"). Although still a none-too-affluent residential quarter, the area through which Ibagu-gil runs is now outfitted with displays about Choryang-dong's history and the notable figures who have lived there, including its favorite son, Na Hoon-a, a singer of trot music (a genre to be discussed in chapter 6) who commands a legendary status in Korea thanks to his remarkably long career. One thus gains an understanding of Busan's past before reaching the hilltop and taking in the panoramic view of the modern seaside city spread out below, though only after climbing its famous 168 steep stairs, or at least riding the funicular that runs beside them.

After such physical exertion, it's only natural—and in Korea, practically obligatory—to enjoy a coffee break. The most newtro place in Busan to have one lies just a few stops north

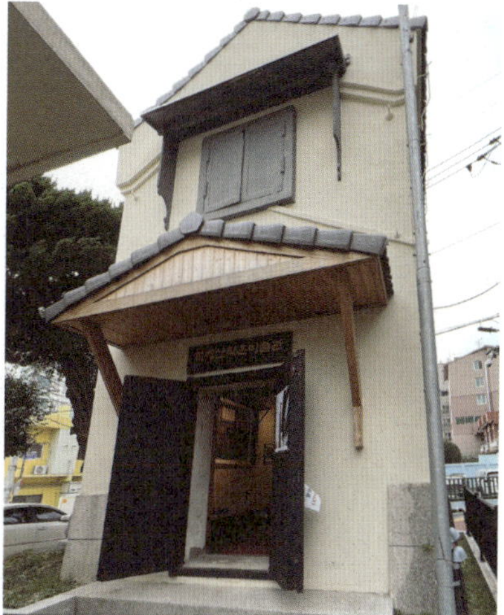

NEITHER HERE NOR THERE
Originally built in a combination of Japanese and Western styles during the colonial period, Busan's Bokbyeongsan Small Art Museum is now run as a cultural center by the district office

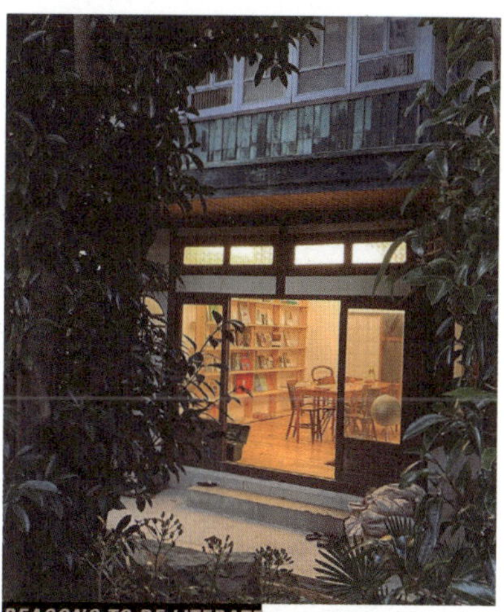

REASONS TO BE LITERATE
Don't leave Busan without visiting its tucked-away bookstores, book cafés, and other literary spaces— but make sure to learn Korean first

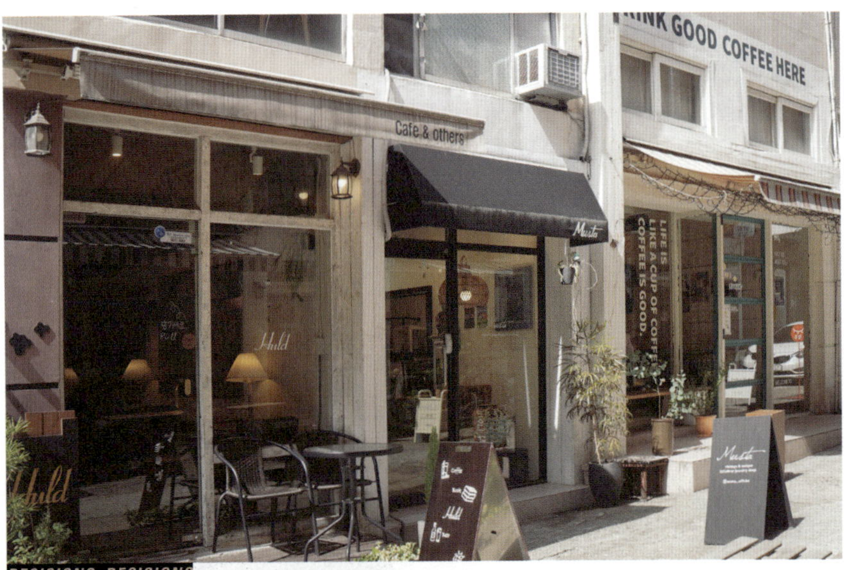

DECISIONS, DECISIONS
You won't have trouble finding a coffee shop on Busan's Jeonpo Café Street, but you may encounter some difficulty picking which one to visit

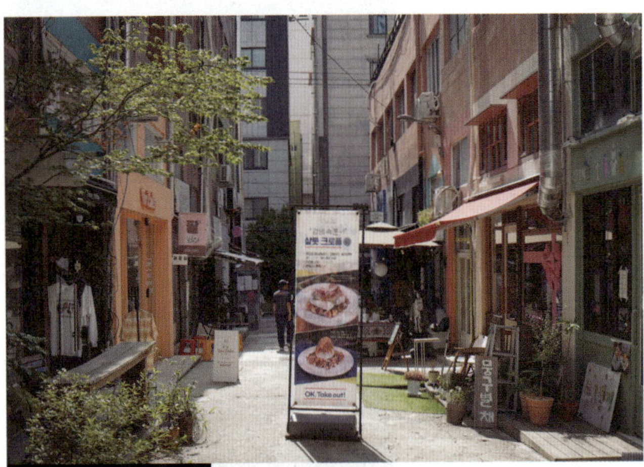

EXPECT THE UNEXPECTED
You'll occasionally encounter surpising establishments on the streets of Jeonpo-dong, like the vegan bakery just down this lane

of Busan Station, in Seomyeon, where the city's two main subway lines cross. Jeonpo Café Street was featured in the *New York Times*' list of "52 Places to Go in 2017," as a visitor will inevitably be reminded even today. "A once-gritty industrial area," wrote contributor Justin Bergman, it had "recently been transformed into a creative hub packed with boutiques like Object, selling handcrafted items by locals." Although few are any longer in prime condition, the buildings of Jeonpo Café Street have been made colorful in every sense by their new commercial occupants, who began appearing in the late 2000s. In fact, the decrepitude is an asset, not least to the photo-snapping members of the MZ Generation (and now, younger cohorts as well) who are invested in what, in the U.S., used to be called "hipster" aesthetics. Apart from cafés, the many small businesses along the street also include memorabilia shops, boutiques, salons, and restaurants serving world cuisines—Thai, Indian, French, Italian, and various hybrids besides—each an expression of its owner's personality. After crossing Seojeon-ro, the first major street to the north, Jeonpo Café Street becomes Jeonpo Tool Street, a name inspired by its past as a center of suppliers for light industry. To this day, a few hardware stores, electronics parts dealers, and workshops still operate here and there, giving passersby reason to wonder whether the ambient noises are coming from the work of a barista or a machinist.

A couple of hours north of Busan is the historic city of Gyeongju, a field trip to which often figures into Koreans' memories of their school days. Formerly the prosperous capital of the Silla kingdom, which lasted from the 1st century BCE to the 10th century CE, Gyeongju offers sights like the Daereungwon Ancient Tomb Complex, final resting place of generations of Silla royals, and Cheomseongdae, an astronomical observatory built in the mid-7th century. Ten minutes' walk away from both of them is a commercial strip that began evolving to attract a younger demographic in 2015. That new wave of its approximately 400 shops, restaurants, and, of course, cafés do business in the street's existing buildings—many of them *hanok*, now in various states of modernization—that were constructed in the '60s and '70s, a fair number putting up newtro-styled signage to match. Within two years, the area became popular enough to be dubbed Hwangnidan-gil, mashing up the names of Hwangnam-dong, the surrounding neighborhood, and Gyeongnidan-

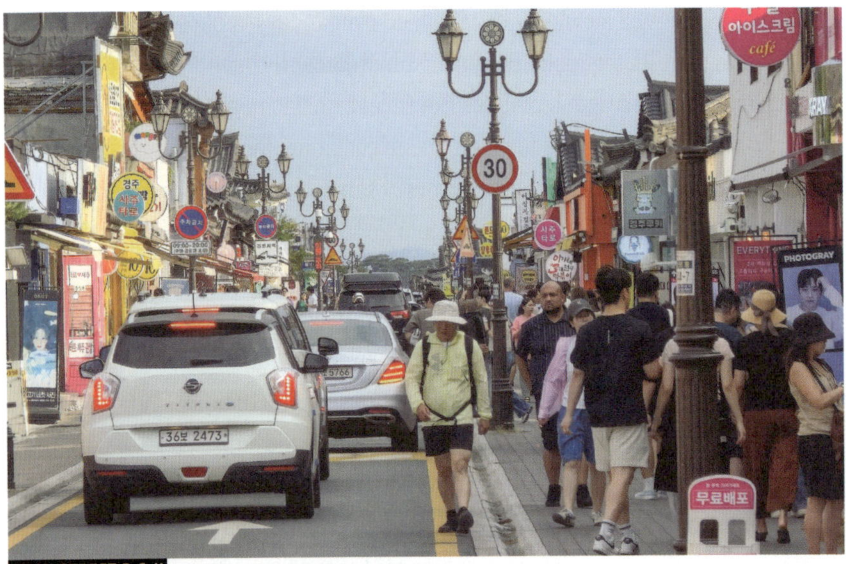

MAIN STREET R.O.K.
Hwangnidan-gil is popular destination for domestic tourists and students on field trips—
at least after they've seen the properly historic attractions nearby

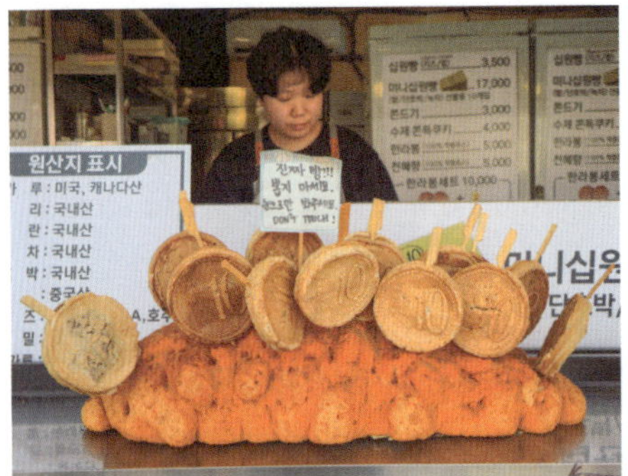

A NUMISMATIC SNACK
Sweet, cheese-filled sipwon bbang, iterally "ten-won bread," are
shaped like a coin seldom used in today's Korea

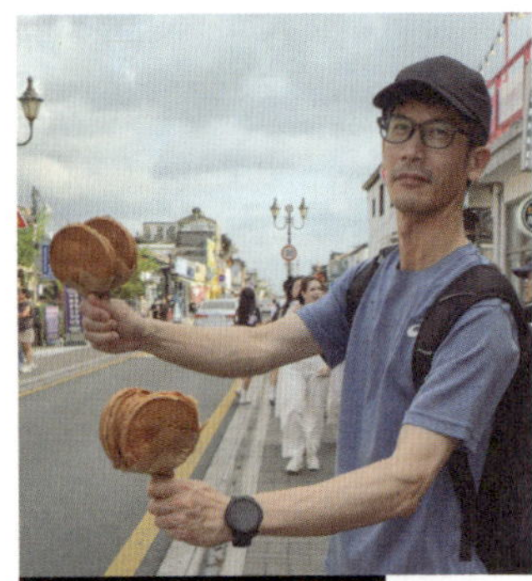

YOU CAN'T HAVE JUST ONE
Sipwon bbang cost much more than ten won,
but it's worth picking up a few if you're in
Gyeongju, where they were invented

gil, a trendy offshoot of Seoul's "foreigner district" Itaewon. A few years later, stores selling "ten-won bread," a cheese-filled snack shaped like the (now practically unused) coin of that denomination, popped up there along with the traditional fortune-tellers, *hanbok* renters, and vintage shops featuring Disney and Peanuts toys in the windows, all of it more than enough to satisfy anyone's senses of both historical and cultural incongruity. (Not far off the main drag, there is even, as of this writing, a place called Newtro Jagae Gallery Café, which will appear in chapter 7.)

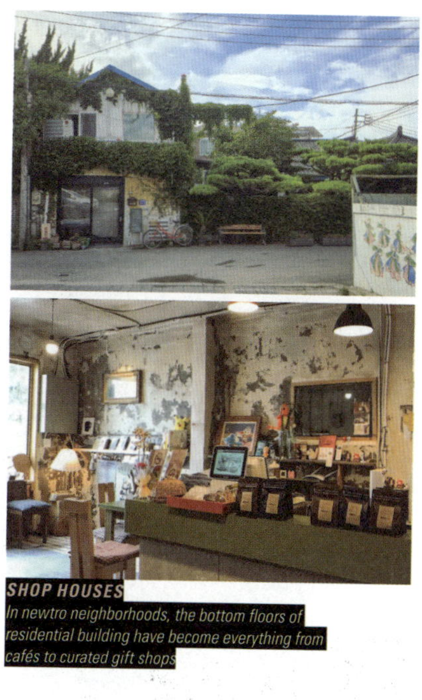

In newtro neighborhoods, the bottom floors of residential building have become everything from cafés to curated gift shops

Much like the more widely known Jeonju Hanok Village, Hwangnidan-gil is by now enough of a magnet for tourists, albeit mostly domestic ones, that, at its busiest, it may not feel entirely different from Seoul. Then again, it would be impossible to confuse with anywhere in the capital due to the height of its buildings, which top out at a limit set by the burial mounds at Daereungwon. Those in search of an equally low-rise, much lower-key newtro neighborhood will find it in Gangneung's Myeongju-dong. Located in Gangwon Province, which occupies the corner of the country up against the North Korean border and the East Sea, Gangneung received its first significant exposure to the wider world, and its first connection to the KTX (Korea's high-speed train network), in the run-up to the 2018 Winter Olympics held in the nearby inland county of Pyeongchang. Myeongju-dong shares much in common with the aforementioned neighborhoods, including aged building stock, a historic Western religious institution (specifically, Imdang-

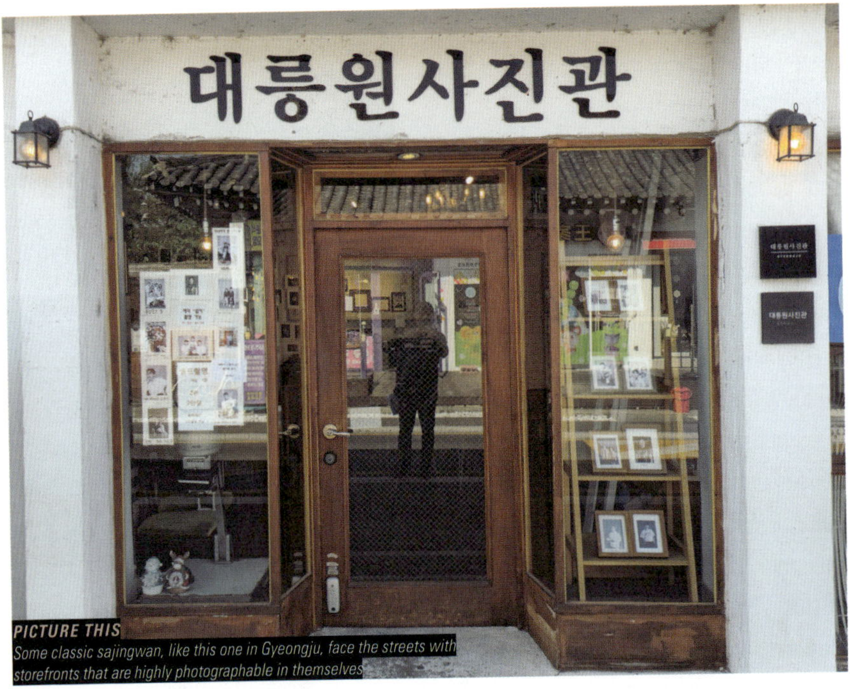

PICTURE THIS

PICTURE THIS
Some classic sajingwan, like this one in Gyeongju, face the streets with storefronts that are highly photographable in themselves

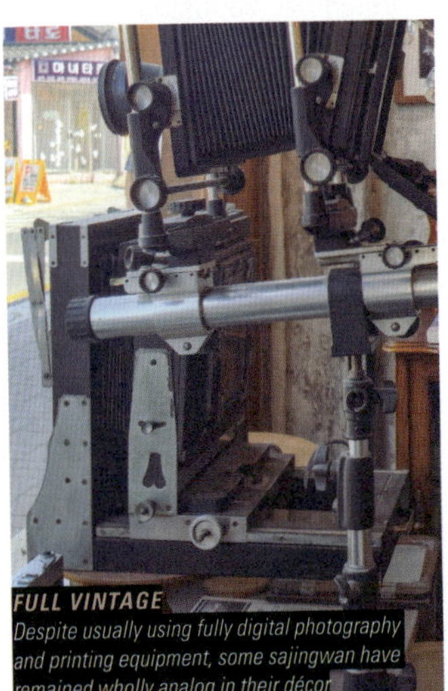

FULL VINTAGE
Despite usually using fully digital photography and printing equipment, some sajingwan have remained wholly analog in their décor

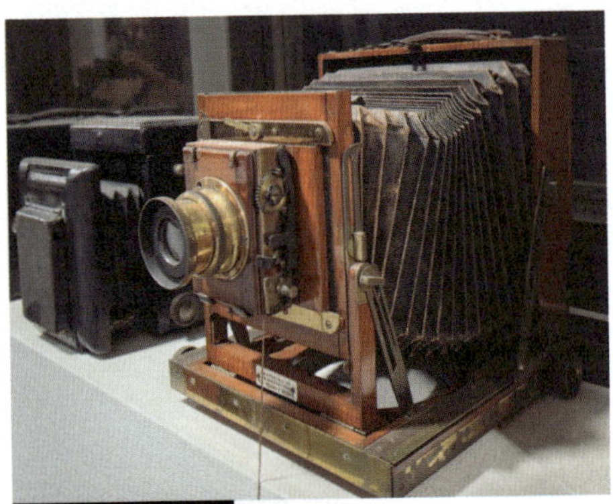

COLONIAL CAMERAS
Film-photography gear has inspired a new generation of hobbyists, though the oldest pieces of hardware tend to be best used for display purposes

dong Cathedral), photographable murals, vintage goods dealers, period clothing rental shops, and third-wave coffee. Once Gangneung's administrative center, Myeongju-dong lost much of its former relevance when the city hall moved away, in much the same manner as Incheon's Gaehang-ro. But the value of its aesthetic was later rediscovered by new arrivals like the former professionals from the Seoul film world and now operators of the abandoned mill-turned-café-gallery Bonbon Roastery. Just a few minutes' walk from there is the Sunshine Museum, a tiny institution, but one full of inspiration for the newtro-minded, displaying as it does objects used by ordinary Koreans over the past century, from stereos to sewing machines and cookware to cigarette packs.

All of these newtro neighborhoods—and indeed, all the others scattered throughout the country—also have *sajingwan* of their own. Here in the 2020s, even the most historically themed among them use digital cameras and computers, almost without exception, to provide their customers with a wider selection of photos from which to choose and the ability to take their prints home right away. Some, however, also employ pieces of older photographic technology as decoration, whether boxlike cameras that date back to Korea's Gaehwagi (or "Enlightenment Period") period of the late 19th and early 20th century or the semi-professional handheld models the MZ Generation remember having seen in their own fathers' hands. Many young Koreans understand the value of film cameras as objets, but some have also taken up the challenge of using them for their intended purpose, learning to negotiate that medium's inherent difficulties and appreciate its special strengths. It may not be the easiest way to take pictures today, but it's certainly the most newtro.

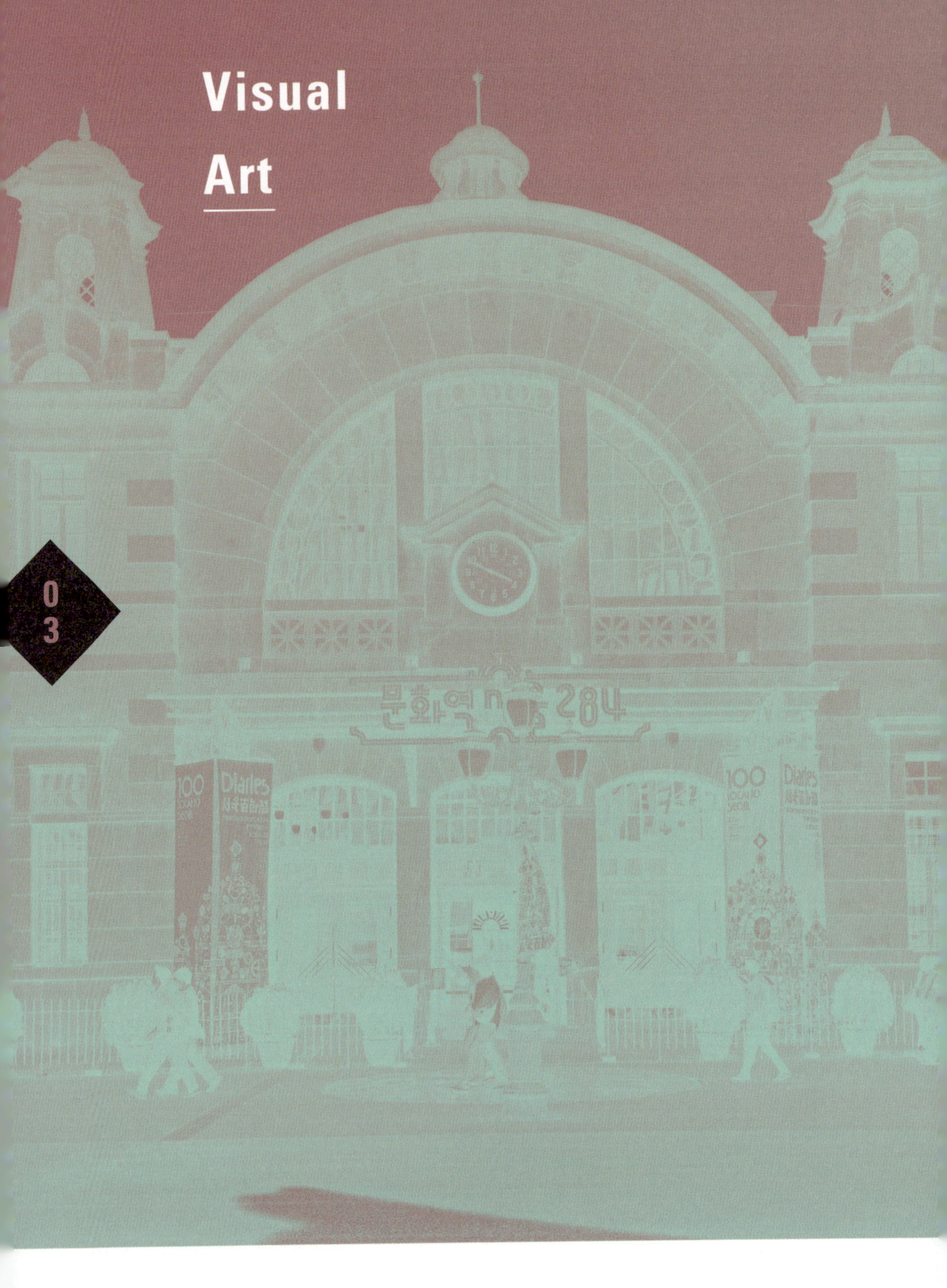

Visual
Art

In several different ways at once, *pilka* is a telling bit of Korean slang. Short for *pilleum kamera*, the Koreanization of "film camera," it exemplifies two common tendencies for vogue terms in this country: to be borrowed from foreign languages, especially English, and to be constructed out of the initial syllables of multiple words, both of which can aggravate the bewilderment experienced by students of the Korean language here for the first time. (For "selfie," incidentally, Koreans say *selka*, a contraction of *selpeu kamera*, "self camera.") Forty years ago, such a word would never have emerged, but then, nor would it have been necessary, since all the cameras available would have been film cameras. That one still hears references to *pilka* in this digital age suggests that they've retained a place in the culture— not least in the culture of newtro.

It isn't particularly hard to buy a *pilka* in Seoul. Dealers operating one next to another on the streets near

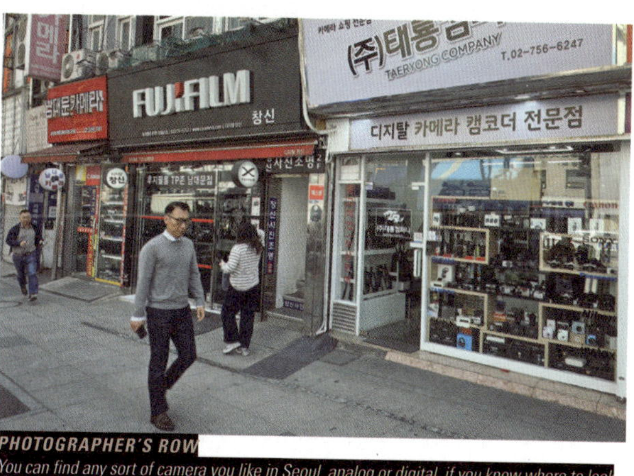

PHOTOGRAPHER'S ROW
You can find any sort of camera you like in Seoul, analog or digital, if you know where to look

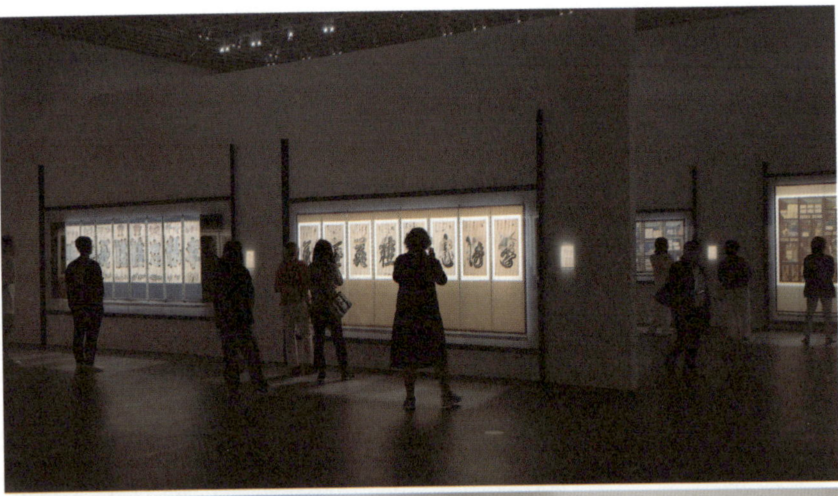

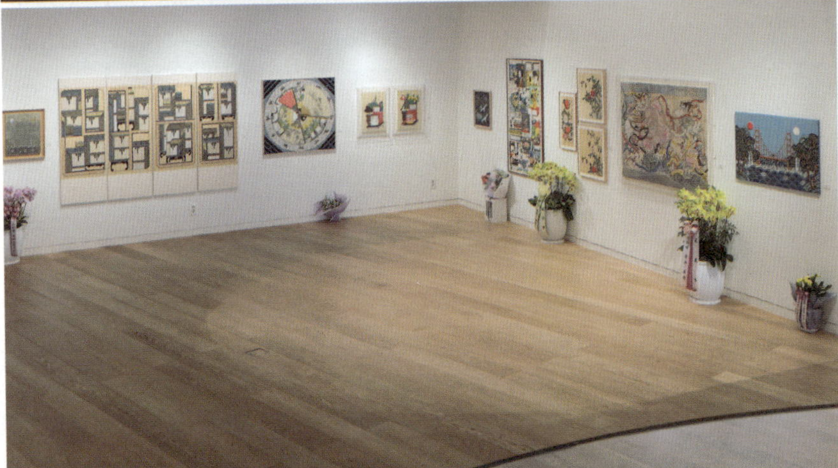

THE PEOPLE'S ART
*Once dismissed as a lesser form, minhwa has come back in a big way,
inspiring popular exhibitions and new generations of practitioners*

Namdaemun Market, to name just one part of town, fill their storefront windows with used makes and models of every kind. What's trickier is finding a *sajingwan* to develop film, to say nothing of mastering the ins and outs of operating a camera with no digital forgiveness of trial and error. But for the MZ or 1020 generation member who takes an interest in film photography, that's part of the attraction. All around the world (but especially in Korea, one comes to believe after living here long enough), smartphones have made everyone into a kind of photographer. But with a *pilka*, taking as many shots as possible first and picking the best one later—let alone performing digital touch-ups and applying filters—is hardly a viable strategy.

For anyone too young to have started taking pictures in the analog age, the awareness of a roll of film's finitude, as well as of the cost of purchasing and developing that film, introduces a certain pressure. The inability to evaluate a picture before taking it, and indeed until the whole developed roll comes back, adds uncertainty to the mix. But along with these feelings comes another, more positive one: that of *yeoyu*. One of the words I habitually cite as an example of the difficult-to-translate abstract nouns frequently used in the Korean language, *yeoyu* refers to the "breathing room" that comes from having more than enough money, time, or any other resource besides. The more Korea develops, one often hears observed with a note of irony, the less *yeoyu* Koreans enjoy in their lives. Perhaps shooting on film, or pursuing any other newtro hobby for that matter, leads to a small, individual reversion to an earlier stage of technological development (or even national development on the whole).

Film photography isn't especially old, at least as far as art forms go, nor is it especially Korean. That makes for a stark contrast with *minhwa*, literally "people's painting," or "folk painting," which originated in the Joseon period (1392–1910). By the time it matured as an art form in the 17th century, it had developed a rich iconographic vocabulary of animals, fish, flowers, fruits, and other aspects of nature, with particular symbolic value for the commoners who both created and purchased *minhwa* artworks. A kind of Joseon-era pop culture, they were sometimes painted with highly refined techniques, but always with the aim of catching the viewer's eye, their vivid, contrasting colors—often cited as the clearest manifestation of *minhwa*'s Koreanness, distinguishing it from contemporary art forms elsewhere in

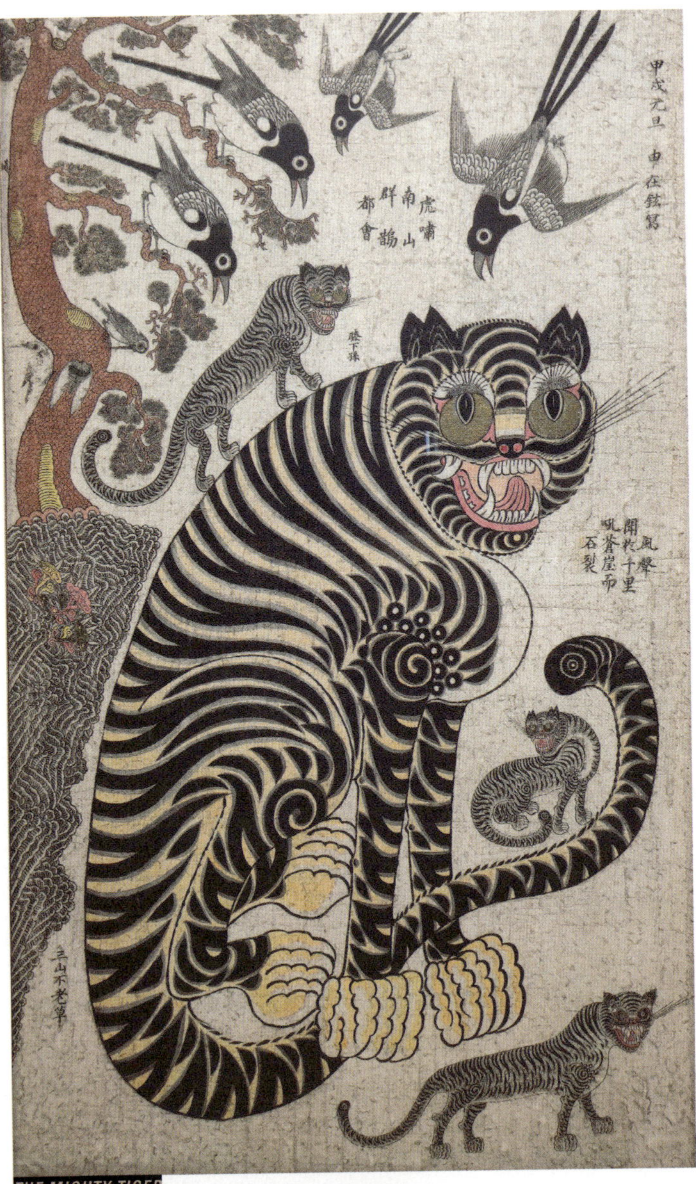

THE MIGHTY TIGER
These fearsome big cats may long since have gone extinct in Korea,
but they survive as a motif in art (and in the design of this book)

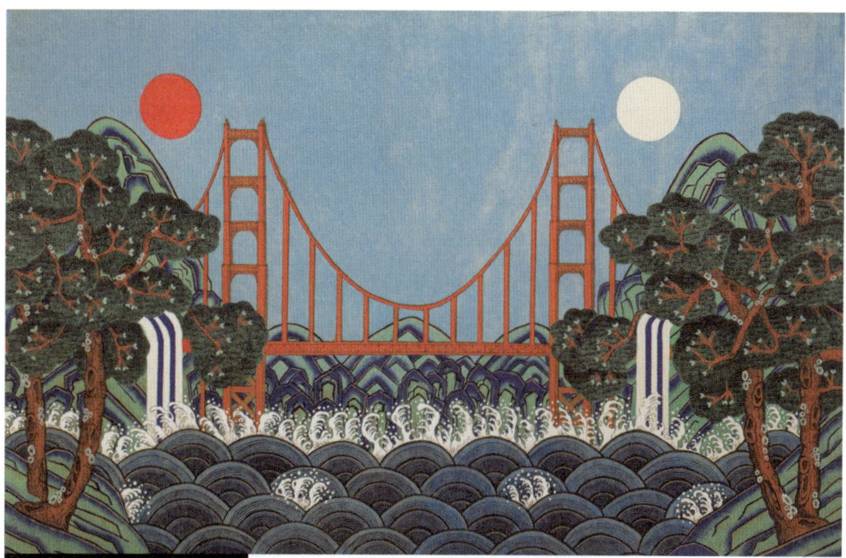

AN UPDATED IRWOROBONGDO
Once installed behind the royal throne, this screen painting of "the sun, moon, and five peaks" remains perhaps the most recognizable piece of Korean art—even with new details added in

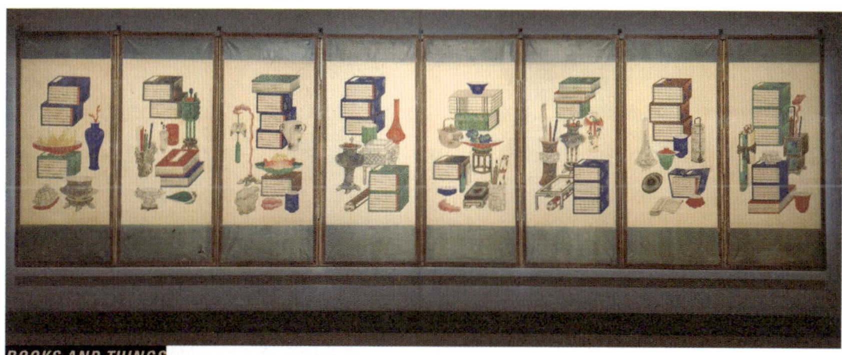

BOOKS AND THINGS
A must-have item in the 19th century, a chaekgeori screen painting sometimes substituted for the prestigious possessions it depicted

Asia—popping right out against usually flat backgrounds.

Another key aspect of *minhwa*'s popularity has to do with its figures being rendered in a style more expressive than strictly realistic. Anyone looking through the more widely known works throughout its history will notice, for instance, how depictions of the tiger, one of the most important creatures in Korean legend, grow ever sillier and wilder-eyed, in contrast to the composed, dignified magpie with which it's typically paired. Taking the tiger and the magpie to be avatars of the ruling class and common people, respectively, reveals a thinly veiled satirical dimension to that subgenre of paintings, but the evident sense of fun on the surface demands no interpretation to enjoy. That, along with the outward simplicity of its compositions, has made *minhwa* a particularly approachable classical Korean art form, a form well-suited for a revival after public interest fell into abeyance during the colonial period and the Korean War.

Ever since beginning a steady comeback in the 1980s, *minhwa* has gone from being a subject of classes for housewives and grandmothers at department store *munsen* (short for *munhwa senteo*, or "culture center") to the basis for entire artistic careers in the 21st century. Whether they label it "modern *minhwa*," "pop *minhwa*," or something else entirely, a new wave of Korean artists now specialize in reinterpreting the people's painting of centuries ago for the present day. While they employ the same compositional techniques and incorporate the same flora and fauna as more traditional examples, their vision also encompasses furniture, products, pets (including breeds of domestic dogs and cats unknown in the Joseon period), symbols, and even brand logos recognizable to viewers of the 2020s, whether Korean or foreign. It should be noted, however, that this does not in any way depart from the fundamental principles of *minhwa*, which was already incorporating the things people actually saw around them half a millennium ago.

Nor did *minhwa* take long to reflect the aspirations of its consumers, most clearly in the genre of *chaekgeori*. The name *chaekgeori* (which has succeeded the earlier *munbangdo*, or "scholar's study painting") is usually translated as "books and things"—and aptly so, since those are just what the images depict. Painted realistically on large folding screens, early examples of the form dating from the late 18th and early 19th century could, at a distance, have been mistaken

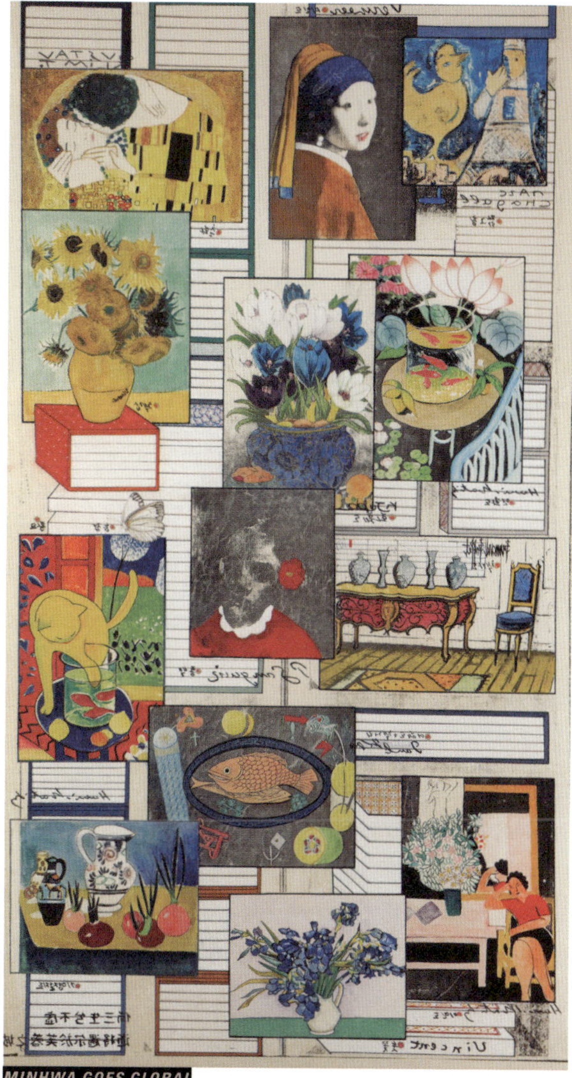

The chaekgeori form has proven versatile, so much so that it can even incorporate pieces of the Western art Koreans love

for actual well-stocked bookshelves. The books may always have been depicted generically, their stacks of bound pages amounting to a repeating motif, but the "things" were more identifiable: teapots, flowers in vases, incense burners, fans, calligraphy brushes, and fruit. Ideally, some of them would be of visibly foreign origin, which spoke to the taste—and more to the point, the means—of the owner having his possessions painted.

Such imports in earlier *chaekgeori* tended to come from China; in later ones, from the West. (One can trace this change through history by the appearance of mechanical clocks, even if the painters evidently had only a vague idea of what the Roman numerals on their faces were supposed to look like.) After the introduction of *chaekgeori*—attributed to King Jeongjo, the reformer who reigned over Joseon from 1776 to 1800—it underwent a steady process of democratization, first spreading through the *yangban* class of aristocratic scholars and then down to ordinary people, by which time it had become a kind of *minhwa*. Its form and content had also changed considerably; books became less common, and, in some cases, even the shelves themselves had disappeared, while the formerly realistic perspective gave way to an artistic license that could approach the edge of abstraction.

Seen today, Joseon-period *chaekgeori* have a clean-lined, startlingly modern quality about them, something that distinguishes them from other contemporary genres of Asian painting. This has made them an attractive prospect for Korean artists looking to bring *minhwa* into the 21st century. Members of the younger generations may have rather fewer possessions than members of the older ones, but they still enjoy putting them on display, especially in forms that can easily be posted to social media platforms. And, as ever in Korea, if some of those possessions bear the mark of certain prestigious other countries, all the better. Hence the inclusion, in new *chaekgeori*-style works of art, of everything from foreign smartphones to coffee cups emblazoned with foreign café logos to dolls modeled on foreign cartoon characters. Some of them even feature items more closely associated with newtro culture, like vinyl LPs, typewriters, and rotary phones.

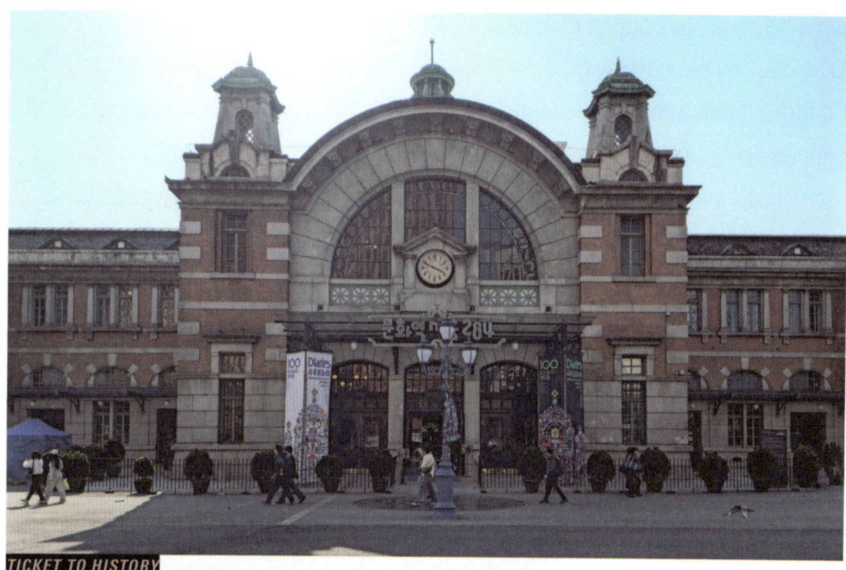

TICKET TO HISTORY

The colonial-era Seoul Station has been restored and converted into an exhibition space (and frequent location for historical film and drama shoots) called Culture Station Seoul 284

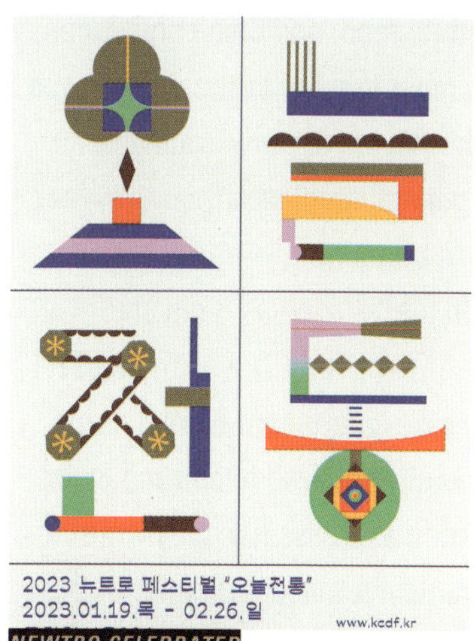

NEWTRO CELEBRATED

Suitably, Culture Station Seoul 284 was the venue for the very first Newtro Festival in 2023

Whether the Korean artists actively updating *minhwa* forms consider their work to be "newtro" is, of course, down to their individual preference. But the word "newtro" has begun to appear as an explicit theme in art and culture exhibitions, most notably the first Newtro Festival, which was held in early 2023 at Culture Station Seoul 284 (a suitable venue indeed, given that it's the repurposed original Seoul Station built in the colonial period). A collaboration between the Korea Craft and Design Foundation and the Ministry of Culture, it was titled "Oneul Jeontong (Tradition Now)," and it focused on re-introducing, in visually stimulating and sometimes participatory ways, certain particularly recognizable elements of Korea's past: folk tales told and children's games played since time immemorial, but also *hanbok* (traditional Korean dress), *hansik* (Korean food), and—perhaps the least widely known of the three—*hanji* (Korean paper).

My own awareness of *hanji* goes back much further than I'd first realized. In fact, it goes all the way back to my high school days in the suburbs of Seattle, Washington. Whenever I felt like a Korean meal, I went over to the small town of Edmonds, which had a large enough immigrant population to support a few Korean restaurants. It was while eating at Hosoonyi, my favorite among them, that I first sensed the depth of the cultural difference between Korea (about which I then knew practically nothing, other than that I enjoyed its food) and China and Japan, the Asian countries with which Westerners were most familiar at the time. It was nothing I could put into words at that point, but the flavors of *hansik* didn't taste much like Chinese or Japanese ones, nor did the general ambience (*bunwigi*) feel similar in any way to that of a Chinese or Japanese restaurant.

Hosoonyi's décor also made an impression on me, striking as it did an intriguingly unfamiliar balance between elegance and rusticity. It was there that I first laid eyes on a curious kind of doll: they could take a variety of human forms, from schoolchildren to senior citizens; they had round, oversized heads and highly expressive faces (not always with the most flattering expressions); they wore clothing, for the most part traditional-looking, minutely detailed with folds and wrinkles; and they seemed to be frozen in a state of exaggerated motion while going about the tasks of ordinary life. What set them further apart from anything I'd seen before was their texture, somehow both rough and smooth at once, that looked like neither wood nor clay. These, I learned much later, were called *dakjongi inhyeong*: *inhyeong* meaning "doll," and *dakjongi* being a compound of *dak*, a kind of mulberry tree, and *jongi*, or "paper."

Some young (or even not-so-young) Koreans may see *dakjongi inhyeong* as the epitome of *chonseureoum*, or "village-like" outdatedness. But to a foreigner such as myself, without memories to associate them with my grandparents' generation, they had a mysterious, almost exotic aura. People still make them, and if the exhibitions I've seen are anything to go by, some do model them after types from modern Korean life (and even after characters from blockbuster movies), but on the whole, the creators of *dakjongi inhyeong* look backward to simpler times— somewhat too simple, it seems, to have yet given the form much in the way of newtro currency. Nevertheless, the material from which they're made has become one of the traditional Korean products most heavily promoted,

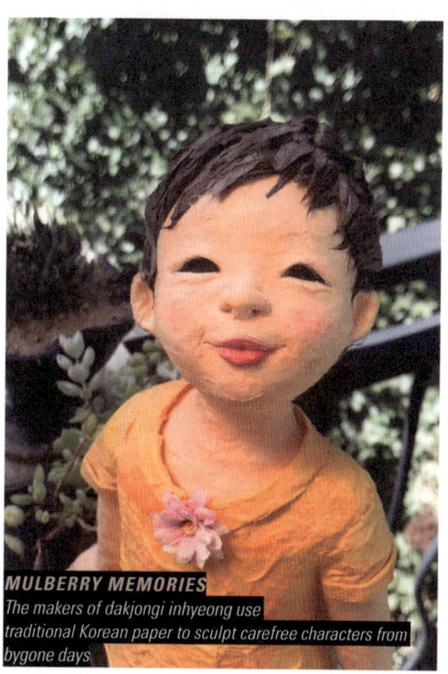

MULBERRY MEMORIES
The makers of dakjongi inhyeong use traditional Korean paper to sculpt carefree characters from bygone days

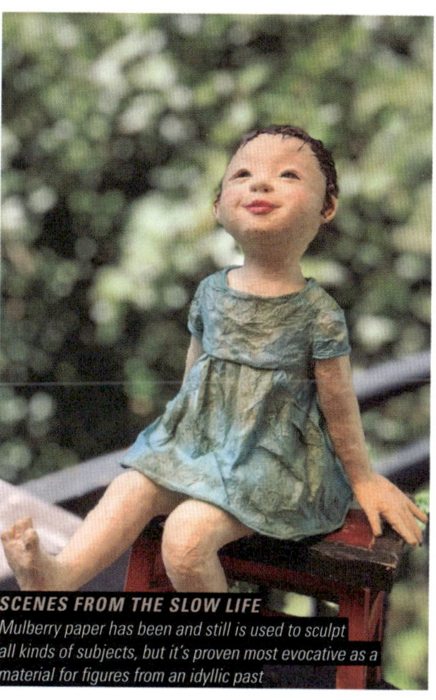

SCENES FROM THE SLOW LIFE
Mulberry paper has been and still is used to sculpt all kinds of subjects, but it's proven most evocative as a material for figures from an idyllic past

and most compelling, to both young Koreans and foreign consumers alike, under the name of not *dakjongi* but *hanji*.

Such is the promise of *hanji* as a sort of traditional brand that the Hanji Culture and History Center, originally founded in 2020 in Seoul's Bukchon Hanok Village by the Korea Craft and Design Foundation and the Ministry of Culture, Sports and Tourism, re-opened after renovations in 2024 as, simply, Hanji House. As its visitors will learn, the technology of papermaking came to Korea from China at some point between the 3rd and 6th centuries. But when made with the bark of this country's native *dak*, or paper mulberry tree, paper became something much more versatile than just a medium for documents. During the Joseon period, *hanji* was used to make a wide variety of goods, including fans, insulation, tobacco pouches, lanterns, decorative flowers, and greenhouses. It even proved to have a military application

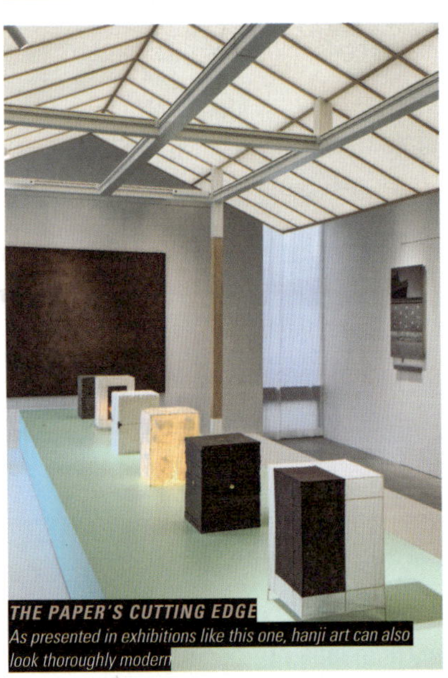

THE PAPER'S CUTTING EDGE
As presented in exhibitions like this one, hanji art can also look thoroughly modern

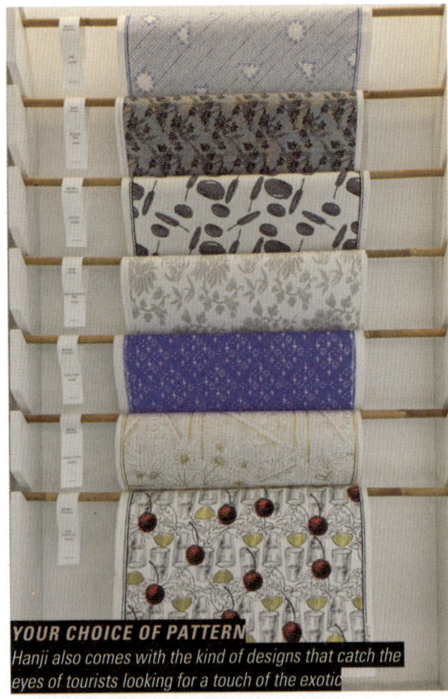

YOUR CHOICE OF PATTERN
Hanji also comes with the kind of designs that catch the eyes of tourists looking for a touch of the exotic

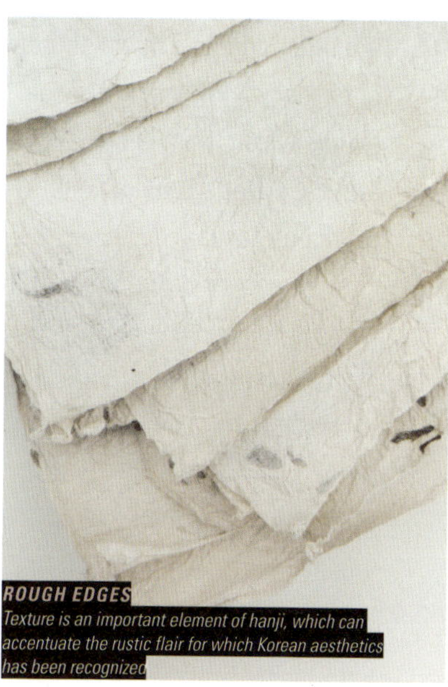

ROUGH EDGES
Texture is an important element of hanji, which can accentuate the rustic flair for which Korean aesthetics has been recognized

FULL SATURATION
These are just a few of the vivid colors hanji-makers can dye their wares

as the material for a light but effective battle armor.

If *hanji* was durable enough for Joseon soldiers, it must surely be durable enough for daily wear in the 21st century. That notion is being put to the test, in any case, by Korean manufacturers of apparel and accessories who make their products out of what's lately been called "*hanji* leather." Although the vegan diet may struggle to catch on in meat-loving Korea—a country where restaurants advertise with images of not only their dishes but also the animals from which those dishes are made—public interest in vegan products (i.e., without any animal-derived ingredients) has proven sufficient to motivate advertising campaigns built around the concept. Perhaps the most effective promotion occurred when South Korea's First Lady appeared at the 2021 G20 Summit in Rome carrying a *hanji* leather handbag that sold out not long after the press photographs circulated. More in

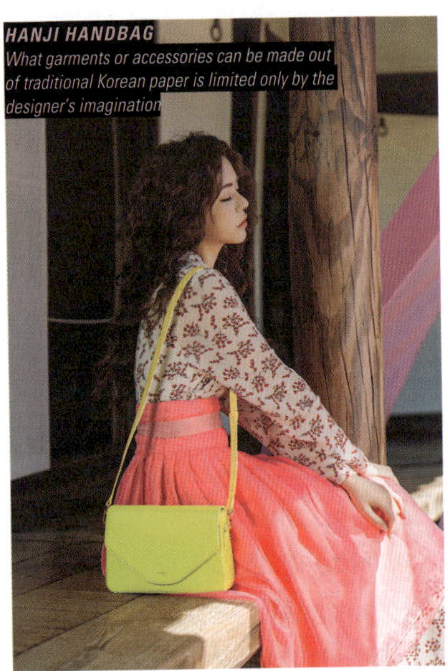

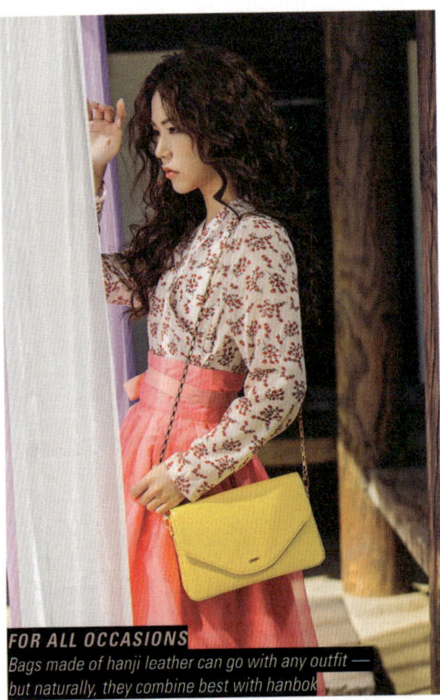

keeping with the newtro style are other products made entirely or partially with *hanji* for casual everyday use, from lamps and storage boxes to wallets and cellphone cases.

Attendees of the first Newtro Festival could examine closely, and even touch, freshly dyed sheets of *hanji*, marveling at the range of brilliant colors they take on (some of which would hardly have been easy to come by for an actual Joseon papermaker). Yet what may have made an even more lasting impression was the pop-up store upstairs, stocked with the work of young artists-entrepreneurs who create their wares with inspiration drawn from traditional Korean culture. If the goal is to bring the elements of the past back into modern-day lives—which, formed by several generations straight of breakneck national development, can now feel as if they have little distinctively Korean about them—it can't be accomplished in galleries and museums alone. Elements of Koreans' common heritage have to shape the things they encounter, purchase, and use on a day-to-day basis, an imperative designers working in the more classically oriented areas of newtro understand instinctively.

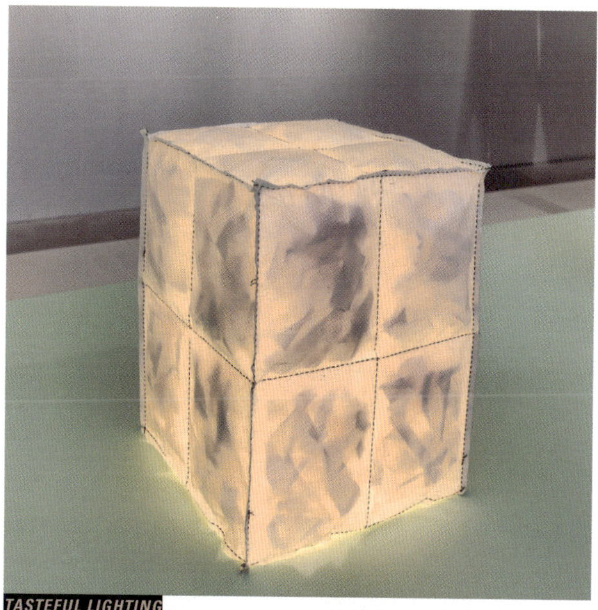

TASTEFUL LIGHTING
As a material for lanterns, hanji works just as well today as it did in the Joseon era

CHEOLSU AND YOUNGHEE
YEONTAN-GUI
OLD BRAND LOGOS
KING SEJONG THE GREAT
TAEGEUKGI
OBANGSAEK
IRWOROBONGDO

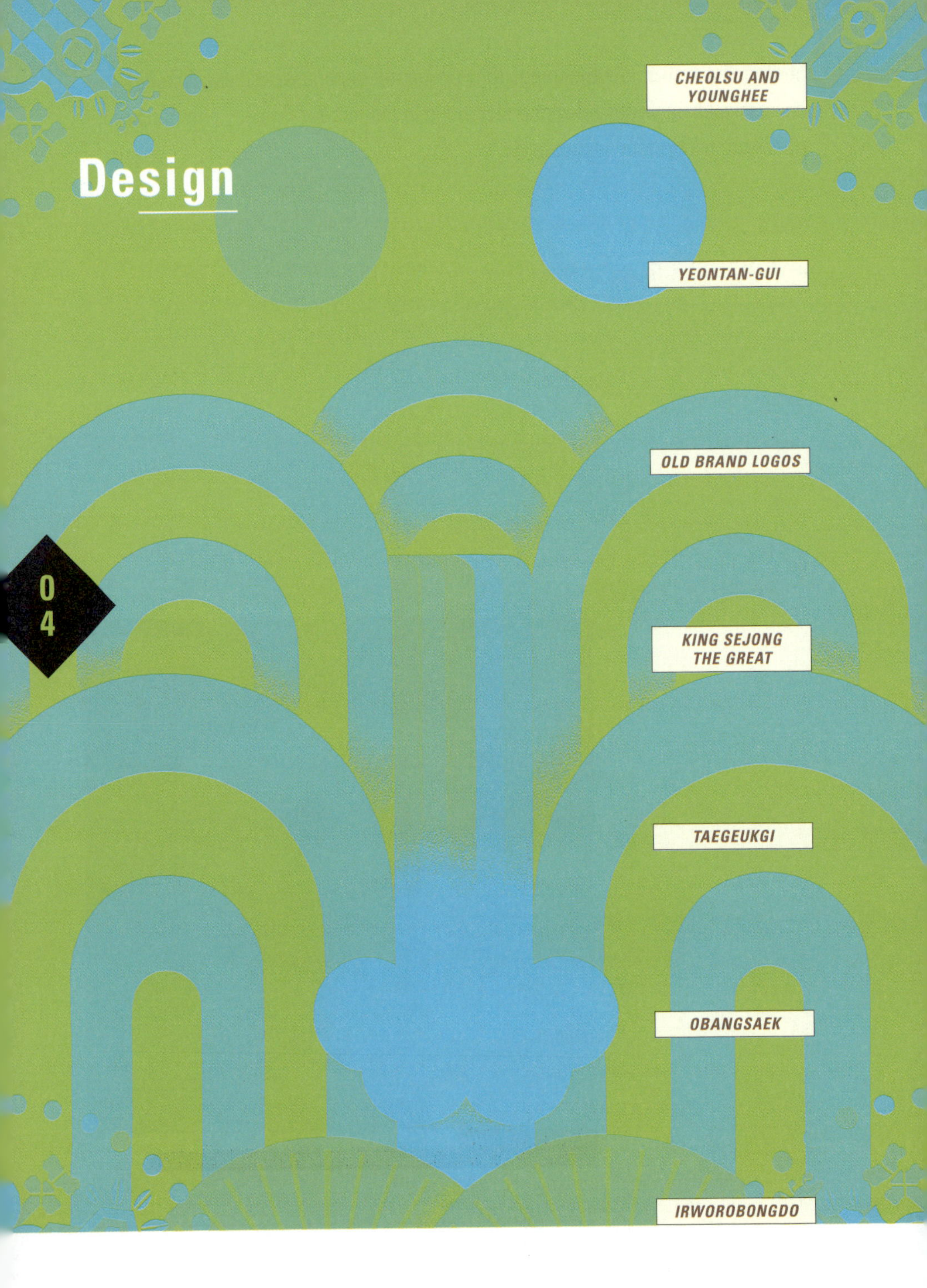

Design

04

Although they may not know their names, foreigners who've spent enough time in Korea have almost certainly seen Cheolsu and Younghee. Rough Korean equivalents of the American characters Dick and Jane, the stars of simplified readers widely used in classrooms of the 1950s, they have an even higher profile in their own country's pop culture. But that hasn't always been the case. Introduced in government-authorized elementary school textbooks in 1948, they enjoyed a nearly 40-year run before being phased out in the late 1980s, and for some time thereafter lived on mainly in the memories of the grown-up former students who had once learned such subjects as reading, arithmetic, and "proper living" through their stories. Here in the age of newtro, however, the rosy-cheeked faces of this young duo have become familiar faces even to Koreans who never once encountered them during their education. And they now appear in contexts never imagined by their creator.

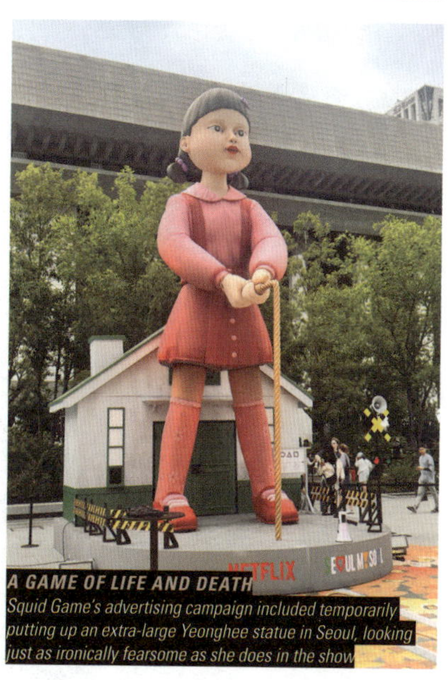

A GAME OF LIFE AND DEATH
Squid Game's advertising campaign included temporarily putting up an extra-large Yeonghee statue in Seoul, looking just as ironically fearsome as she does in the show

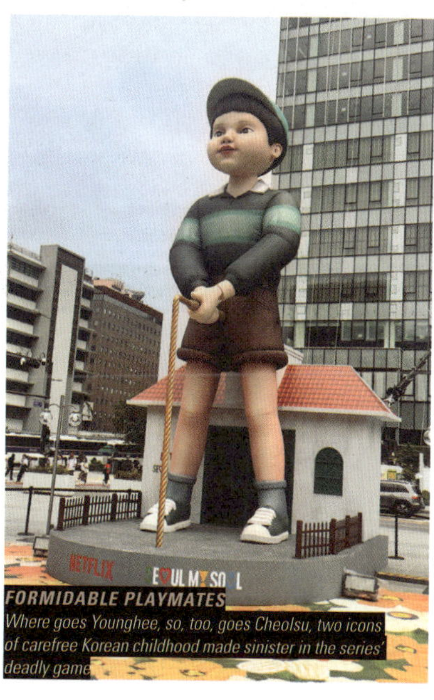

FORMIDABLE PLAYMATES
Where goes Younghee, so, too, goes Cheolsu, two icons of carefree Korean childhood made sinister in the series' deadly game

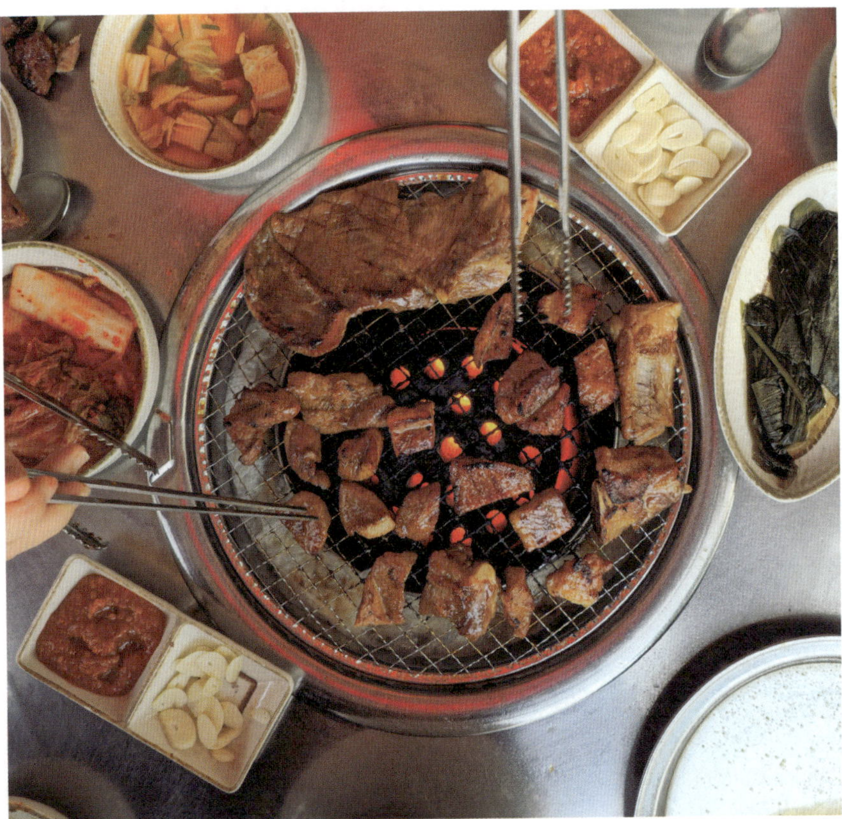

Cylindrical yeontan bricks once heated most every Korean home, but now they're increasingly often used to prepare nostalgic grilled-meat dinners

Cheolsu and Younghee (or characters highly reminiscent thereof) have lately been used to advertise fried chicken, test preparation classes, online shopping services, coffee, and even, despite their eternal youth, alcohol: a veritable rundown of the stuff of modern Korean life. Artists have essayed grown-up 21st-century versions, decked out in streetwear or with smartphones and cigarettes in hand, but even today, Cheolsu and Younghee seem to be most compelling when adhering to their original aesthetic—an aesthetic that might not have stood out half a century ago, but certainly does today. Imagery that could have been taken straight out of one of their textbooks has been appearing for years on stickers, calendars, notebooks, and other items at stationery or design shops geared toward young customers: too young, in fact, to ever have encountered those textbooks in the classroom.

As with so much that can be labeled newtro, Cheolsu and Younghee, figures created in the same year as the Republic of Korea itself (1948), are thus, in some sense, not old but new. So, by the same token, are the products widely advertised back in their original heyday. I'm reminded of this whenever I pass a *yeontan-gui* restaurant that opened just a year or two ago near where I live in western Seoul. Grilling meats with *yeontan*, the cylindrical, beehive-like charcoal briquettes once near-universally used for heating and cooking in Korean households, creates something of a retro atmosphere all by itself. But for interior decoration, the proprietors have also opted for murals, photographs, vintage magazines, and collectibles that evoke the time when stacks of depleted *yeontan* (makeshift toys for passing children inclined to smash things up) were an everyday sight on the street, which is to say, broadly speaking, the often-reminisced-about *yetnal*, or "bygone days."

These days, this sort of aesthetic isn't so unusual for an eating or drinking spot. More tellingly, newtro, in this particular case, is the sign outside, which features large, illuminated reproductions of venerable brand logos, most of them now retired. The beaming sun of Lotte Confectionery, with its Cheolsu-and-Younghee cheeks; the swirly-haired, bow-tied face of Binggrae (makers of a still-beloved banana-flavored milk found in every convenience store in the country); Seoul Milk's monochromatic rendition of the *taegeuk* symbol from the South

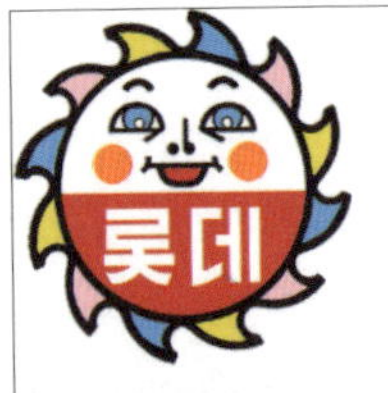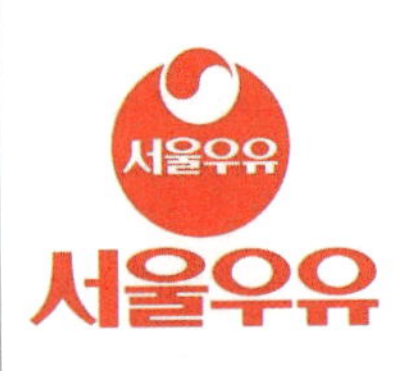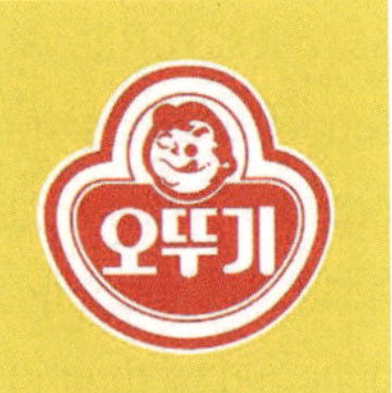

Korean flag: these have a renewed eye-catching quality, but also a kind of charm uncommon in the branding of recent decades. The sign also includes a couple of liquor bottle labels from Jinro, a company most widely known as a manufacturer of *soju* and one of the brands that has most embraced its own newtro image, with marketing campaigns that restore its trademark toad to his iconic two-dimensional simplicity.

Korean consumers have turned out to be especially receptive to newtro marketing of drink as well as food, so much so that companies have brought long-discontinued products back onto the market—*ramyeon* (or "ramen" as it's spelled in English dictionaries) noodles, custard cream pastries, ice cream bars—with not just the taste but the very packaging that older generations remember. Certain brands in that industry had changed little enough over the years that they happened to be well-placed to capitalize on the newtro craze as soon as it came along. Everyone had, at one time or another, seen the contented polar bear on bags of Gompyo wheat flour, but few would have imagined that staid emblem becoming anyone's idea of cool. Yet a series of collaborations beginning in 2020 with a canned beer rolled out to great success in a chain of convenience stores, drawing serious enthusiasm from consumer demographics not known for their frequent purchases of flour.

By the time of the brand's 70th anniversary a couple of years later, there was everything from Gompyo cookware to Gompyo tortilla chips to Gompyo toothpaste to Gompyo cosmetics to Gompyo winter jackets, all designed with

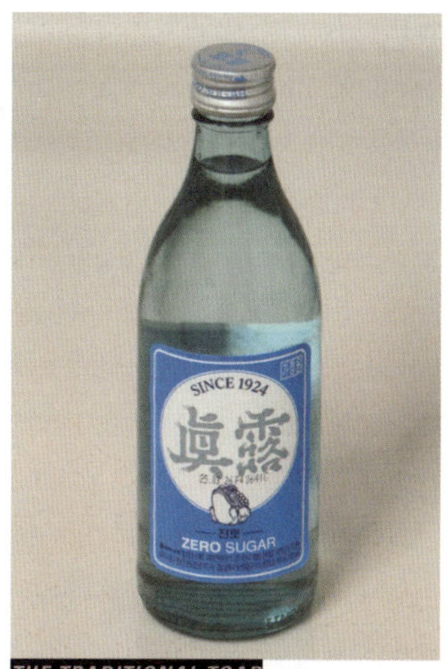

THE TRADITIONAL TOAD
Jinro soju has always been set apart by its blue bottle, and lately its signature amphibian has reverted to his classic look

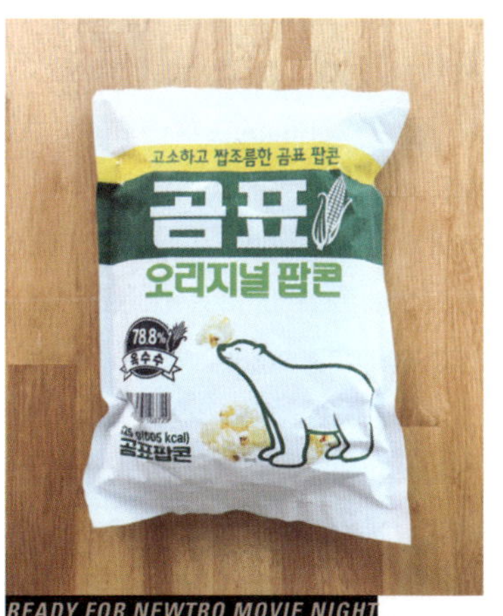

READY FOR NEWTRO MOVIE NIGHT
Even young consumers who've never bought Gompyo's flour have enjoyed its more recently introduced convenience-store snacks

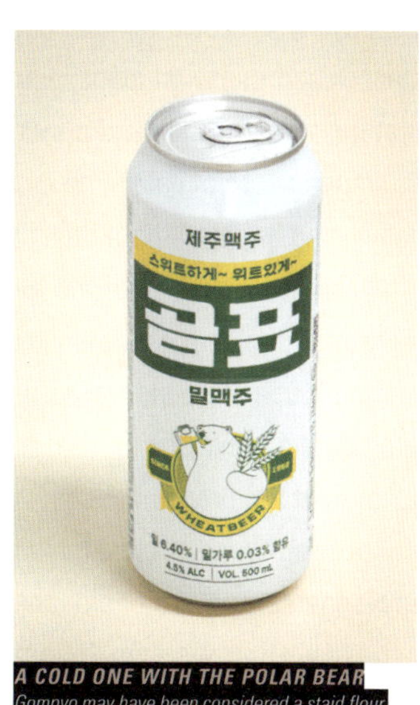

A COLD ONE WITH THE POLAR BEAR
Gompyo may have been considered a staid flour brand, but its long-unchanged logo was more than ready to turn cool

the same distinctive green-and-yellow color scheme and stark white mascot. Always a canny choice for the recognizability of its silhouette and its associations with a pure, uncontaminated landscape, the polar bear has translated easily into a variety of other commercial contexts—and to the design landscape established over the past 15 to 20 years, internationally subject as it's been to the almost overwhelmingly strong influence of concepts like "minimalism" and "flat design," which favor clean lines and uncluttered arrangements. Even marketers and graphic designers for brands without much history behind them have looked to the past, attempting to imbue their work with the counterintuitive allure of the newtro aesthetic. This tendency was evident even at the Seoul Design Festival 2018, with its theme of "Young Retro: Design Reversing Back to the Future." There, amid displays that included rotary phones and printing presses—equally unfamiliar devices to its 1020 or even MZ Generation attendees—exhibitors showcased products, some of them as simple as matchboxes, pencils, and calendars, designed in the newtro style before the term was even coined.

With today's digital tools, used in Korea as everywhere else, any image imaginable can be turned into a limitlessly reproducible graphic. That wasn't true in the days when Lotte Confectionery, Binggrae, Seoul Milk, Jinro, and Gompyo commissioned their first logos, whose now-sought-after graphical style owe to the limitations of the design and printing technologies of the day. Hence, for example, their limited range of colors, no more than two or three in total, and those colors' usually being bright without being too deeply saturated. That quality is exemplified by the long-standing logo of the food company Otoki, with the face of its delectating young boy rendered in red against a yellow background. Also typical is the round frame surrounding that face, which echoes the more or less round form of the entire graphic and, if it's not too much of a stretch, the initial circular Korean letterform of the brand name.

Spotting those circles, incidentally, is one way that foreigners who can't read Hangeul, the Korean alphabet, visually distinguish it from the Chinese and Japanese writing systems. It speaks to the growing international popularity of Korean culture that more and more non-Koreans have put in the effort to learn Hangeul, but it's just as noteworthy how many who haven't can still recognize

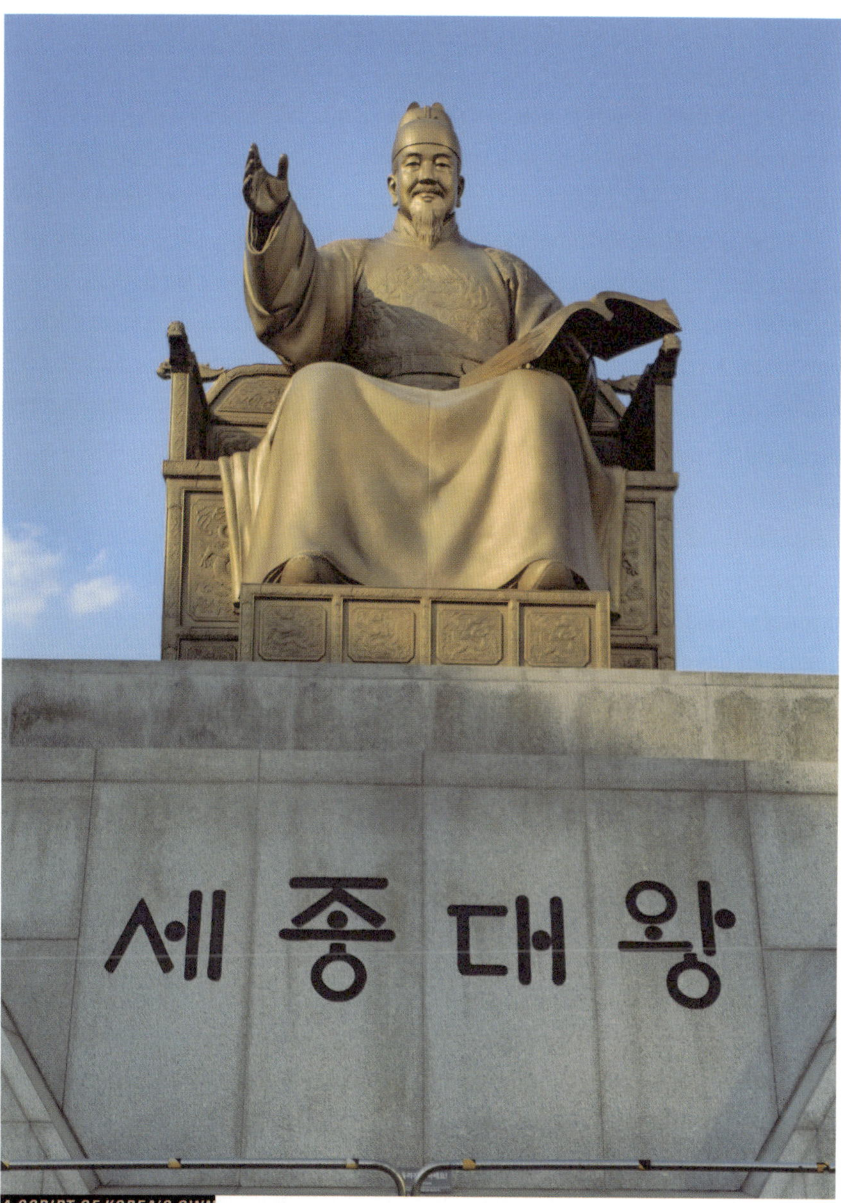

A SCRIPT OF KOREA'S OWN
Originally commissioned by King Sejong the Great in the 1430s, Hangeul has since become an integral element of Korean graphic design.

it. What surprises some of the foreigners who come to Korea is how often it isn't used here. There are any number of explanations for the preponderance of signs in English (or at least in the Latin alphabet), most of which involve a desire to project an image of international modernity. For a time—at least outside of historic quarters like Seoul's Insa-dong, which mandates the use of the local alphabet, even for foreign chains—a sign written in Hangeul alone was thought unsophisticated.

Now, it could be said that the essence of the mid-century logos and package designs currently being revived and imitated is their very lack of sophistication—or, rather, their lack of a need for sophistication as it was understood around the turn of the 21st century. To use Hangeul instead of English constitutes something of a newtro choice in itself, but the past few years have also seen the introduction of explicitly "newtro" fonts, many of which replicate the look of hand-painted or stenciled signs still visible, if somewhat worse for wear, on old buildings all around Korea. Whether sharp-edged, soft and rounded, or tapered in the manner of calligraphy, these varieties of new-old Hangeul tend to have a chunky, unabashed boldness—and to exude a mixture of old-school playfulness and seriousness—that had more or less gone missing from the typography of recent generations of Korean graphic design.

As every Korean schoolchild knows, the history of Hangeul goes back to the year 1443, when King Sejong the Great commissioned its creation as a tool to bring about universal literacy in a society whose relatively few lettered members all wrote in a modified form of classical Chinese (China having been the world power to which Korea looked at the time, even more so than the United States today). Its progress was fitful, however, until the late 16th century, when it was used to compose the ascendant genres of *gasa* and *sijo* poetry, and the 17th century, when it became a textual medium for novelistic stories. Official documents weren't written in Hangeul until 1894, the year after Gojong, the second-last king of Korea (Sunjong being the last), officially adopted what's become an even more widely recognized symbol of Korea than its script, the national flag, referred to as the Taegeukgi, which now represents the Republic of Korea.

The origin point of modern Korean graphic design, the Taegeukgi centers on a

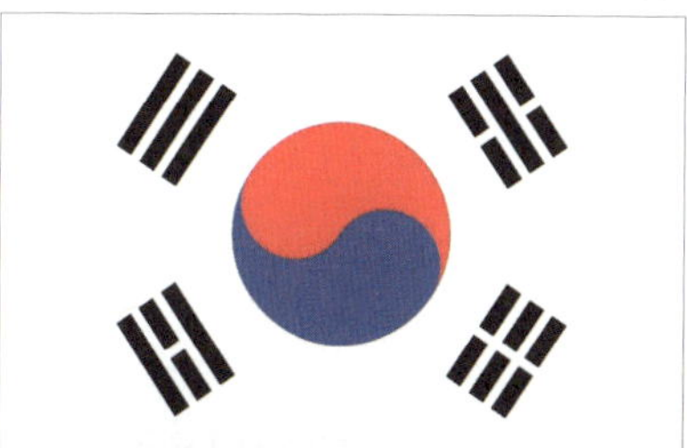

HEAVEN, EARTH, WATER, FIRE
Introduced in 1893, the Taegeukgi is now a globally recognized symbol of South Korea—and the origin point of modern Korean design

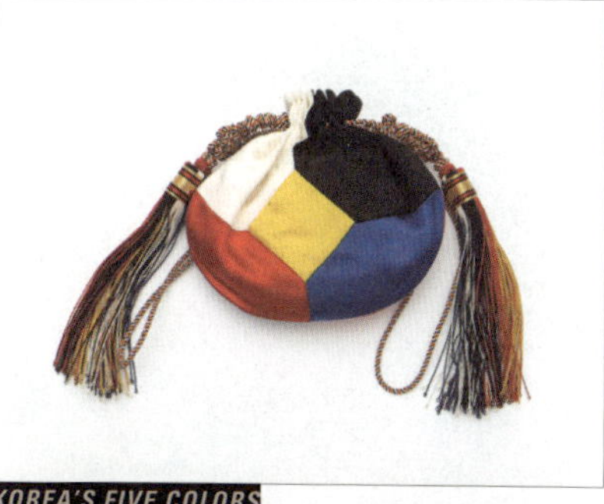

KOREA'S FIVE COLORS
The obangsaek are at the center of the traditional Korean worldview, and they remain a source of inspiration for current Korean artists and designers diving deep into their culture

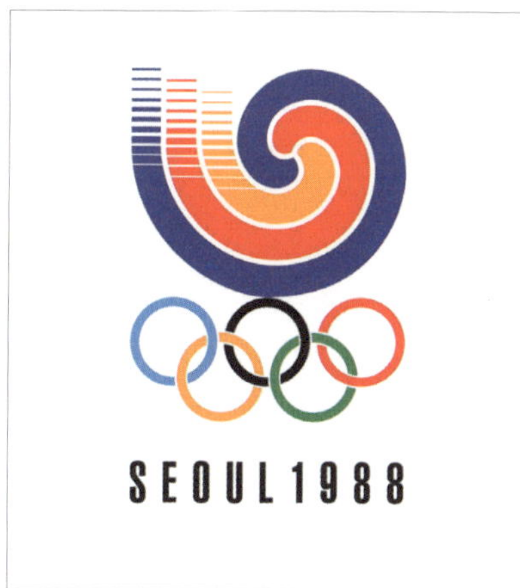

THE GAMES COME TO KOREA
The 1988 Summer Olympics gave South Korea the chance to debut on the world stage, but also to show off traditional Korean aesthetics in a sleek, stylish way

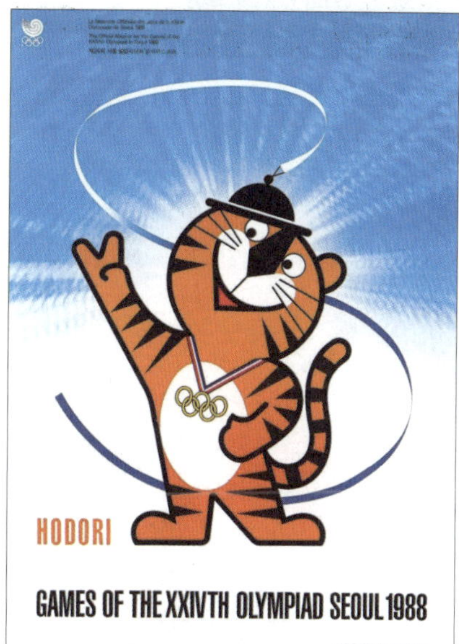

A SPORTING TIGER
Designed by Kim Hyun, creator of more than one beloved Korean mascot, Hodori can still be seen here and there in Seoul nearly 40 years after the Olympics

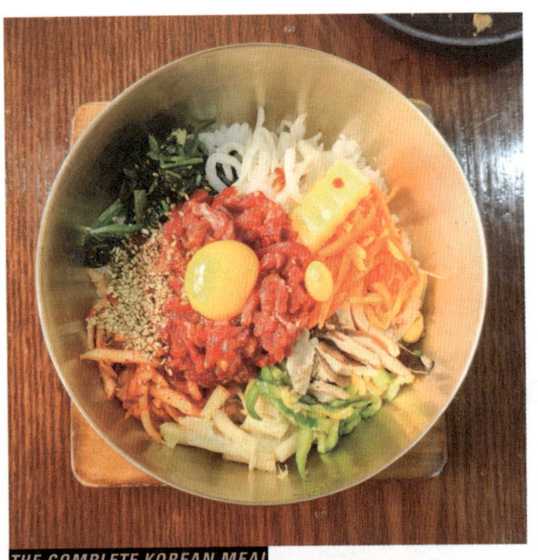

THE COMPLETE KOREAN MEAL
Bibimbap has become one of the most globally recognized Korean foods thanks not just to its flavors, but also its colors

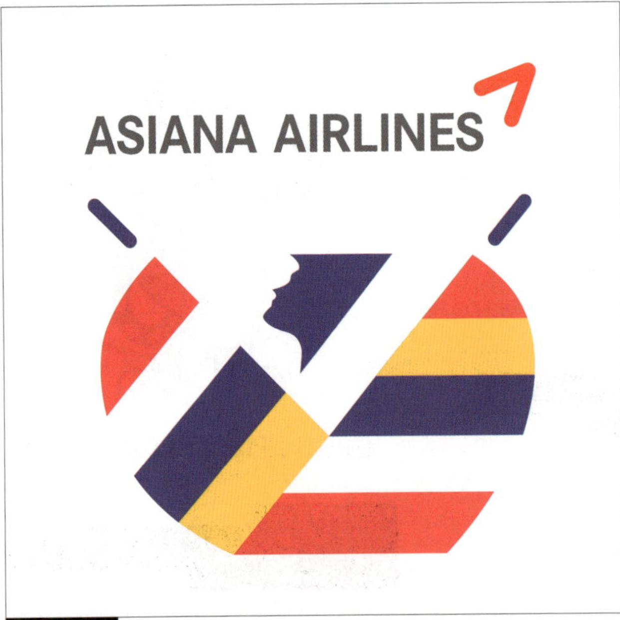

FLAG CARRIER
This previous Asiana Airlines logo incorporates certain national colors from the obangsaek and Taegeukgi

taegeuk, a circular symbol whose red and blue halves represent earth and heaven, as well as positive and negative energy, respectively; the four trigrams surrounding it stand for the classical elements of heaven, earth, water, and fire, as well as their corresponding seasons, virtues, family members, and heavenly bodies. A tri-colored variant of the *taegeuk* called the *sam taegeuk,* which includes a swath of yellow representing humanity, constituted the basis for the logo of the 1988 Summer Olympics in Seoul, an event that also produced the adorable tiger mascot Hodori (whose female counterpart, Hosoonyi, was the namesake of my Korean restaurant of choice back in high school in America) and a series of influential posters whose use of both high-tech graphic design tools and classical Korean iconography made their aesthetic the newtro of its day.

Together, the Taegeukgi and *sam taegeuk* use four of the *obangsaek*, or "five direction colors," whose importance to classical Korea could hardly be overstated. Each color is associated with a different element and direction, in accordance with a scheme adapted from China when Korea drew a great deal of influence from Confucianism. *Baek*, or white, stands for metal and the west; *heuk*, or black, for water and the north; *cheong*, or blue, for the sky and the east; *hwang*, or yellow, for earth and the center; and *hong*, or red, for fire and the south. The *obangsaek* are visible in practically all well-preserved areas of traditional Korean culture, from the architecture of temples and palaces to the costumes of *samulnori* percussionists and *mudang* (or shamans) to popular dishes like *bibimbap*. Even Koreans uninterested in history can't help but feel a deep familiarity with these five colors.

To some modern Korean artists, the *obangsaek* have offered a means of connecting their work more directly with their heritage. In 2023, Mokgyenaru Culture Space in Chungju used it as a uniting theme for a group show that promised *saeroun gomisul*, or "new antique art," under an apt title: *Newtro*. Although it may draw most conspicuously from the visual culture of the 1960s through the 1990s, the newtro movement has also demonstrated the potential to reach much deeper into the past, if sometimes in a second- or third-hand manner. Certain colors of the *obangsaek* jump out from the most memorable *yetnal* logos (at least four of them are evident in the one Asiana Airlines used in the '80s and '90s), and though graphic designers may have an infinitely wider palette available to them today, they've

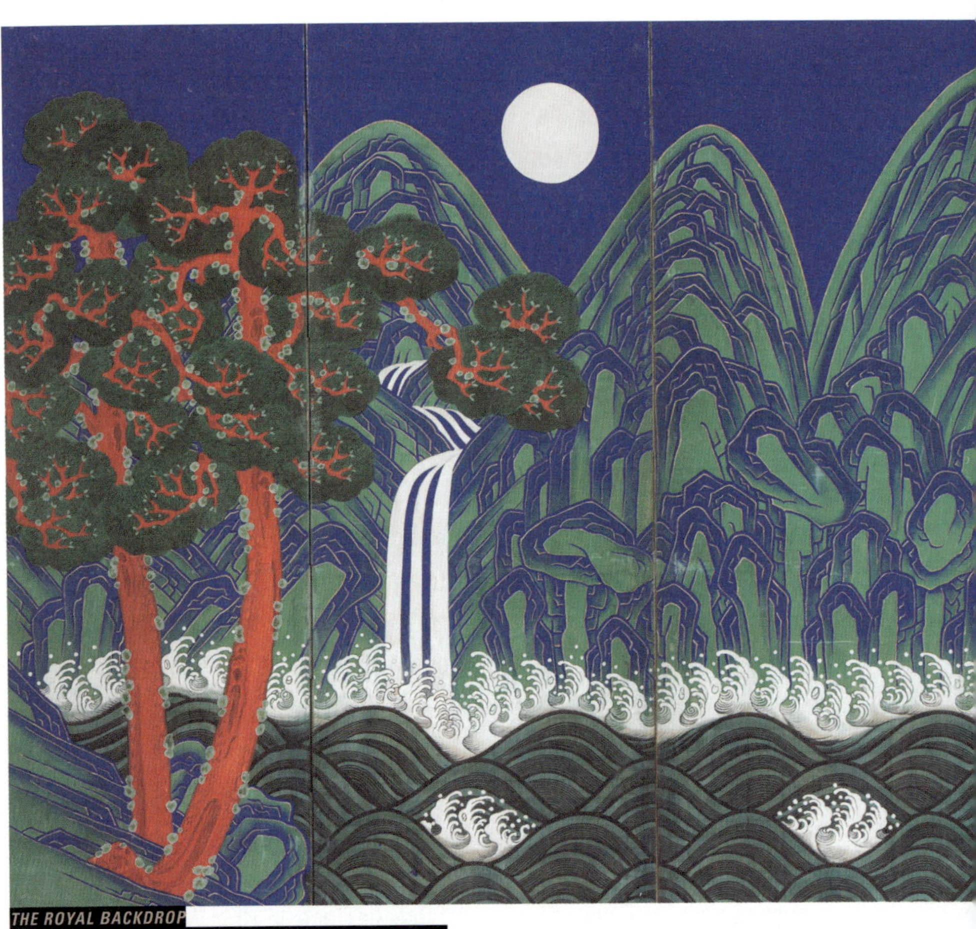

THE ROYAL BACKDROP
Irworobongdo in full—missing only a Joseon monarch seated before it

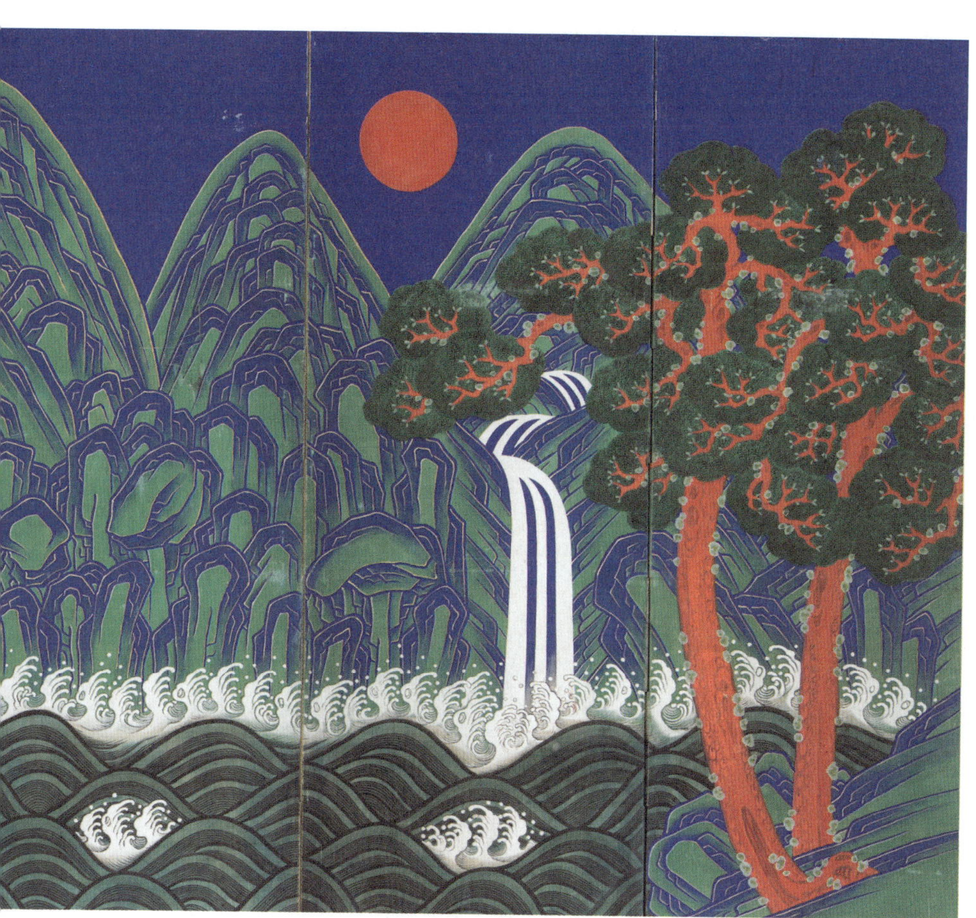

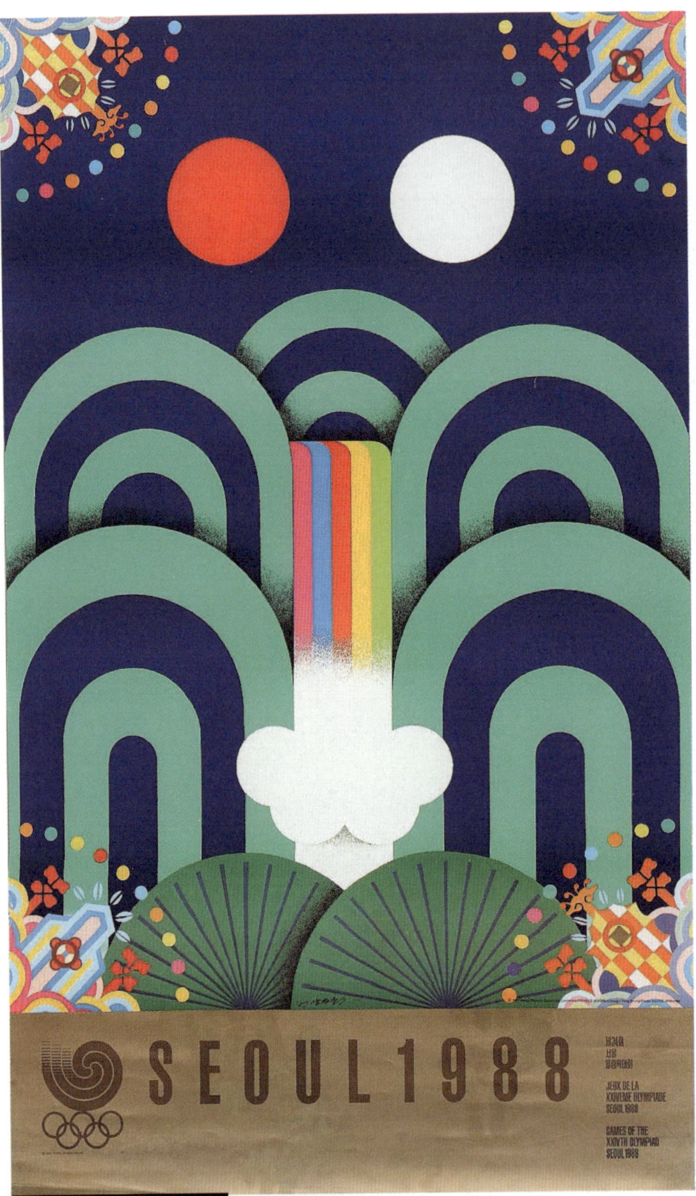

RETURN TO THE FIVE PEAKS
This Seoul Olympics poster abstracts Irworobongdo in
an aesthetic that holds up still today

clearly found white, black, blue, yellow, and red useful in making a newtro impact.

The same goes for designers in the world of high fashion. On runways in Seoul and other world capitals besides, garments have now and again made striking use of the *obangsaek*, or indeed specific works of Korean art. I often find myself looking appreciatively at the classical painting *Irworobongdo*, an image of—as its name suggests—"the sun, the moon, and five peaks" painted on the folding screens that were placed behind the royal throne during the Joseon period. Reproduced in countless different contexts, it also, adapted into a design even more stylized than the original, became one of the posters for the 1988 Olympics. Later, in 2022, it even appeared embroidered on an extravagant, almost Disney princess-esque dress by the London-based Korean designer Miss Sohee. While that particular item never found its way to the shops, a keen eye on the streets of Seoul can spot subtler reinterpretations of past styles and, in some cases, centuries-past styles.

Fashion
and
Beauty

05

HANBOK

HANBOK
RENTAL SHOPS

MODERN HANBOK

CHANEL CRUISE
COLLECTION

K-POP STARS
WEARING HANBOK

UGLY SHOES

GYEONGSEONG STYLE

K-BEAUTY

On any day with reasonably good weather, central Seoul's Gyeongbokgung Palace, the grandest of all palaces that were built in Korea during the Joseon period, is filled with wearers of *hanbok*, or Korean traditional dress. Most of them will be tourists from other countries; almost all of them will have picked out their outfits at the numerous rental shops that do business in the nearby neighborhoods of Seochon and Bukchon. The palace waives its already-nominal admission fee for anyone in *hanbok*, regardless of nationality. But that's only a partial explanation of why visiting Gyeongbokgung Palace in rented period costume—and, often, with a selfie stick in hand—has become a *de rigueur* tourist activity here. Another, more important factor is the country's having discovered the unlikely fashionableness and marketability of its own distant past.

Long a popular form of entertainment in Korea, historical films and television dramas set in the Joseon times or earlier

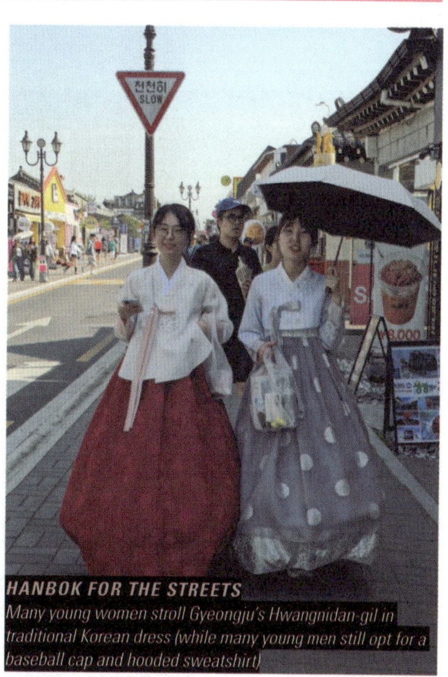

HANBOK FOR THE STREETS
Many young women stroll Gyeongju's Hwangnidan-gil in traditional Korean dress (while many young men still opt for a baseball cap and hooded sweatshirt)

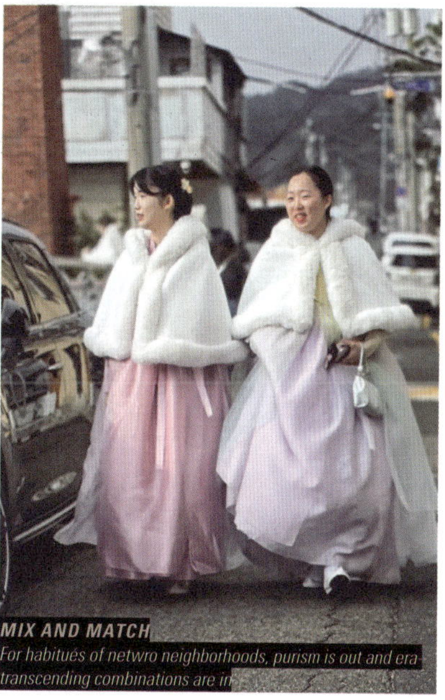

MIX AND MATCH
For habitués of netwro neighborhoods, purism is out and era-transcending combinations are in

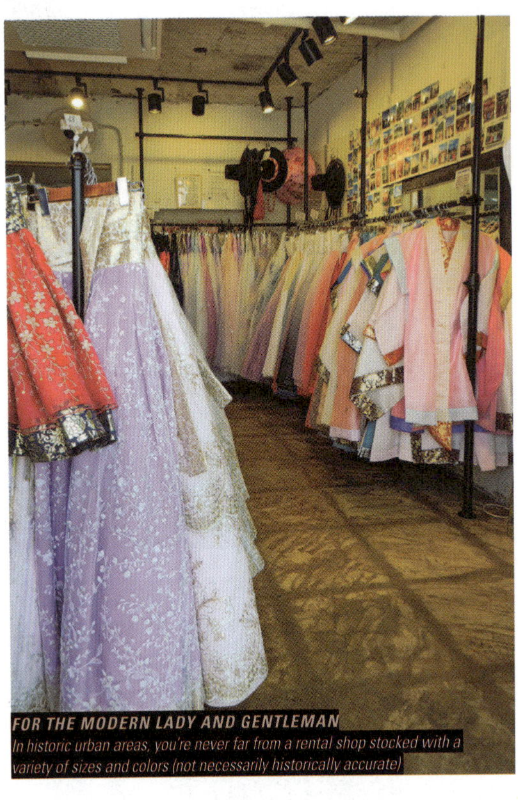

have more recently gained audiences in other parts of Asia, and even, to a certain
degree, in the West as well. That's not to say that they necessarily adhere to
the highest standards of historical accuracy—nor, in truth, do the *hanbok* rented
out in the streets around Gyeongbokgung Palace. Although modeled on the
splendid attire worn by mid-to-late-Joseon nobility and royalty, their vivid colors
are often achieved by being made with curtain fabric, which, according to one
purist objection, adds considerable volume to the women's skirts by employing an
incongruously rigid Victorian-style understructure. Traditionally created from two-
dimensional patterns, skirts or any other element of *hanbok* should ideally flow in

a manner more naturally dictated by the body of the wearer (even if mediated by several layers of undergarments).

Foreigners could be forgiven for failing to notice the anachronistic qualities of the *hanbok* they've rented for a single afternoon of their trip. It's not as if the Koreans making their own similarly costumed strolls through Gyeongbokgung Palace visibly object to such inaccuracies either, perhaps because of how much distance modern life has put between them and their country's traditional dress. For many, *hanbok* has always been reserved for special occasions, and then only certain special occasions; some wear it for the celebration of their *dol*, or first birthday, and never again until the formal photos taken after their wedding ceremony. Its retreat from public life dates to Korea's Gaehwagi, the "Enlightenment Period" mentioned in chapter 2, which began in the 1870s. Only then did it even acquire the name *hanbok*, literally "Korean clothing," such a term having become necessary to distinguish it from the Western apparel, or *yangbok* (though today this word usually refers only to a man's suit), fast coming into vogue—and soon thereafter becoming practically obligatory—as the country opened up to a greater volume of international trade.

Although *hanbok* has re-emerged in new forms and contexts in the 21st century, it's done so independently of the newtro phenomenon. Many Western fashion enthusiasts got their first glimpse of it in 2015, when the German designer Karl Lagerfeld filled his travel-oriented Chanel Cruise collection with *hanbok*-inspired pieces—incorporating the colors of the *obangsaek*, discussed in the previous chapter, as well as the patterns of *jogakbo* patchwork wrapping cloth—and presented it at Seoul's own Dongdaemun Design Plaza. The previous year, the young, self-taught Korean designer Hwang Yi-seul launched the label Leesle, which specializes in *saenghwal* (or "everyday") *hanbok*, adapting recognizably traditional lines to the dress sense and lifestyle of young people in the 21st century. She also published a memoir whose title translates to "*I Go to Hongdae in Hanbok*," Hongdae being the perpetually trendy Seoul neighborhood that surrounds the renowned art college of the same name.

Just as it makes sense that Leesle would have been founded in the historic city of Jeonju, which is famous for its village of *hanok* (traditional Korean houses),

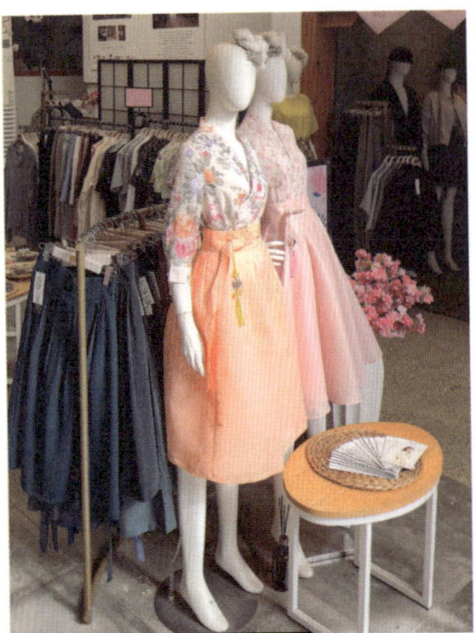

NO NEED TO GO FLOOR-LENGTH
Today's hanbok designers cater to today's tastes, not least with skirts that end below the knee—or higher

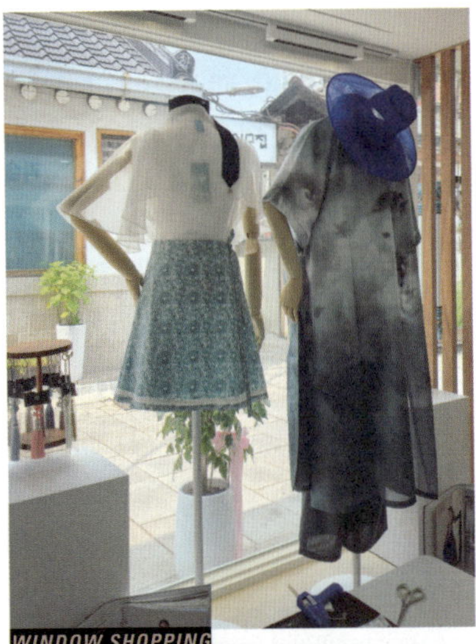

WINDOW SHOPPING
Whether designed for women or men, hanbok always look that much more appealing in a hanok

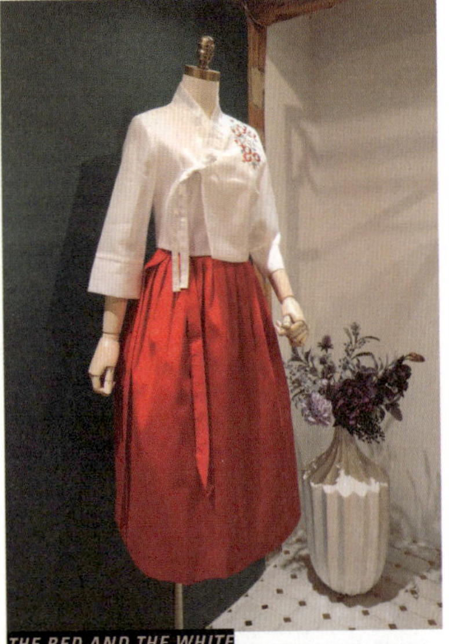

THE RED AND THE WHITE
Everyday hanbok can also adhere to a more classic style, and without looking frumpy

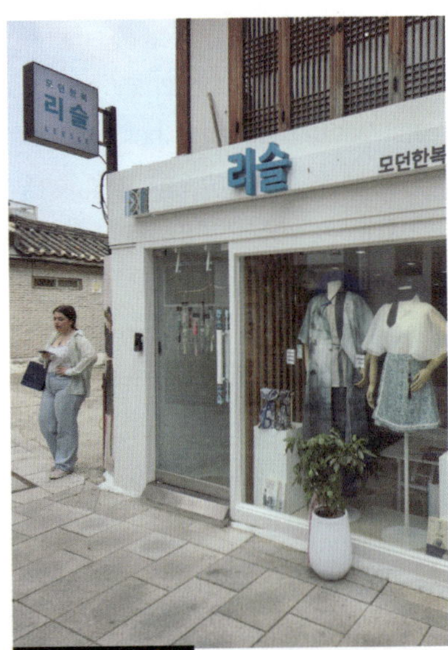

HANBOK-CURIOUS?
Younger designers like Hwang Yi-sul, founder of the label Leesle, draw even Westerners to their boutiques

it also makes sense that the brand would open up its first Seoul store in Hongdae. That's also a prime part of town in which to see everyday *hanbok*—from Leesle, Teterot Salon, Soosulhwa, AHHORN, or any of the other labels founded in recent years—as it's actually worn today. Not that an eye accustomed to the conspicuous looks available in Gyeongbokgung Palace-proximate rental shops would notice it right away, but everyday *hanbok* designers tend to go in for more muted hues (some of which were actually worn by non-aristocrats in the Joseon era), subtler decorative touches, and shapes easily combinable with articles of modern Western clothing.

Social media style influencers wear their favorite everyday *hanbok* pieces—not just *jeogori* and *chima*, the short jacket and long skirt, respectively, that define the classical female outfit, but also long *magoja* jackets, *baeja* vests, *jokduri* headdresses, and *norigae* knotted pendants—with everything from trench coats to blouses to jeans. It is the girl group NewJeans, incidentally, who most recently drew wide public attention to *hanbok* through K-pop. In the spring of 2024, they performed at the Korea Heritage Service's Korea on Stage event at Gyeongbokgung Palace wearing custom-designed costumes that reinterpreted the *dansam*, a kind of unlined *jeogori*; skirts like the pleated *seuran* and billowing *daeran*; and even *beoseon* socks. Such a spectacle would have been difficult to imagine in the Korea of 30 years ago, yet the clothing worn by NewJeans and their backup dancers underscored a continuity with at least a millennium and a half of Korean civilization.

NewJeans weren't the first K-pop stars to turn heads with looks inspired by *hanbok*, nor even the first girl group to do so. When it came out in the summer of 2020, the music video for Blackpink's "How You Like That" (which set a record with the number of views it racked up on YouTube within 24 hours of its release) presented the group's members in a stylistically dizzying variety of outfits, some of them created by the modern *hanbok* studio Danha, whose designs draw from classical artifacts and architecture. When they performed the song shortly thereafter on The Tonight Show Starring Jimmy Fallon in the United States, their skirts may have been far too short to qualify as *chima*—or, perhaps, even to qualify as skirts—but what caught even more eyes were the traditional motifs emblazoned on their (also-abbreviated) *jeogori*. Reportedly, Google experienced a surge in searches for "*hanbok*" as a result.

Headlining California's Coachella music and arts festival in 2023, Blackpink took the stage in full-length *hanbok* designed by the mother-daughter team Lee Il-soon and Chang Ha-eun. Although engineered to be removed before the dancing began, they weren't without attention to detail. Based on the *cheollik*, a type of overcoat worn by military officials in the Joseon period and the Goryeo before it, they incorporated brooches of *najeon chilgi*, or mother-of-pearl-inlaid lacquerware (about which more will be discussed in chapter 7) and different hand-embroidered traditional patterns for each member: *sipjangsaeng*, the ten symbols of longevity, for instance, or *dancheong*, the colors used to decorate wooden buildings such as those that comprise Gyeongbokgung Palace. As Chang explained in an interview, whereas older Koreans might find these elements a bit too familiar or associate them with excessive formality, younger ones see them as fresh enough to incorporate into their own wardrobes, thus bringing tradition back into mainstream culture.

That may go mostly for younger female Koreans, in this country where women tend to occupy the cultural vanguard, but many designers of everyday *hanbok* produce garments for men as well. In their own 2020 series of appearances on The Tonight Show, the boy-band-turned-cultural-phenomenon that is BTS opted to perform their song "Idol" entirely in *hanbok*-inspired outfits, just as Blackpink had with "How You Like That," Gyeongbokgung Palace featuring prominently in the background of their set. In the music video for "Idol," originally released in 2018, they'd worn *hanbok* just as naturally in some shots as they did school uniform blazers, cartoon character sweaters, and deliberately garish '70s-style suits in others: an unironic historical mix-and-match aesthetic that surely did its part to prime the interest of a generation in what would soon be defined as newtro.

The members of BTS were born in the 1990s, and their fans skew even younger; for them, the turn of the millennium holds just as much

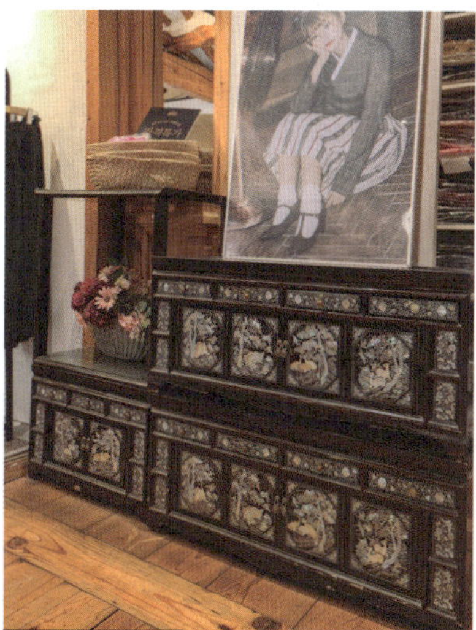

GLITTERING PRIZE
Najeon chilgi furniture is a popular—and apt—form of decoration for hanbok shops

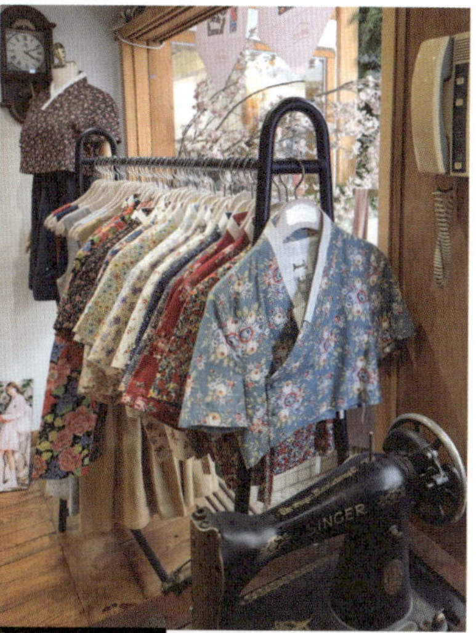

NEVER TOO LOUD
Riotously colorful patterns aren't just for grandma's generation anymore, especially when tailored in elegant cuts

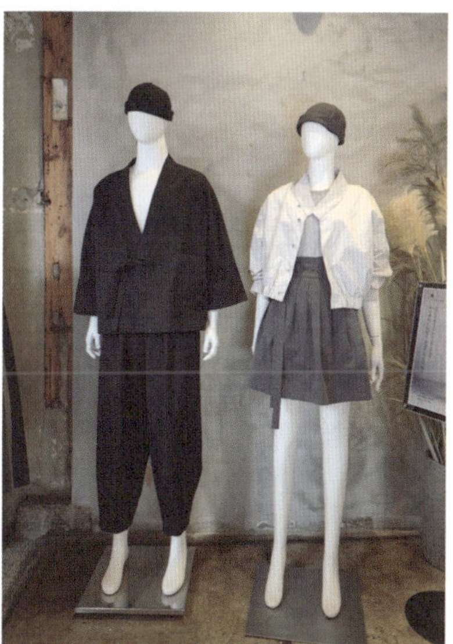

HEAD-TO-TOE MONOCHROME
There's no law against adapting hanbok to 21st-century minimalism

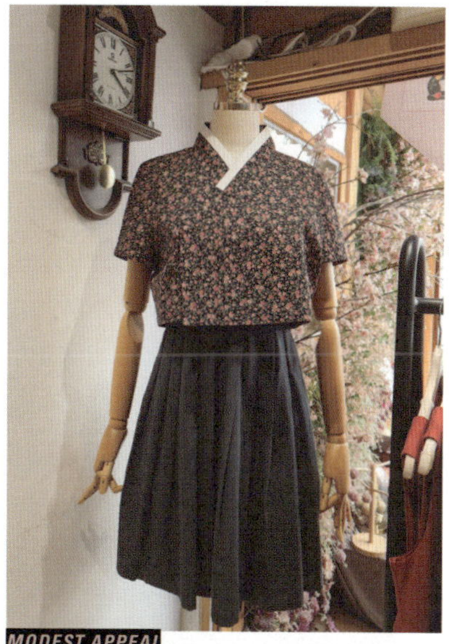

MODEST APPEAL
As dress styles on the streets of Seoul's youth-oriented neighborhoods grow ever more brazen, there's much to be said for subtler displays

retro fascination as the era of disco. This made itself memorably clear to me a few years ago, on a Korean travel company's group tour of Taiwan. One of the participants had brought along her teenage daughter, who turned up every day dressed like a member of the girl groups I remembered from the early 2000s, when I first became aware of Korean pop culture thanks to the emergence of early music download programs. As it manifested in Korea and elsewhere, "Y2K fashion"—cropped T-shirts, cargo pants, *cheongcheong* (or denim-on-denim)— seems to have become viable again for those too young to have worn it during its initial popularity. (Having been a teenager during Y2K myself, I do confess to mixed feelings about it.)

To an extent, the revival of retro looks has been a part of the worldwide fashion cycle since at least the 1970s. What puts a newtro twist on the story in Korea is the revival of vanished domestic brands. Take TIPI COSI, whose colorful casual wear made it the highest-profile youth-oriented Korean fashion label of the '90s, as did its endorsement by a variety of rising young stars of the day, including Seo Taiji and Boys, the group now widely considered the progenitors of K-pop. At its height, the brand operated more than 200 stores across Korea, a number that diminished during and after the 1997 Asian financial crisis (a period referred to in Korean as simply "IMF," in reference to the austerity conditions placed upon the local economy by the International Monetary Fund), and was finally reduced to zero amid further economic difficulties brought about by the Great Recession, which began in 2008.

It was in 2023 that TIPI COSI re-launched, targeted at not the grown-up Gen Xers who remember it from their teenage years, but their children: the "1020" cohort in their teens and 20s now, for whom its baggy, neon-hued, streetwear-inspired fashions would be a novelty. In any event, the revival failed to draw as much interest from the backward-looking youth of today as some had imagined it would, and it withdrew from the market within a year. There are several possible explanations of why TIPI COSI couldn't manage to ride the newtro wave: that its clothing didn't stand out on the much more crowded commercial landscape of the 2020s; that it relied more on tapping into nostalgia than on creative reinterpretation; or that, popular though the brand may have been in its time, it had never attained enough cultural cachet to grant it iconic status.

More successful, and perhaps more surprising, is the example of Fila, a brand that was actually founded in Italy. Originally a maker of underwear for the market proximate to the Italian Alps, it successfully shifted its focus in the 1970s to athletic wear intended for Europe more broadly, to that end securing an endorsement deal with tennis star Björn Borg. Later, in the late '80s and '90s, it grew larger still in the United States' footwear market by repeating its European strategy with American basketball players. Soon, Fila shoes were everywhere to be seen in Korea as well, but by the early 21st century, their chunky, often pure-white designs came to be associated with the dreaded *chonseureoum*—the quality of passé "village-likeness" discussed in this book's introduction—despite not being identifiably Korean.

At about that same time, Fila's financial situation had grown dire. With its once-popular shoes beginning to be dismissed as "dad kicks," in the parlance of sneaker enthusiasts, maintaining its costly endorsement deals became a burden. In 2003, an American hedge fund bought the company, but not Fila Korea, an independent operation that had licensed the brand for domestic use; four years later, the relatively robust Fila Korea acquired the ailing Fila brand and all its subsidiaries. It was thus well positioned to ride the wave that would arise in Korea a decade later: in 2017, its sales rose an astonishing 162 percent over the previous year. Now, Fila's sneakers, and especially the blunt Disruptor II model, with its distinctive serrated-looking sole, are widely regarded as the spearhead of the broader Korean retro fashion trends still underway.

They may be ugly shoes, but they've found a firm place in the Korean style lexicon as *eogeulli shujeu*—a term

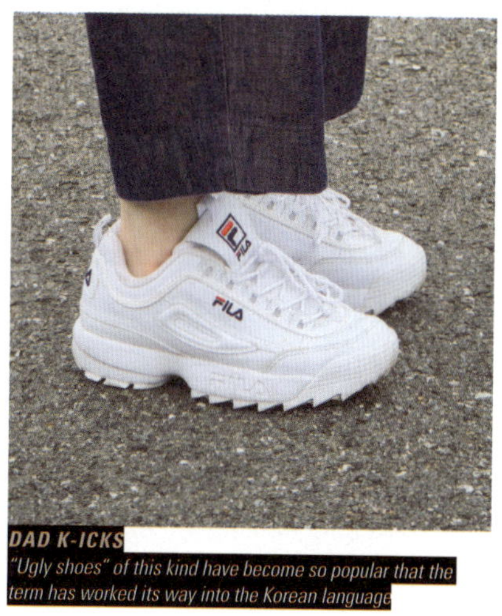

DAD K-ICKS
"Ugly shoes" of this kind have become so popular that the term has worked its way into the Korean language

that plainly means "ugly shoes." Whether Disruptor IIs that look unchanged since the '90s or newer but similarly ungainly offerings from high-fashion brands like Balenciaga, their sheer lack of sleekness or elegance has become, for young people in this country, a viable element to combine into outfits with things both newer and older. This habit of mixing and matching is true to the ethos of newtro, which—as distinct from retro—is less about reviving the styles of specific eras than about finding new contexts for various pieces of the past. Even so, a line has to be drawn somewhere: I've always cringed at the clash between the *hanbok* tourists wear and the modern footwear they usually insist on keeping on their feet, but *hanbok* with *eogeulli shujeu*—that's simply going too far.

The fashions of newtro reflect the postmodern condition in which 21st-century Korea finds itself, where an unprecedentedly wide variety of time periods and cultures have all come to feel immediately accessible. But this era is hardly the first in which Koreans have dressed in a manner that draws at once from East and West, new and old. The modernization process set underway during the aforementioned Gaehwagi, which spanned the last few decades of the 19th century and the beginning of the 20th, extended not only to Korea's infrastructure, economy, education, social structures, and form of government but also to the clothing seen on the streets of its cities—and in no city more vividly than Seoul. Having opened to trade and influence not just from the rest of Asia but from the West as well, Korea would never again be a "hermit kingdom."

Nor would Koreans ever again wear only *hanbok*. The late Gaehwagi gave way to the culturally heady 1920s and '30s, when short-haired "modern boys" and "new women" stepped out in local versions of the attire of Western ladies and gentlemen: long-sleeved velvet dresses, lace gloves, pearl necklaces, and jauntily angled hats on the former; three-piece suits with suspenders, bowties, and pocket watches on the latter. This was Korea's own "jazz age," and to extend the musical metaphor, just as PSY's viral song from 2012 made "Gangnam style" a household phrase, we can now also speak of "Gyeongseong style," into which MZ Generation members have looked to immerse themselves by visiting period costume rental shops. Such establishments have been popping up in not just Ikseon-dong, but also other areas across the country that have retained architectural traces of the early 20th century,

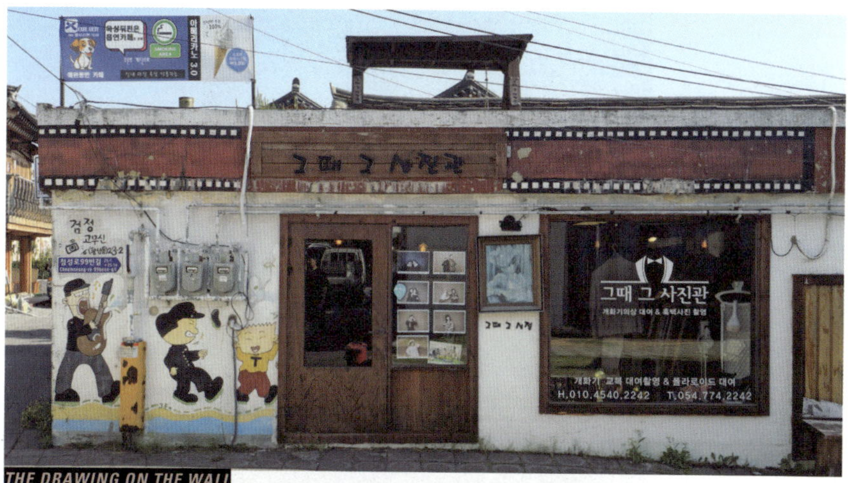

THE DRAWING ON THE WALL
Cheerful murals have been key to revitalizing down-at-the-heels neighborhoods all across Korea

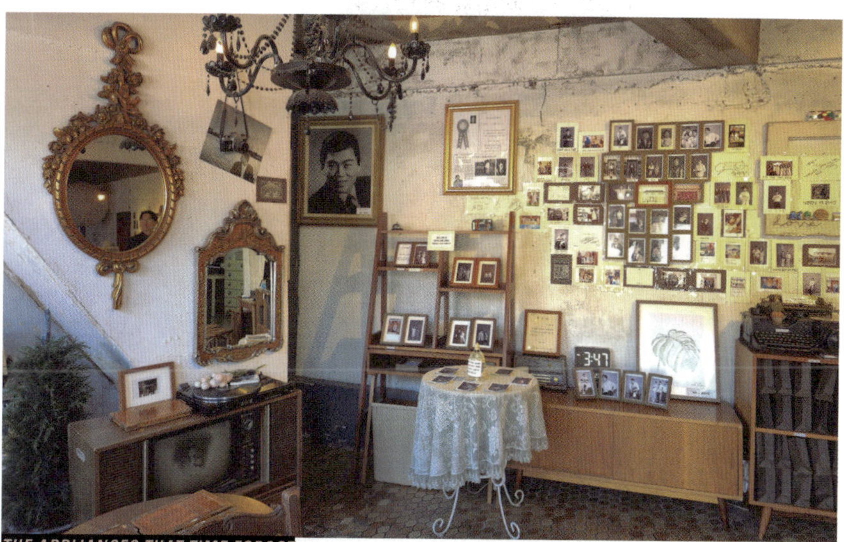

THE APPLIANCES THAT TIME FORGOT
In newtro interior design, obsolete televisions and typewriters go nicely with even older mirrors and chandeliers

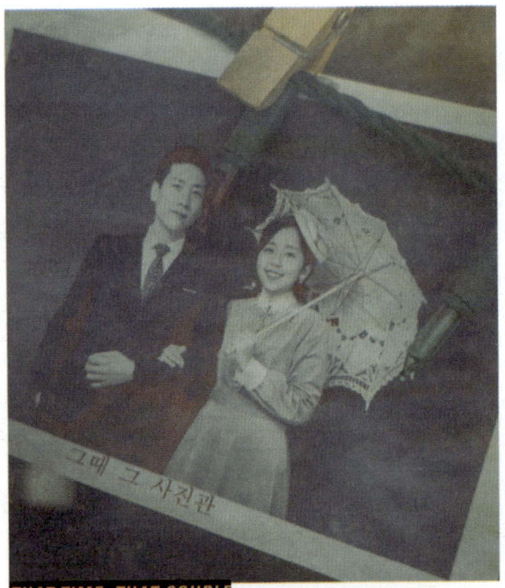

THAT TIME, THAT COUPLE
The colonial period may now be considered a dark time, but its trappings are enjoyed in costumed studio shoots

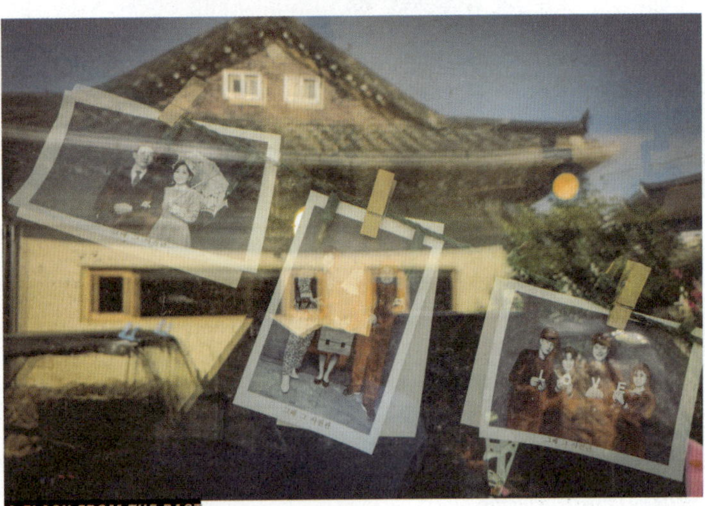

A FLASH FROM THE PAST
Photographic time travel isn't just about romance; friends and family take yetnal sajin of their own

like Jeonju Hanok Village and the historic southeastern city of Gyeongju.

These locations share the all-important quality of Instagrammability, but they've also proven popular for more formal kinds of photography, especially pre-wedding portraits. Their range of possible concepts has become quite diverse, in style, of course, but also the time periods from which they draw: no longer is it a surprise to visit a couple's home and see a large framed portrait of man and wife wearing Joseon-era or Gaehwagi attire in a modern style in what's clearly 21st-century Seoul. As for the wedding itself, Korean tastes have diversified; no longer does everyone opt simply to buy a package at a "wedding hall," those full-service, highly regimented providers of a brief ceremony followed by a somewhat more leisurely buffet. Whether their faux-European ostentation, at times accented by lasers and fog machines, will one day be incorporated by the smaller venues now specializing in "newtro weddings" remains to be seen. Another option is to go further back in time by booking at the Korean Folk Village in Yongin, a large complex that recreates rural Joseon life. The last time I went down there, I happened to see one such wedding ceremony underway, and the groom was a Westerner, dressed in *hanbok* and all. With international enthusiasm for Korean culture at a high point, it's not even unheard of for a wholly non-Korean bride and groom to wear *hanbok* at the altar in their own country.

An international "K-wedding" industry surely has growth potential, but it will have a long way to go before catching up to the juggernaut of K-beauty, given the number of foreign shoppers now flocking to Seoul primarily or wholly to purchase local cosmetics. They descend on areas like Myeongdong, where nationwide chains like Olive Young (which could be described as a Korean version of American Sephora, albeit with a wider, faster-changing selection of products) have set up extra-large branches and staffed them with clerks fluent in English, Chinese, and Japanese. K-beauty brands like The Face Shop and TIRTIR have put out elegantly designed and explicitly newtro-branded box sets, while Romand went so far as to create one with the theme of Anne of Green Gables, who as "Red-Haired Anne" has been a beloved animated character for generations here in Korea, all packaged to resemble a VHS tape. Even Gompyo, the flour brand with the polar bear logo discussed in the previous chapter, has, in collaboration with SWANICOCO, put out its own makeup base, cleansing foam, and sunscreen. This all makes sense not just because of the Korean cosmetics industry's responsiveness to trends, but also because of its connections to a deeper kind of "newtro"; the emphasis evident in the industry's marketing efforts is not only on scientific and technological developments but also the resonances between traditional Korean culture and health, natural ingredients, and slower, more *yeoyuroun* rhythms of life that now seem so enviable this deep into modernity. Whatever the profitability of O'Sulloc, for example, the Jeju Island-based tea company established by Suh Sung-hwan, founder of K-beauty giant Amorepacific, the connections to newtro can hardly be bad for the brand.

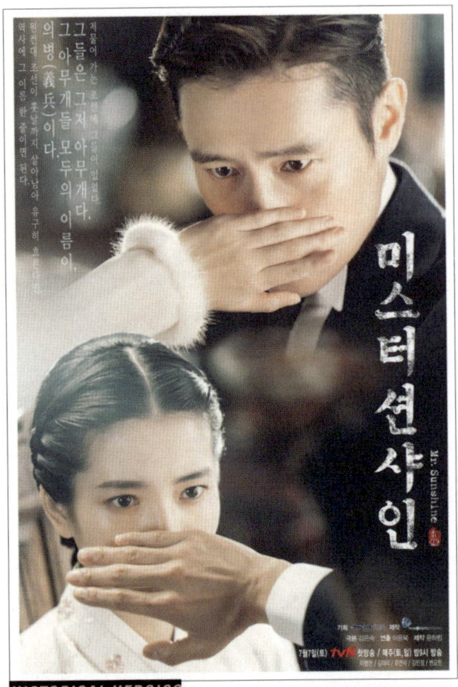

HISTORICAL HEROICS
The hit television drama Mr. Sunshine popularized turn-of-the-century gaehwagi style, though some accused it of romanticizing the colonial period.

Old and new currents of Korean fashion and beauty run together at many of the country's *sajingwan*, the photo studios mentioned in chapter 2, which now also cater to the revival of interest in the aesthetic of urban Korea as it was a century or so ago. Some maintain their own libraries of era-appropriate costumes, offering their visitors the chance to replicate the kind of portraits for which their great- or even great-great-grandparents' generation would have sat. But whatever the charms of that time, it was also one of Japanese colonial rule, an era of Korean history whose romanticization has drawn criticism, given the potential for its upper-class splendor to overshadow its widespread suffering and depredations in cultural memory. Perhaps that explains the popularity of one Gyeongju rental shop whose customers can pose, outfitted like a freedom fighter—rifle and all—in front of an oversized Taegeukgi.

Korea's struggle for independence has also been a common theme for films and television dramas set between the early Gaehwagi and the end of the Second World War. The prime example of the newtro era has to be *Mr. Sunshine*, which aired on the cable network tvN in the summer and fall of 2018 (and was subsequently distributed worldwide by Netflix). Its highly aestheticized story centers on a perilous romance between a Korean-American U.S. Marine Corps captain and a young noblewoman-turned-freedom fighter during the years preceding Japan's official annexation of Korea, an underused setting in dramas by comparison to the earlier Joseon era or the actual colonial period itself. Having ended its run as the third highest-rated series ever broadcast on Korean cable television, Mr. Sunshine bears more responsibility than any other single production for the popularization of dress styles from the late 19th and early 20th century.

In France, that same span of history is called *la Belle Époque*, a phrase that evokes economic prosperity, artistic and technological flowering, and thoroughgoing civilizational optimism. Although these qualities were hardly absent from contemporary Korea, its colonial status prevents the period from being considered truly equivalent. I once read a Korean blogger's argument that Korea's *Belle Époque* was, in fact, the 1990s, when the country was flourishing after the end of its military dictatorship, and the possibilities for its future seemed limitless—at least until the IMF had to step in. Korea may have been poorer in that decade than today, the blogger granted, but it enjoyed a freedom from the kind of existential anxiety that besets it now. "Those were good times," some Koreans have said, not without a note of surprise, while reflecting on the '90s—or, even more so, while seeing them reflected on television.

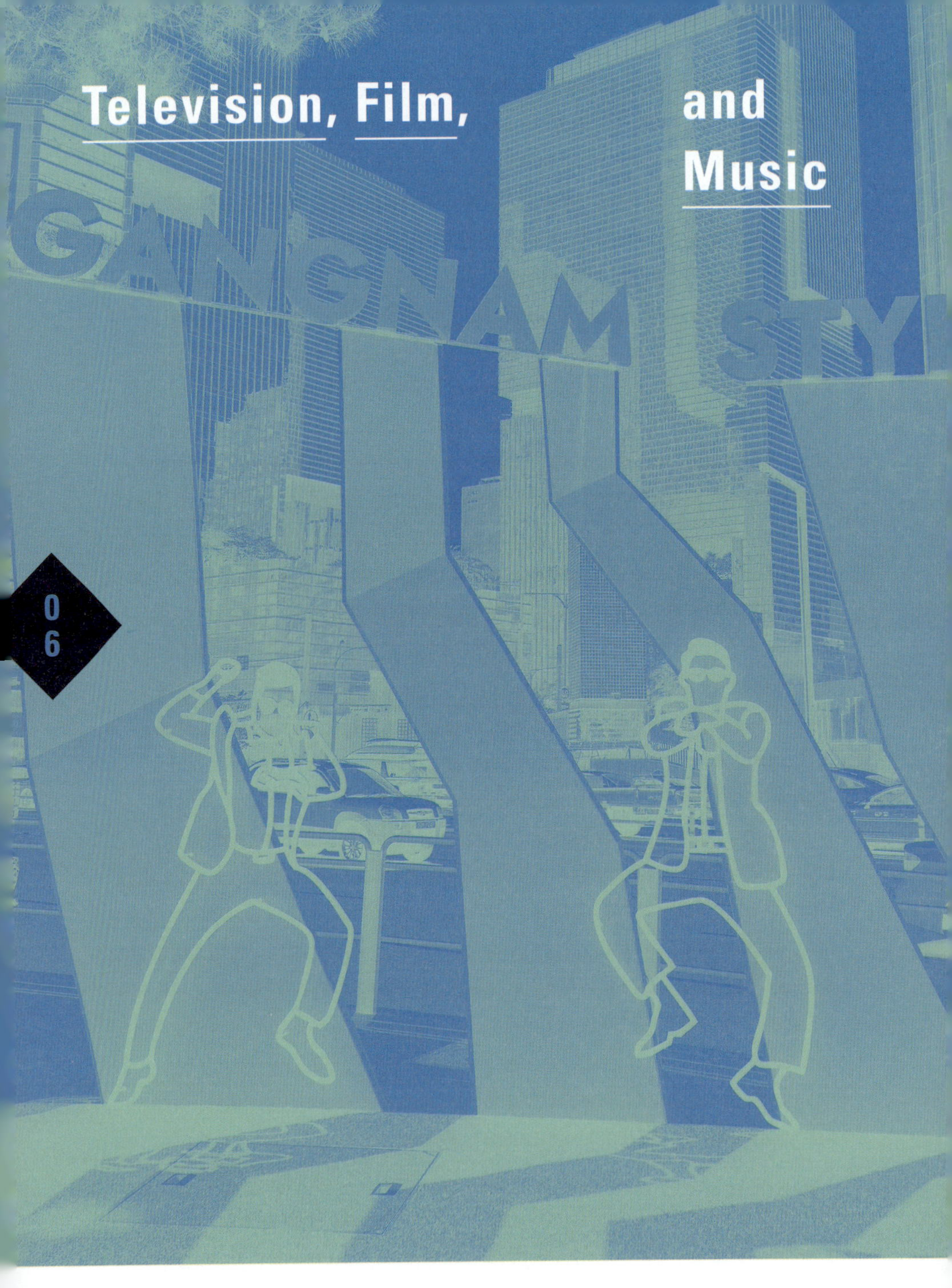

Television, Film, and Music

REPLY SERIES

MYMY

CITY POP

GIMBAB RECORDS

GANGNAM STYLE

MINYO ROCK

TIGER IS COMING

SEOPYEONJE

TROT

Not even the oldest among Mr. Sunshine's viewers could have lived through its time period, but that wasn't the case at all with tvN's earlier drama, *Reply 1997*, much of which takes place in the titular year. For many Koreans who watched the series when it was first broadcast in 2012, the era it recreates was the one in which they came of age, and thus one they remembered with a special vividness. Faced with such high expectations of authenticity, *Reply 1997* exceeded them, drawing acclaim for its recreation of both the general feeling and specific details of Korean life in the mid-to-late-1990s, right down to the burgeoning K-pop idol culture in which its young protagonists participate as fans. The series' success is now seen as the starting point of Koreans' large-scale interest in things retro from their own country, which would evolve into newtro culture over the following years.

More immediately, it stoked demand for a sequel: *Reply 1994* premiered in 2013, with a narrative oscillating between the present day and a time slightly deeper into the past than the first series. From its own brief but eventful period in Korean history, the series incorporates everything from the catastrophic collapse of the Sampoong Department Store in Gangnam to the rise of Seo Taiji and Boys, the group mentioned in the previous chapter as endorsers of the youth fashion label TIPI COSI. Nor would it have been possible to exclude the TIPI COSI label itself; every Korean viewer who had lived through the '90s themselves would recognize its logo on the two characters' long-sleeved his-and-hers T-shirts, or *keopeul ti* (literally "couple tee [shirt]"). (The brands may have changed in the past three decades,

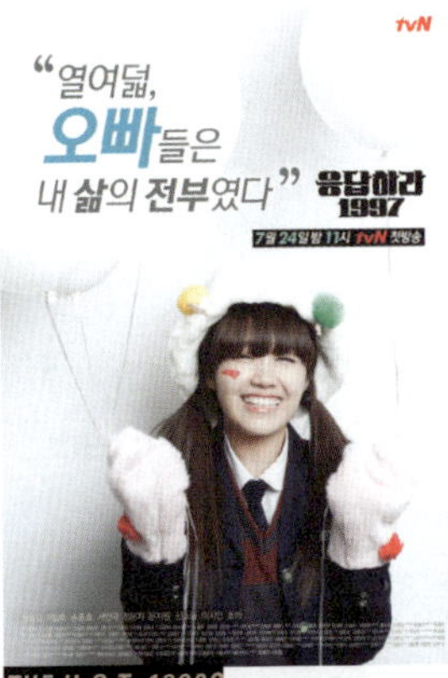

THE H.O.T. 1990S

When it debuted in 2012, the drama Reply 1997 brought back viewers' memories of their own schooldays — and the pop music they loved back then

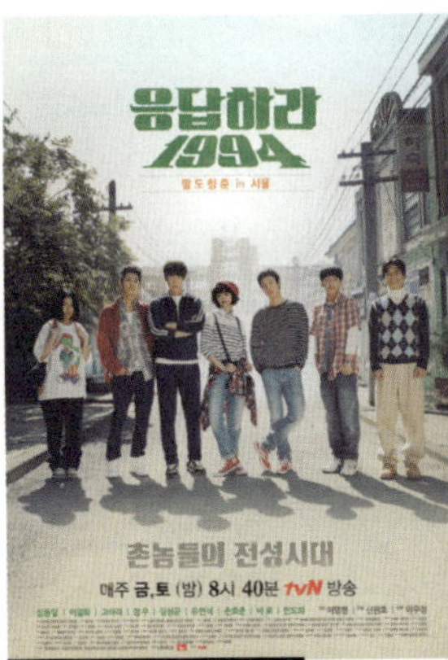

BRIGHT COLLEGE DAYS

The second series Reply 1994, aired in 2013, follows a group of students in the heyday of Yonsei University's neighborhood of Sinchon

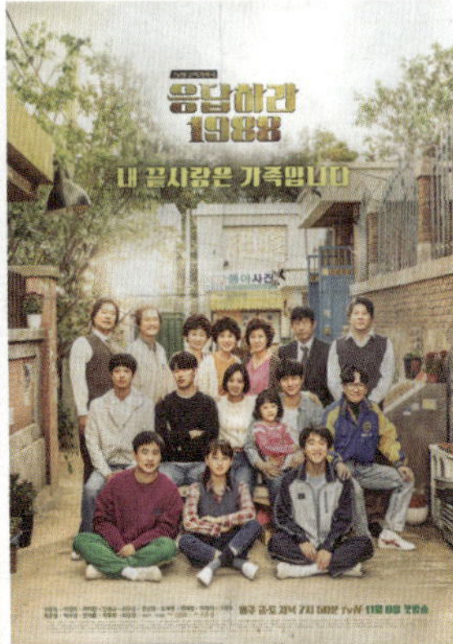

THAT 80S SHOW

The third and final series, Reply 1988, was the biggest hit of all, and has been described as a precipitating factor in the newtro boom

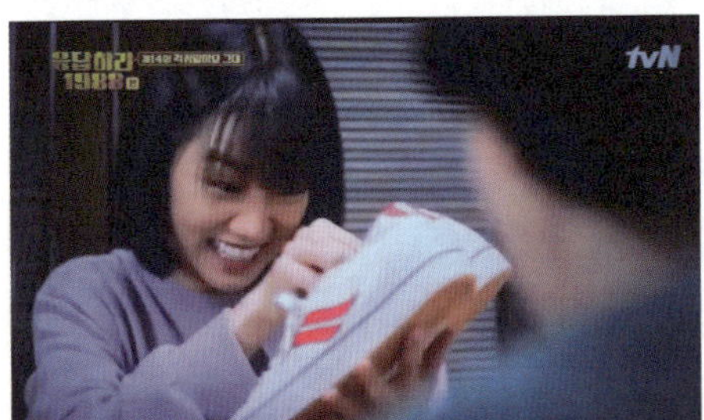

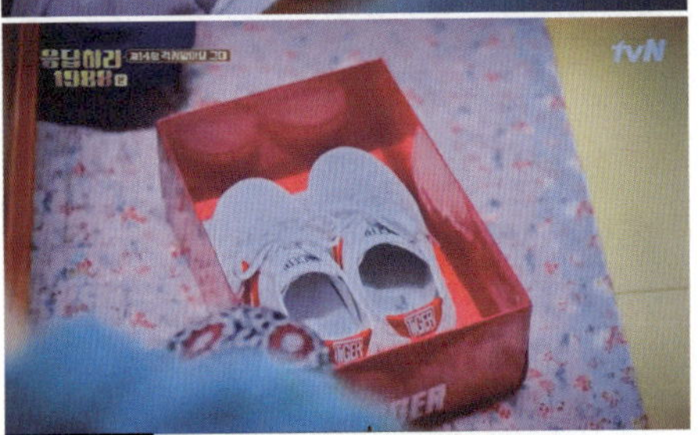

NEW SHOES

In the 80s, nothing felt quite like a fresh pair of Tigers, and Reply 1988's writers knew it

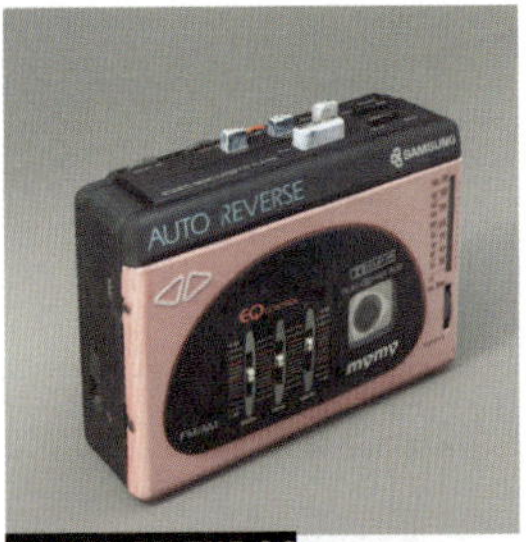

TUNES ON THE GO

The Mymy, Samsung's answer to the Sony Walkman, was one of the first electronic gadgets Korean teenagers couldn't do without

but such matching "couple looks" are still often seen today in Korea, much to the surprise of visitors from the West.)

Throughout *Reply 1997* and *Reply 1994*, the series' creators, director Shin Won-ho and writer Lee Woo-jung, had been steadily raising their own bar of historical detail. That ambition reached its peak in *Reply 1988*, which aired in 2015 and 2016, evoking its most distant period yet through not just the clothes worn by its cast of young neighborhood friends—the raglan shirts, denim jackets, berets, horn-rimmed glasses, and sneakers from domestic brands like Arthis, Cavallo, and Tiger—but also their forms of family and neighborhood life, the media they consume, and the music they listen to. Its storyline makes use of the Summer Olympic Games in Seoul, an event regarded as South Korea's official debut on the stage of the developed world, as well as the country's transition to a democratic political government and the political protests that continued thereafter.

The *Reply* series may well have primed the viewing public's appetite for more recent historical productions, including less lighthearted ones like Jang Joon-hwan's *1987: When the Day Comes*. That film came out in 2017, thirty years after the events it dramatizes—events that shaped the June Democratic Uprising and led the South Korean government to adopt democratic reforms. Of some importance to its story is a Mymy, an early Walkman-like personal cassette player from Samsung, on which a teenage character listens to the song "Hidden Road" by Yoo Jae-ha. While the Mymy was indeed an important piece of consumer electronics at the time, Yoo's *Because I Love You*, the album that contains "Hidden Road," wasn't released until August of 1987, after the time period covered by the movie. Jang has acknowledged the anachronism, explaining his decision to use the song anyway as a matter of dramatic effectiveness, thematic appropriateness, and personal taste.

It certainly suits my personal taste: not just a singer but a multi-talented musician and composer, Yoo Jae-ha remains my favorite Korean recording artist, despite the fact that his death in a car wreck in the fall of 1987 meant that he never put out a second album. Had he lived, Korean pop music could well have taken a slightly different direction in the 1990s and 2000s. In recent years, some musicians here—many of them born in those same decades—have crafted their own such alternative musical futures by using the sounds of Yoo's time and the years thereafter in combination with modern technology. Take, for example, the versatile singer, composer, and producer Park Moonchi, whose dissatisfaction with the similarity of new songs to one another led her to discover a freshness in older ones, and subsequently to identify herself closely with the newtro movement.

Given her dedication to not just reinterpreting the sounds of the recent past but fusing them with elements of the present, it came as no surprise when Park Moonchi participated as a producer on a 2021 EP by the Japanese actress and singer Yukika. Despite her singing in the Korean language, Yukika's music is some of the most credible in the ongoing revival of "city pop," a genre that originated in the economically high-flying Japan of the 1980s. City pop has become known worldwide over the past 15 to 20 years thanks to YouTube, which has made instantly accessible recordings that had once fallen into obscurity even in Japan. (Perhaps the most notable international example of city pop's influence on non-Japanese music is Canadian singer-songwriter The Weeknd's sampling of Aran Tomoko's 1983 song "Midnight Pretenders" on his "Out of Time," which was also a hit in Korea when it came out in 2022.)

Lush and energetic, but not without its shades of reflectiveness, city pop has proven so inspiring to this country's newtro-minded musicians of the MZ Generation and younger that "Korean city pop" has begun to gain recognition as a subgenre unto itself. Bands like Adoy or singer-songwriters like KIMSAN, both active since the late 2010s, have recorded

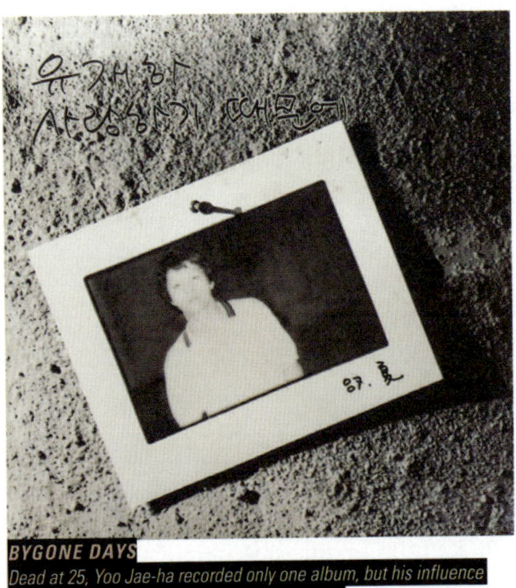

BYGONE DAYS
Dead at 25, Yoo Jae-ha recorded only one album, but his influence reverberates through Korean ballads to this day

almost exclusively in a city pop style. Some performers have also paid homage to the music Korea was making during city pop's heyday: when Stella Jang (a member, along with Park Moonchi, of the newtro concept girl group CSVC) covered Yoon Sooil's hit "It's Beautiful" in 2018, it came out sounding, in some respects, even more '80s-like than the 1984 original. Around the same time, beats and electronic textures of a similar vintage appeared in the work of artists with one foot in the indie world and the other in the mainstream, like IU and Baek Yerin.

Songs by full-on K-pop acts like TWICE and SHINee soon came to incorporate city pop-like sounds, or to show the general influence of newtro, an influence the girl group DIA made explicit in 2019 by putting out an EP titled, simply, *Newtro*. The following year, it could be heard even more strongly on singles like "We Ride"

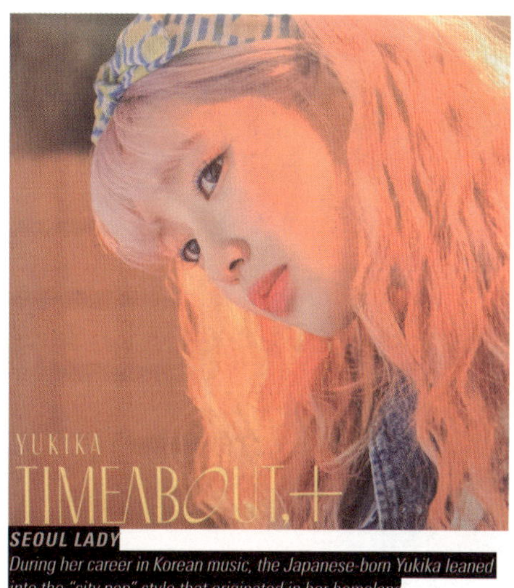

SEOUL LADY
During her career in Korean music, the Japanese-born Yukika leaned into the "city pop" style that originated in her homeland

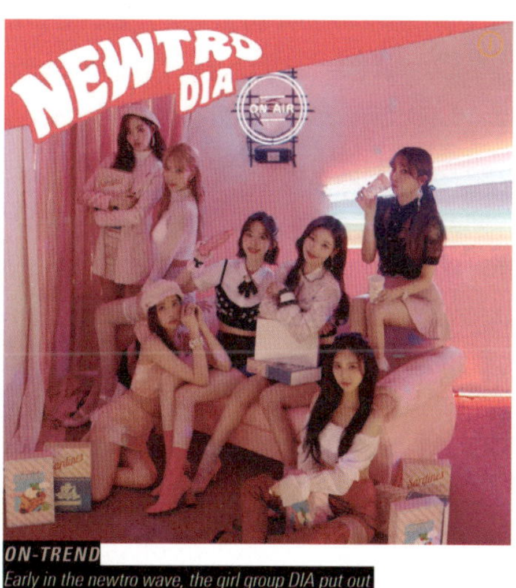

ON-TREND
Early in the newtro wave, the girl group DIA put out an EP named after it

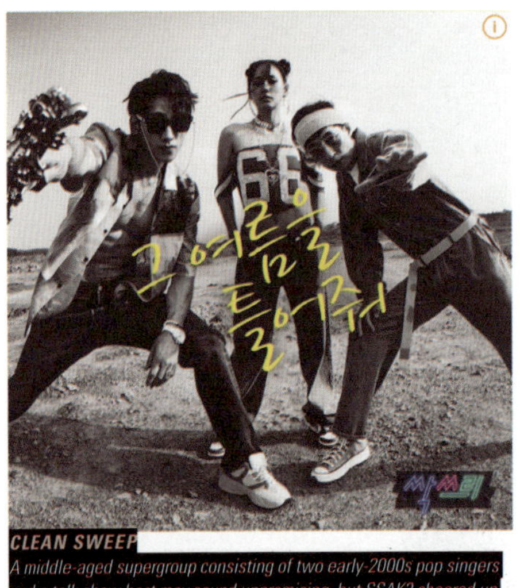

CLEAN SWEEP
A middle-aged supergroup consisting of two early-2000s pop singers and a talk show host may sound unpromising, but SSAK3 cheered up listeners during the pandemic

by Brave Girls (now BB Girls) and "Lovesick Girls" by Blackpink (whose use of *hanbok* was discussed in the previous chapter). Such was the fascination in 2020 with musical trends from before the turn of the millennium that the charts could be topped by SSAK3, an unlikely one-off supergroup consisting of '90s girl group star Lee Hyo-ri, 2000s idol singer Rain, and Korea's most popular television host, Yoo Jae-suk. During that COVID-19-dominated summer of 2020, SSAK3 paid humorous homage to the carefree sensibility of the kind of hip-hop-adjacent pop music that topped the charts in the '90s.

SSAK3 also released a mini-album as a CD, a digital download, and even a cassette tape. Long assumed obsolete, the humble cassette has attracted a generation of analog-curious listeners who'd never before had the chance to hit a rewind button. SHINee, in perhaps the earliest of K-pop's attempts to exploit this trend, put out an album on cassette in the fall of 2016. Four years later, BTS made a bigger splash by releasing their disco-inspired single "Dynamite" in the same format, which no doubt motivated members of the vast ARMY (as the group's fans collectively refer to themselves) to dig their parents' disused Mymys out of the closet. Independent music shops like city pop-oriented Gimbab Records in Hongdae—that same neighborhood where you might well see 20-somethings in *hanbok*—now sell tapes alongside their selection of vinyl records, an even more abundantly revived format. (I took note of how far the trend had gone when I passed a Hongdae coffee shop that rented out personal cassette players by the

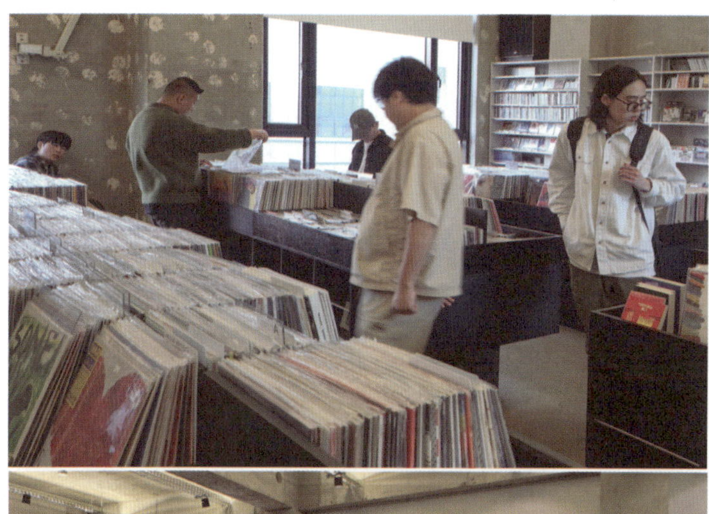

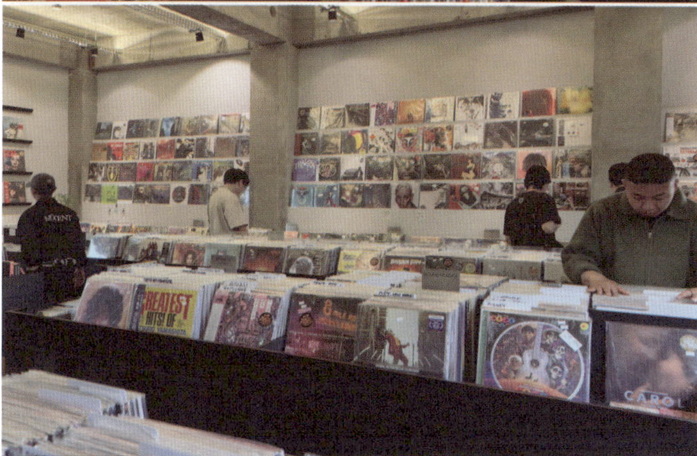

CRATE-DIGGING
Record shops were dying in Korea, as in most countries,
but then made a comeback in a more curated, specialist form.

hour, city pop tapes included.)

In the early 2000s, Japan became the first country in which Korean pop culture cultivated an enthusiastic foreign audience, sending such flagships across the East Sea as the television drama *Winter Sonata* and the singer BoA. Those were just two phenomena involved in the first phases of the "Korean wave," or Hallyu, which went on to spread across Asia, and within a decade it was at least lapping the shores of the West. Due to its viral music video filled with bizarre (but to Koreans, immediately recognizable) imagery satirizing life in the nouveau-riche parts of Seoul, PSY's 2012 novelty hit "Gangnam Style" swept the world—including the United States, which to that point had seemed impervious to Hallyu's musical charms. Even today, despite the inroads made by the likes of Blackpink and BTS (six of whose songs have topped the Billboard 100 chart), a suspicion of K-pop lingers throughout the West in general, and the U.S. in particular, where some see its direction by producers and entertainment companies as giving it an unappealingly manufactured quality.

To Western listeners who prize a sense of authenticity in the foreign cultural products they consume, K-pop can also sound insufficiently Korean. Hence, perhaps, the interest raised in 2017 when an act called SsingSsing performed on Tiny Desk Concerts, a video series produced by the U.S.' National Public Radio network. SsingSsing's music has been described as "*minyo* rock," *minyo* meaning Korean folk songs. (The word shares its first syllable, *min*, which refers to a people, with *minhwa*, the term for the folk art discussed in chapter 3.) However, it could just as well be called *minyo* glam rock, considering the extravagant androgyny employed by lead singer Lee Hee-moon. That would seem to conflict with the received image of Korea as a conservative society—still believed, in some quarters, as late as the 2010s—but in fact, it draws from tradition: Lee has compared his performances to the folk religion rites still led by Korea's predominantly female *mudang* (or shamans).

Lee's singing styles may be age-old—one of them, the regional *Gyeonggi sori*, is even officially designated as an Intangible Heritage of Gyeonggi-do—but SsingSsing's instruments are standard equipment for rock-and-roll: electric guitar, drums, bass. Coreyah, another Korean band featured on Tiny Desk Concerts,

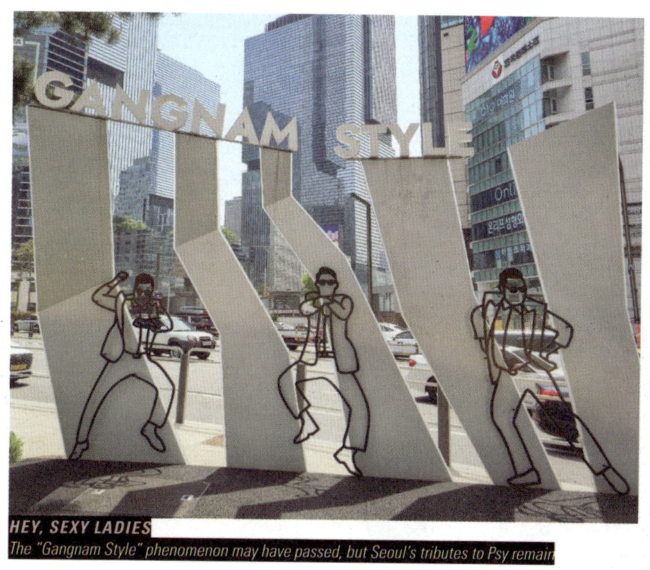

HEY, SEXY LADIES
The "Gangnam Style" phenomenon may have passed, but Seoul's tributes to Psy remain

accompanies such universally recognizable pieces of musical gear with others that are much more culturally specific. When they appeared on that series, they gave many of their foreign viewers their first chance to hear the bamboo flutes known in Korean as the *daegeum*, *sogeum*, and *tungso*. What must have looked and sounded most exotic, however, was the *geomungo*, a six-string box zither (sometimes called a "black zither") used in Korea since the time of the Goguryeo kingdom (37 BCE– 668 CE). (Korean viewers, for their part, registered their surprise at seeing a video from NPR with a box of *mikseu keopi* visible in the frame.)

The *geomungo* is one of the two most recognizable traditional Korean stringed instruments, the other being the *gayageum*. Introduced in the 6th century, the *gayageum* has at least 12 finger-plucked strings that make brighter, higher suited modern melodic lines. Unlike the *geomungo*, which was primarily heard in Confucian courts in its day, the *gayageum* was a popular instrument used in a wide variety of social contexts, including performances of folk music for common people. Both of

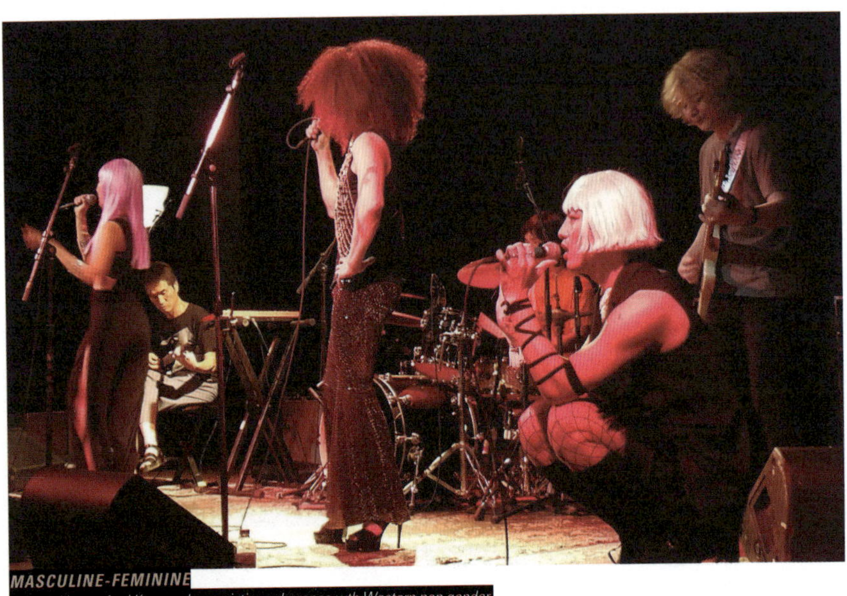

them have proven adaptable to 21st-century musical genres. Bands like Jambinai,
Black String, and Tori Ensemble have incorporated the *geomungo* into their heavy
rock, jazz, and avant-garde sounds, while the *gayageum* has been brought into
new contexts by solo players like Jung Mina, who's known as the instrument's first
singer-songwriter, and the U.S.-based Luna Lee, who has gone viral with her videos
covering classic rock songs by Jimi Hendrix, Dire Straits, and AC/DC.

Much like *hanbok*, the *geomungo* and *gayageum* have found their way
into K-pop, first in the work of several boy bands. In 2014, Topp Dogg used the
gayageum on "Arario," promoting the song with a video loaded with classical
Korean imagery. Three years later, VIXX put out an even more gayageum-forward
single called "Shangri-La." In 2019, ONEUS made not just one music video laden
with art, architecture, and accoutrements straight from the Joseon period for their
own *gayageum*-featuring song "Lit," but also a special "taekwondo version," with

dance moves evocative of that Korean martial art. Going solo in 2020 under the name Agust D, BTS member Suga released the rap song "Daechwita," which takes its name from a form of traditional royal military music sampled in its construction. Its video resembles a quick-cut Joseon drama, albeit with such newtro elements as a 1990 Hyundai Grandeur drifting in a palace courtyard.

A *geomungo* solo figures prominently in a version of "I'm a B" from 2021 by singer Hwasa, who rose to fame with the girl group Mamamoo. Blackpink's "Pink Venom," released the following year, opens with a *geomungo* passage played in the video by member Jisoo herself. These traditional instruments stand out in such an ultra-modern musical context, but for a purer sense of the potential in the hands of young musicians, listen to the work of acclaimed *geomungo*-and-*gayageum* duo Dal:um, much of which would sound familiar to Koreans of centuries past—at least on the surface. The interplay of Hwang Hyeyoung on the *geomungo* and Ha Suyean on the *gayageum* produces compositions quite unlike the canon of *gugak* (or Korean classical music), though they do draw from it: their most recent album, *Coexistence*, contains their own interpretation of *Suyeonjangjigok*, a Joseon-era court song that was once played for the longevity of the king.

Perhaps no adaptation of a piece of classical Korean music has caused as much of a sensation as "Tiger Is Coming." It was the lead single from *Sugungga*, the 2020 debut album by Leenalchi, a band whose sound has the newtro characteristic of using multiple pasts at once: in this case, hybridizing disco and *pansori*, a form of musical storytelling that took shape in the 17th century. Registered not only as a piece of Korea's National Intangible Cultural Heritage but also as one of UNESCO's Masterpieces of the Oral and Intangible Heritage of Humanity, *pansori* has become a great source of national pride. Yet it had a much lower profile as recently as the early 1990s, before it was brought back to public consciousness by the unexpected domestic success—and, just as important, positive arthouse reception abroad—of the film *Seopyeonje*.

Directed by Im Kwon-taek, one of Korea's longest-working and most prolific filmmakers, *Seopyeonje* portrays a makeshift family of itinerant *pansori* performers in a fast-Westernizing mid-20th-century Korea that offers them ever more scant means of making a living. Its story, and especially the character of Song-hwa, a young woman blinded for her art, did much to associate *pansori*—despite the happy endings of the intact *madang*—with the deep-seated, historically inflicted sorrow known as *han,* one of a suite of emotions held to be unique to the Korean people. As interpreted by Leenalchi, however, it feels closer to *heung,* a kind of spontaneous collective joy. The same could be said of the *pansori*-inflected songs by SsingSsing (in which Leenalchi's founding bassist and drummer both played), or the frequent collaborations between Korean reggae band NST & The Soul Sauce and famed *pansori* vocalist Kim Yul-hee.

These and other projects have done their part to let younger generations hear *Joseon*-period music as more *meotjyeo* than *chonseureoweo,* to put it in the terms laid out in this book's introduction. A slightly harder sell is *teuroteu,* or trot, a style of popular song that dates back to the Japanese colonial period. In fact, its signature faintly militaristic two-beat rhythms, vibrato and "voice-breaking" *kkeok-kki* singing techniques, and unabashedly sentimental lyrics have enough in common with the Japanese ballad style known as *enka* to have sparked a few controversies since then. But like most foreign cultural forms that have taken root here, trot has been thoroughly Koreanized, to the point of incorporating instruments like the *gayageum,* the *janggu* drum, and the fiddle-like two-stringed *haegeum,* while its songs have long dealt with such culturally specific themes as the division of the Korean Peninsula into North and South after World War II.

It was during the postwar decades that trot steadily gained popularity, reaching its zenith in mainstream entertainment in the 1970s. From then on, however, though its star singers have always drawn big crowds—albeit composed of fans not much younger than themselves—the music itself came to be regarded as ever more old-fashioned. This was perhaps inevitable in the age of Seo Taiji and Boys, to say nothing of the K-pop idols who succeeded them. When I initially got to Korea in the mid-2010s, I first came to know trot as the music senior citizens would blast out of their portable speakers while cycling along the Han River. Yet soon its revival among the relatively young would be underway, owing in part to the women's singing competition show *Miss Trot,* which premiered on TV Chosun in 2019, followed by the male version, *Mr. Trot,* the next year.

With their penchant for loud colors and sequins, classic trot singers have never been known for their understated elegance. But even the most garish

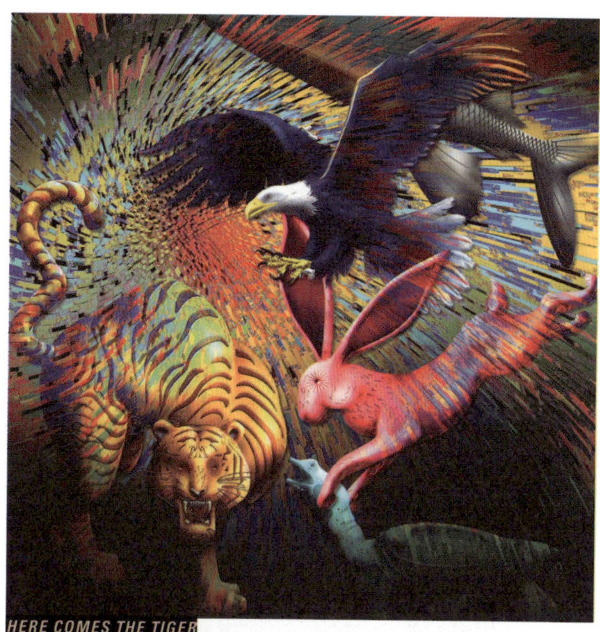

HERE COMES THE TIGER
With their debut album, Leenalchi brought the pansori story *Sugungga* to a wider audience than it had ever reached before

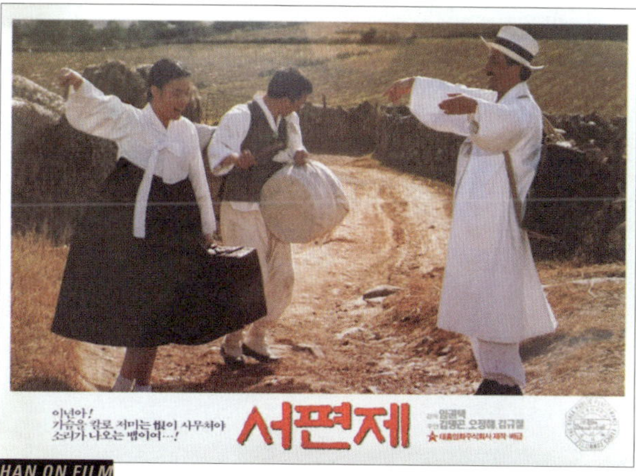

HAN ON FILM
A surprise art-house hit, Im Kwon-taek's *Seopyeonje* generated a good deal of curiosity about pansori among not just foreigners, but also Koreans themselves

aspects of their look, and even the most synthetic-sounding electronic touches in their music, have become unironically viable newtro material. A new generation of trot singers, most famously the balladeer Lim Young-woong, has shown an inclination to hybridize that music with other popular genres, and even to inject it with the energy of K-pop. More recently, 2024 brought the unprecedented launch of a trot boy band, created in a collaboration between TV Chosun and SM Entertainment, the agency whose acts were on the vanguard of Hallyu (and which, true to form, has included one foreign member, in this case from Japan). Whether Mytro, as they're called, can popularize trot outside Korea remains to be seen, but never has there been a more potentially receptive global audience.

Like any art form, music benefits greatly from being experienced in the right context. Trot must have resonated with the joys and sorrows felt by Koreans living through the '50s, '60s, and '70s, and to that same degree it came to sound irrelevant to their children and grandchildren coming of age in what was practically a different country by the end of the century. At this point, even the most bubblegum-inclined members of the MZ Generation may have begun to feel alienated by the relentlessly adolescent-focused—and, it must be said, relatively narrow in a stylistic sense—world of K-pop. Trot, if not in its original form then perhaps in its newtro revival, could well have a place in their lives. But what's the right place in which to listen to it? While one can encounter trot anywhere in Korea, I personally find that it always sounds best in a *dabang*.

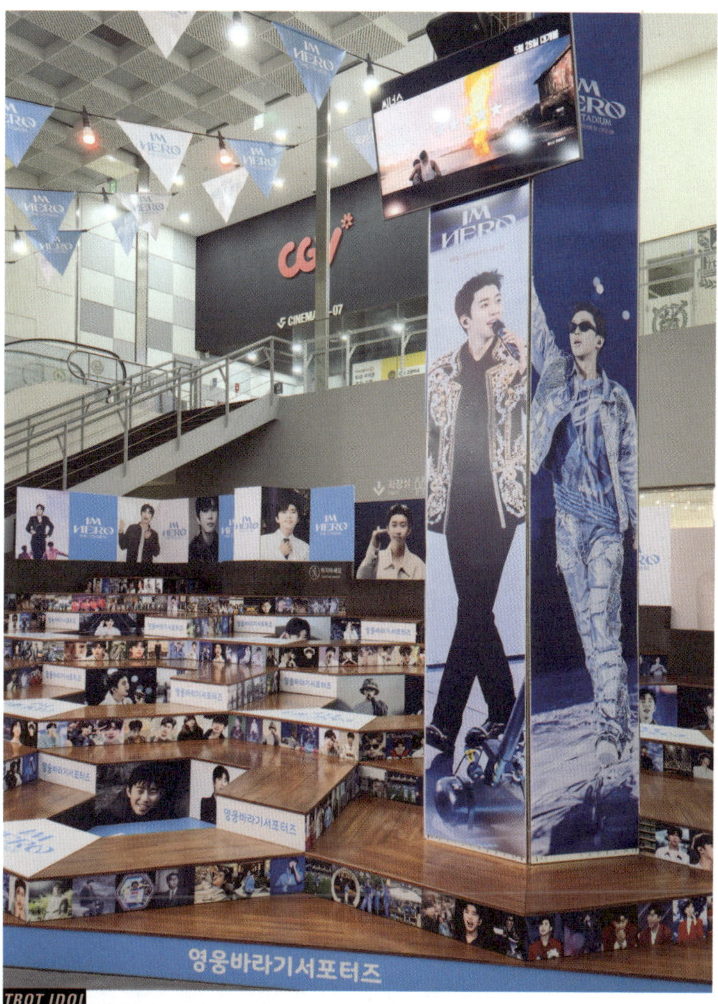

TROT IDOL
A new generation of singers like Lim Young-woong has begun to blur the line between K-pop and genres that preceded it

Architecture and Interior Design

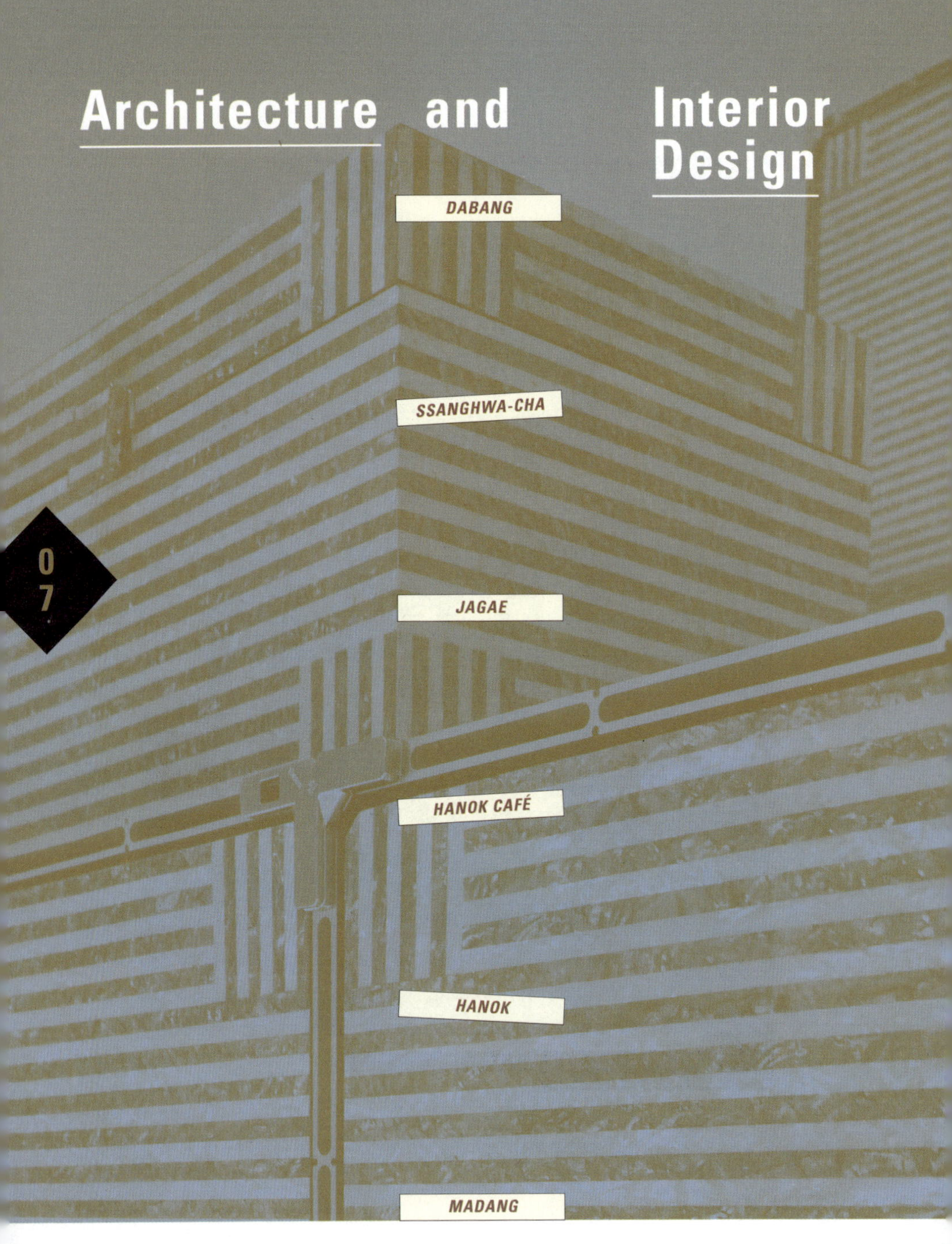

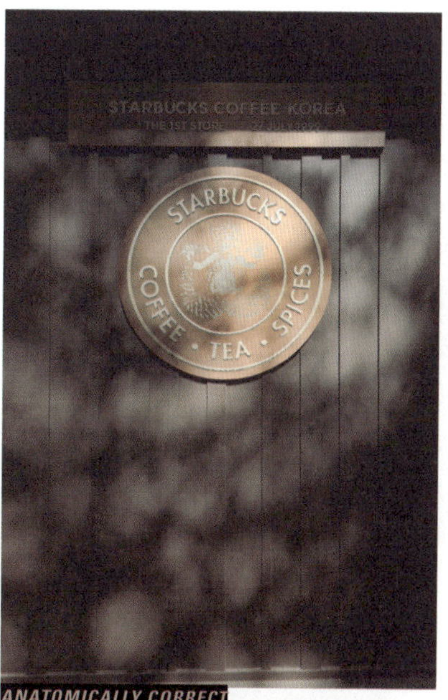

ANATOMICALLY CORRECT
Korea's very first Starbucks now bears a commemorative plaque, as well as the original mermaid logo used when the chain was founded in 1971

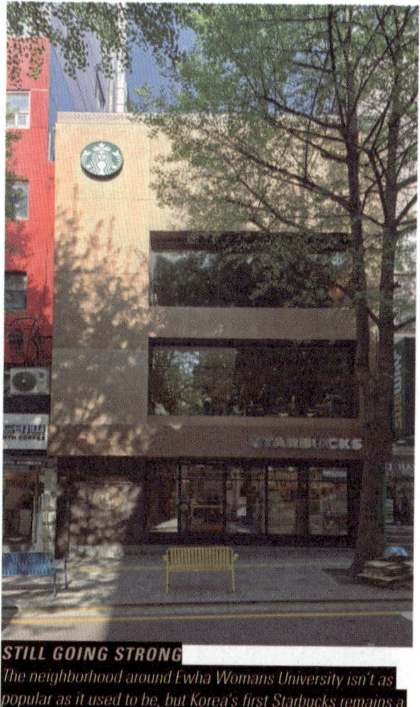

STILL GOING STRONG
The neighborhood around Ewha Womans University isn't as popular as it used to be, but Korea's first Starbucks remains a reasonably "hot place"

Despite being a foreigner, I spend as much time as any Korean in cafés, the sheer number and variety of which was one of the qualities of Seoul that convinced me to move here. My first apartment happened to be in the neighborhood of Ewha Womans University, where Starbucks opened its first store in Korea in 1999 (a date commemorated by a plaque on the building's exterior). Around that time, I learned that the South Korean capital was the city with the most Starbucks locations per capita in the world, a fact that didn't surprise me all that much: in Seattle, the hometown of that world-famous coffee chain in whose suburbs I grew up, people used to joke about one Starbucks opening across the street from another; in Seoul, it actually happens. But its international chains are outnumbered by domestic ones, and even more so by the countless independent cafés found in practically every neighborhood of every Korean city.

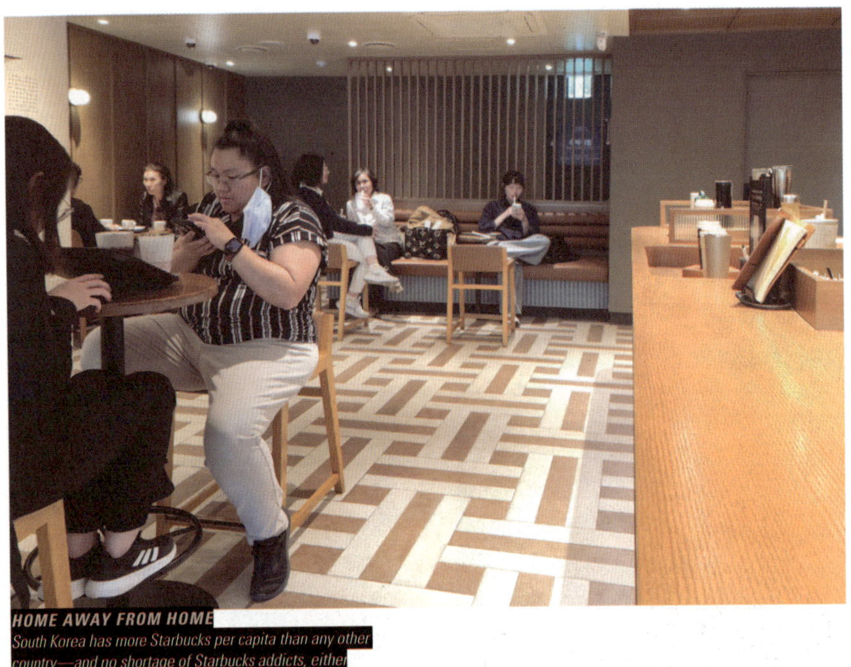

HOME AWAY FROM HOME
South Korea has more Starbucks per capita than any other country—and no shortage of Starbucks addicts, either

Although many Korean cafés are basically modeled on Starbucks, they do tend to cater to local tastes: offering elaborate desserts, for example, or building their menu around the Americano, by far Korea's caffeinated beverage of choice. Yet before Starbucks, there was the humble *dabang*, a coffee shop, usually small, that was often tucked away on the second or third floor of a building, or even in its basement. On its dark-wood walls would hang a miniature grandfather clock, swinging pendulum and all, or maybe a first-generation digital clock with glowing, chunky red numbers. The antimacassars on its low padded chairs would bear the establishment's logo and phone number, almost always consisting of only six or seven digits, rather than the eight used today. The coffee served therein, even when not of the instant *mikseu* variety, probably wouldn't please anyone used to this century's "third-wave coffee" movement, with its focus on high-quality beans and roasting methods.

But then, coffee wasn't the only item on the menu, and for some older *dabang* habitués, it wasn't what they'd come to drink in the first place. They would have been more likely to order *ssanghwa-cha*, a traditional herbal tea made from a variety of roots and barks with a faintly medicinal taste (and, according to its most enthusiastic drinkers since the Joseon period, medicinal effects). It's served with a small spoon on the side, the better to eat the ingredients floating around in the cup: seeds, bits of dried jujube, and—in *dabang* that serve the deluxe option—a whole raw egg yolk, whose inclusion is liable to come as a surprise even to the adventurous foreigner. While today's Western travelers might take such a beverage as bracingly authentic, *ssanghwa-cha* wasn't the hippest thing for younger Koreans to be drinking by the '70s and '80s.

I saw the *dabang* of that era many times before I'd ever set foot in Korea, thanks to their frequent inclusion in Korean movies, and

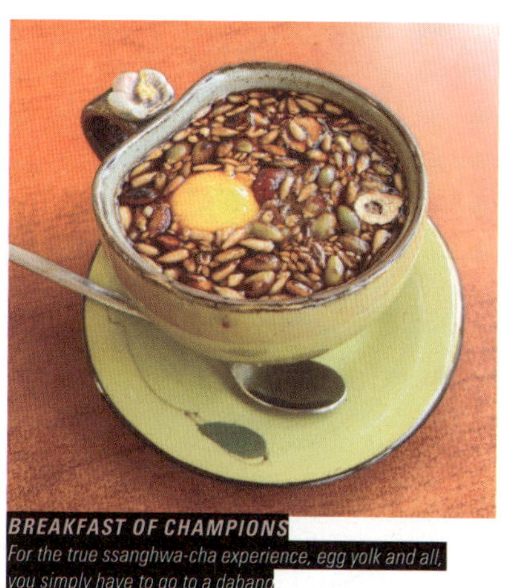

BREAKFAST OF CHAMPIONS
For the true ssanghwa-cha experience, egg yolk and all, you simply have to go to a dabang

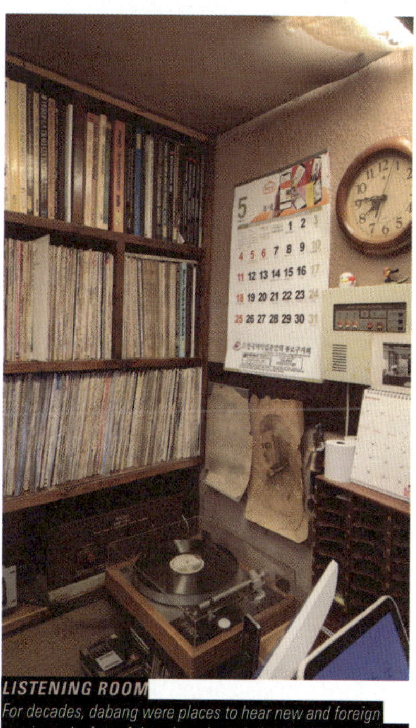

LISTENING ROOM
For decades, dabang were places to hear new and foreign music, and a few of them have kept their record libraries intact

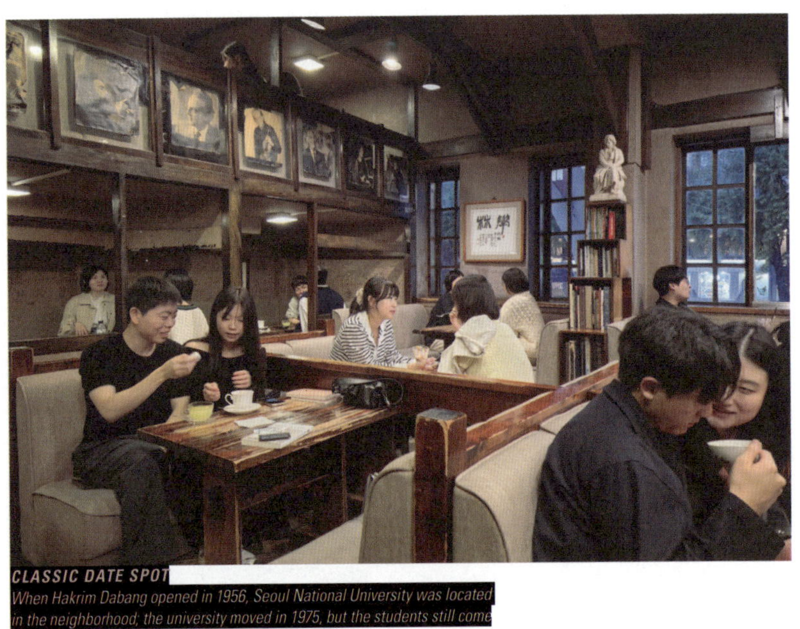

When Hakrim Dabang opened in 1956, Seoul National University was located in the neighborhood; the university moved in 1975, but the students still come

came to associate them with a certain romance. That made sense, given their tendency to be used as the setting for scenes of confessions of love, as well as breakups and exchanges of confidential information. Koreans who came of age between the '60s and '80s will remember frequenting *eumak dabang*, or "music cafés," expressly to hear their house DJs spin the latest (usually imported) hit songs. The first *dabang* I actually visited must have been Hakrim Dabang, a veritable cultural institution of the Seoul neighborhood Daehangno, literally "College Road," which was once the location of Seoul National University. In operation since 1956 (which, by some reckonings, qualifies it as Korea's oldest coffee shop), Hakrim Dabang maintains its signature ambience with a menu of whipped cream-topped European-esque coffees and walls adorned with displays of vintage classical music LPs that contribute to its nostalgic charm. My mother-in-law, who hung out in Daehangno in the '70s, once asked if its stairway still

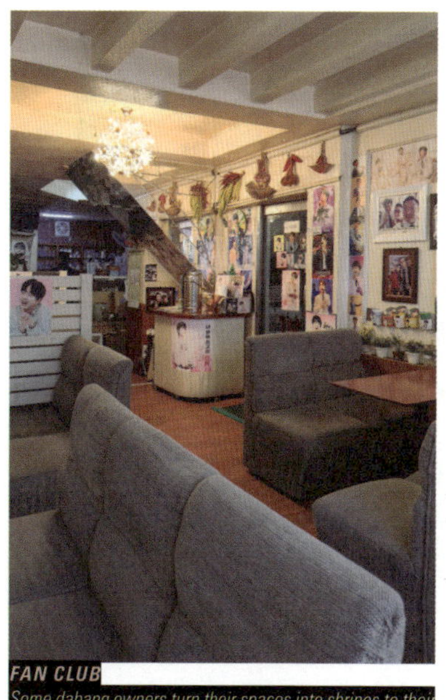

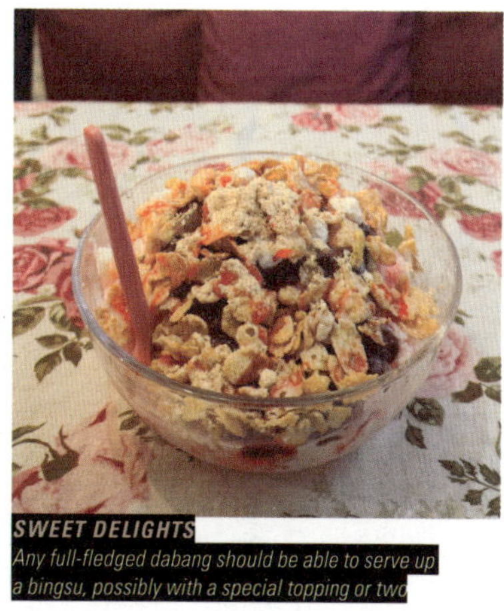

squeaks, and sure enough, it still does.

Although the numbers of original *dabang* have been severely reduced in the 21st century, survivors persist here and there around Seoul and other Korean cities, usually in less-than-prepossessing locations. Some have been visited by unexpected fame, and in certain cases literally: when the boy band powerhouse BTS shot their newtro-inflected 2021 season's greetings video at Eulji Dabang, it became a site of pilgrimage for members of ARMY. As its name suggests, it's located in the neighborhood of Eulji-ro, whose transformation to "Hipjiro" was discussed in chapter 2. For me, Sewoon Sangga, the megastructural electronics market complex from the 1960s, was where I happened to discover my own *dabang* of choice. Known for its own *ssanghwa-cha*, as well as its hazelnut-scented iced coffee and its *bingsu* (a classic Korean dessert made of shaved ice and sweet red beans), Sol Dabang gives the impression of having changed very little indeed

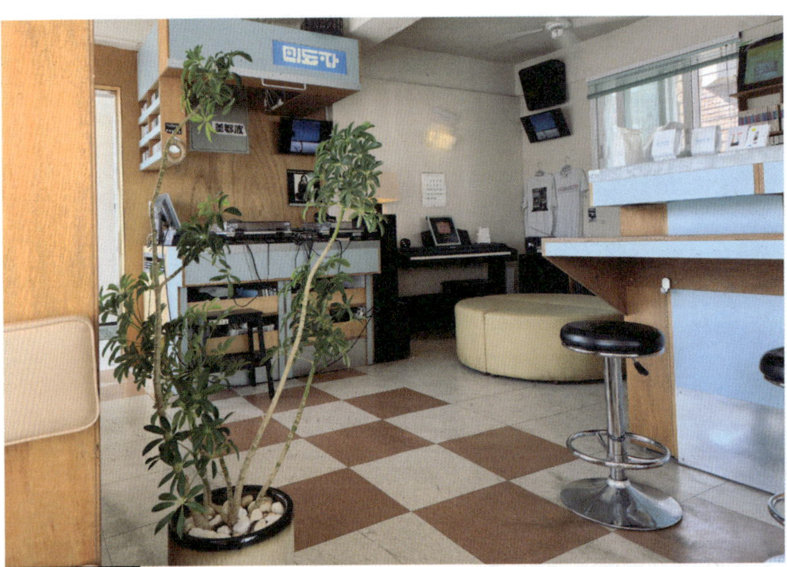

PULL UP A STOOL
It may look old, but Midopa Coffee House in Yeonhui-dong is all new—
or rather, all newtro

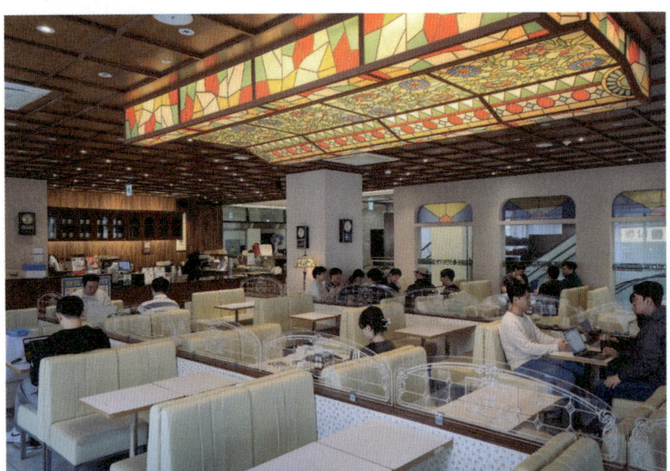

THE PROGRESSION OF THE SIMULACRUM
Pyeonghwa Dabang brings in the young denizens of Gangnam,
even if they've never set foot in a real dabang before

over the past 40 years, apart from the ever-accumulating fan memorabilia of the owner's favorite MZ Generation singer.

Earlier in this century, the very word *dabang* would have exuded *chonseureoum*. Now, what with newtro having evolved from a fad into a seemingly long-term trend, old-fashioned names are fashionable again, such as, for restaurants, Chinese-derived ones ending in syllables like *dang*, *ok*, and *hoe*. Even *dabang* has been appropriated by cafés opened in recent years, such as Midopa Coffee House, which takes the first word of its name from one of downtown Seoul's grand department stores in the second half of the 20th century. It opened in Yeonhui-dong, a part of town very nearly in Eulji-ro's league of hipness and thus receptive to its immaculately newtro aesthetic, one tinged with mid-century European modernism. Elsewhere, in even more expensive parts of Seoul, like the business center of Yeouido and the luxury brand-stocked Garosu-gil, branches of Pyeonghwa Dabang (or Peace Coffee House), the first conceptually newtro Korean chain café, have popped up.

Despite the attention to detail evident in everything from the solid shapes, clean lines, and restrained color palette of its branding to the faux stained-glass fixtures in its wood-paneled ceilings to the vintage radios, fans, and telephones used as decorations to the timeless offerings on its menu—right down to *ssanghwa-cha*, complete with yolk—Pyeonghwa Dabang has contracted, not expanded. When the chain first launched, young Korean bloggers enthused over its fresh feel that captured the ambience of a *dabang* (while in many cases acknowledging that they'd never actually been to a *dabang*), but perhaps its look and feel ultimately seemed too deliberate, too of-a-piece, and even too artificial. Hardier examples of newtro cafés have grown more organically, like Eulji-ro's Coffee Hanyakbang, which really feels as if it's come to occupy both sides of its tight mural-lined alleyway in the manner of a living organism.

Coffee Hanyakbang opened in 2013, before Eulji-ro was Hipjiro, and indeed before newtro itself had even been given its name. But almost every one of its physical components feels much older, beginning with the building itself, which dates to the 1940s. The café's founder, a former stage actor named Kang Yun-seok, opened it as a kind of tribute to the area's bohemian character in recent history, and in more distant history its function as the center of Korea's medical establishment. The word hanyakbang literally means "Korean medicine room," a reference to its standing on the same site where renowned late 15th- and early 16th-century royal physician Heo Jun, author of an influential compendium of herbal remedies, once treated his patients. This is also reflected in the décor, which, besides the newtro-standard analog LP sound system and Tiffany-style lamps, includes pieces of vintage medical equipment (albeit not quite of Heo Jun's vintage).

In true newtro fashion, Coffee Hanyakbang has created its own kind of temporally and culturally blended past, whose ambience evokes Gaehwagi Korea and 1950s Hong Kong in equal measure. What will most catch the eye of first-time visitors, Korean or foreign, is less its ragged concrete, exposed rebar, and narrow passages—the sort of thing certain commentators have indicted as newtro cafes' perilous tradeoff for Instagrammability—than its well-used antique fixtures and furniture, and especially the *jagae* surfaces everywhere you look. If that pure Korean word sounds unfamiliar, the same material is also known as *najeon*, a Sino-Korean word derived from the same Chinese characters used across East Asia. In English, it would be called nacre, or more colloquially mother-of-pearl, and for over a millennium it's been used to adorn armoires, chests of drawers, vanities, folding screens, and other pieces of furniture in Korean households.

Thinly sliced from the inner layers of clam and abalone shells (only five or six of Korea's 600 species of which are suitable for

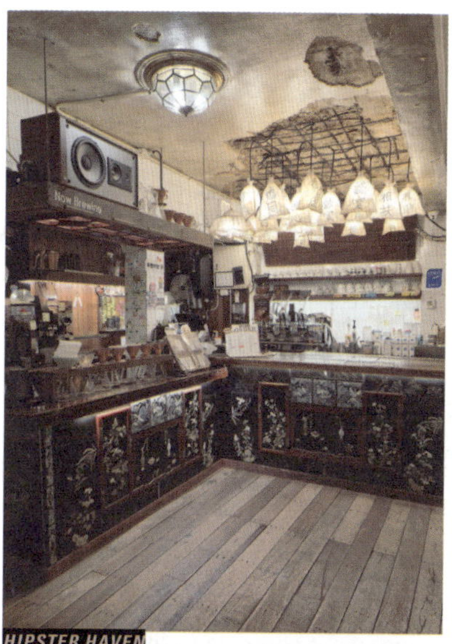

HIPSTER HAVEN

It may be some way down a narrow alley, but by now Coffee Hanyakbang is less a hidden gem than an Eulji-ro institution

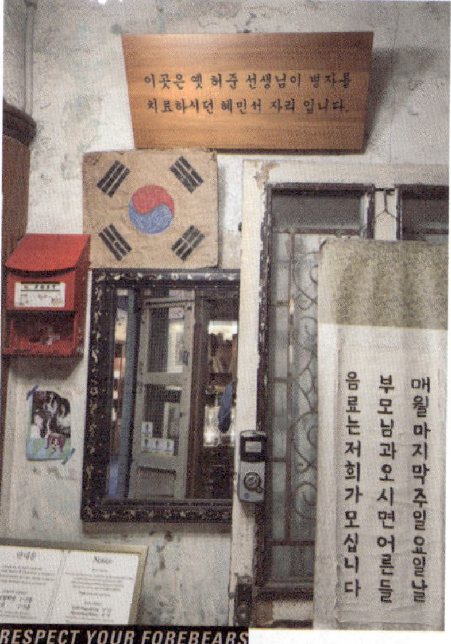

RESPECT YOUR FOREBEARS

One sign explains that the royal physician Heo Jun treated his patients where Coffee Hanyakbang now stands (and the other, that customers who bring their parents get a free drink on the last Sunday of each month)

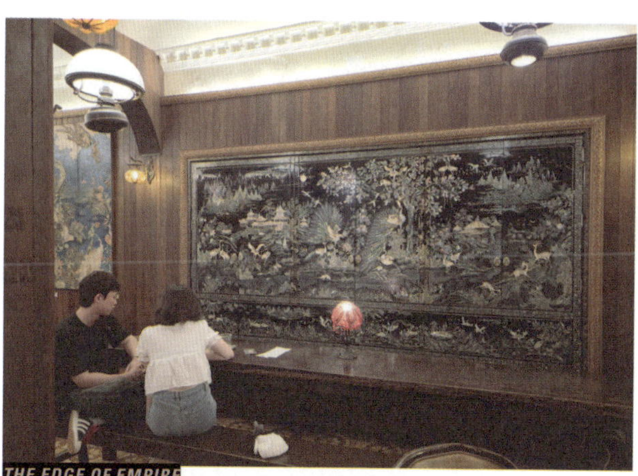

THE EDGE OF EMPIRE

Sprawling jagae fantasias, among many other forms of decoration, create an atmosphere part 21st-century Korea and part 1920s Shanghai

use), the brilliant, swirling colors of *jagae* are painstakingly applied to heavily lacquered wood in order to create elaborate—and, to the Western eye, classically "Oriental"—fantasias full of trees, waterfalls, birds, animals, palaces, and noblemen and noblewomen. It was only aristocrats, in fact, who could afford *jagae* pieces during the form's golden age in the pre-Joseon Goryeo dynasty (918–1392), but during Korea's wealthier periods, they became more available to well-off commoners. As Korea struggled its way out of desperate postwar poverty in the 20th century, *jagae* became a clear symbol of wealth again, and indeed became practically required for the household of any family that had arrived in the country's fast-expanding middle class.

By the 1980s, the market for *jagae* had grown sufficiently overheated to make collecting it unaffordable again. What's more, it was aesthetically anathema to the international millennial minimalism that arose early in the following century, in whose cultural context it looked not just kitschy but also bulky and burdensome. Members of Korea's MZ Generation have long instinctively described *jagae* furniture as looking like it came from their grandmother's house, and while that was once a way of dismissing it, it's now,

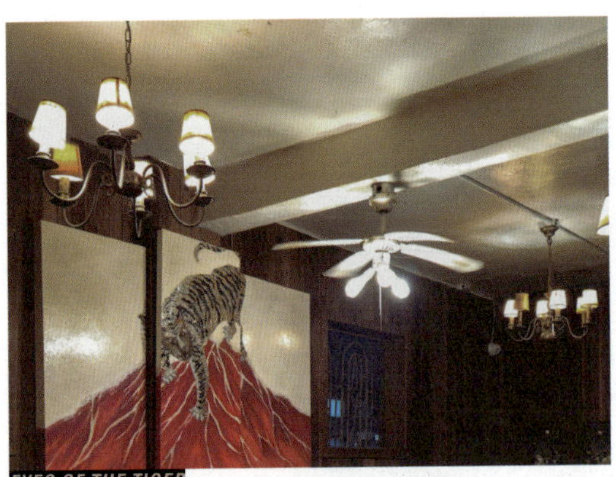

EYES OF THE TIGER
This kind of interior decoration may feel exotic, but it doesn't lack traces of Koreanness

in the age of newtro, a form of high praise. This is even truer in the view of the *halmennial* described in chapter 1, for whom a trip to Gyeongju, with its famously rich historical and cultural heritage, wouldn't be complete without a stop at the Newtro Jagae Gallery Café, where an Americano or a *bingsu* can be enjoyed in surroundings that practically constitute a *jagae* museum.

With the Korean economy not growing today at quite the same breakneck pace as it was in the '70s, many young Koreans have found it difficult to achieve and maintain middle-class lifestyles. But even if they lack the means to purchase a home, much less to outfit it with full-scale antique furniture, they can still introduce a bit of *jagae* into their lives with the more modest newtro products that incorporate it, from modern coffee tables and coasters to earrings and watch faces to cases and grips for their cellphones—the sorts of items available for purchase at Donuimun Museum Village, which was included in the rundown of newtro neighborhoods in chapter 2. Even Starbucks put a *jagae*-patterned version of its trademark mermaid on the keychain payment card it produced to commemorate the 20th anniversary of its arrival in Korea in 2019.

Around that same time, the small homegrown chain Fritz Coffee Company

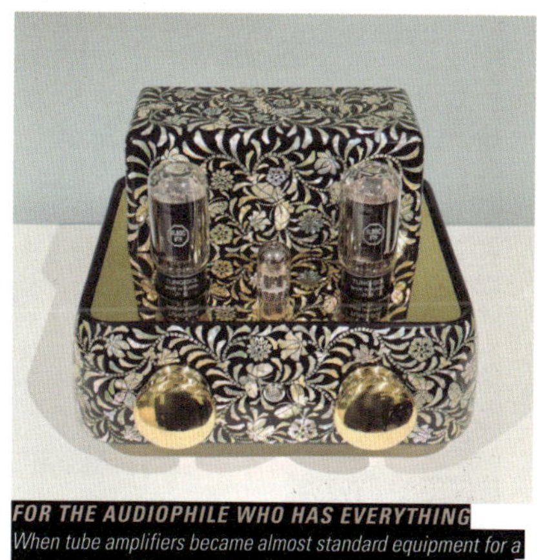

FOR THE AUDIOPHILE WHO HAS EVERYTHING
When tube amplifiers became almost standard equipment for a certain class of Korean café and LP bar, it was only a matter of time before someone would make one with jagae

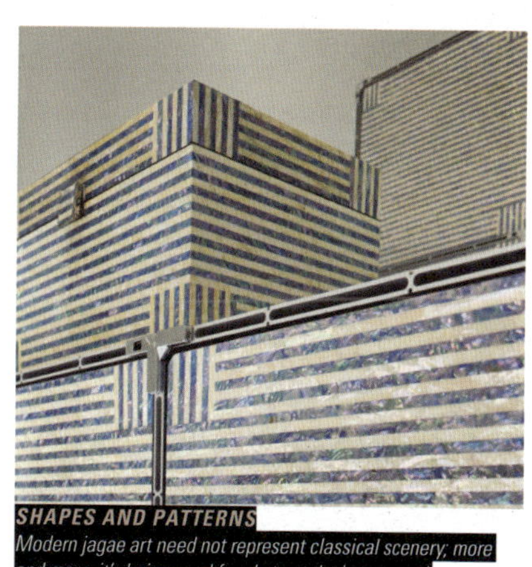

SHAPES AND PATTERNS
Modern jagae art need not represent classical scenery; more and more, it's being used for abstract designs as well

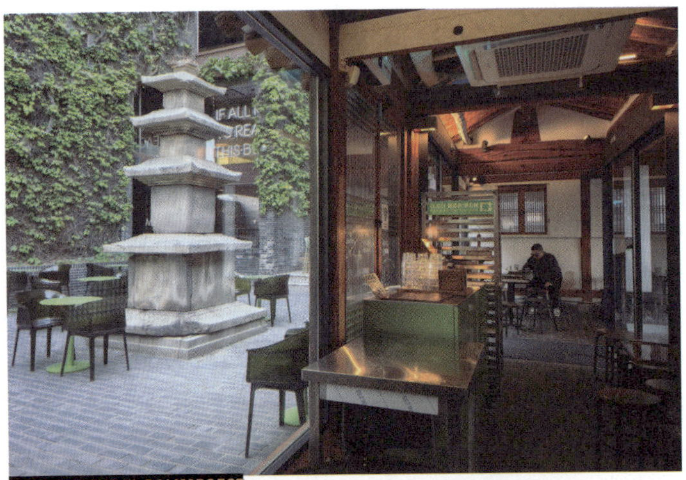

ARCHITECTURAL PALIMPSEST
Seoul's Arario Museum, originally built in the 1970s as the headquarters of famed architect Kim Swoo-geun's Space Group, now includes a Fritz Coffee in its courtyard hanok

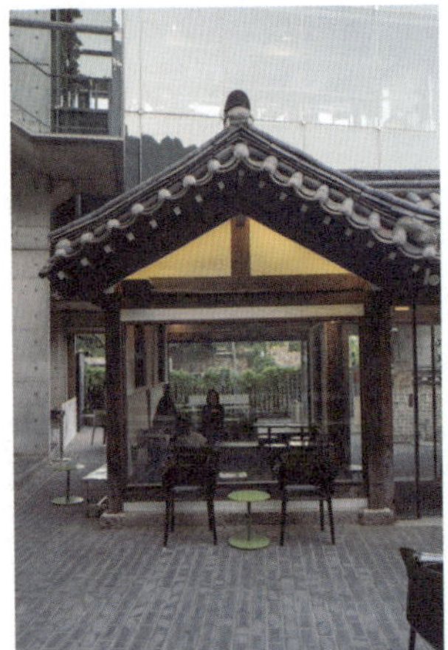

A STUDY IN CONTRAST
The diminutive hanok stands between Kim Swoo-geun's brick Space Group Building and the glass wing added to the Arario Museum by Kim's disciple Jang Se-yang in 1997

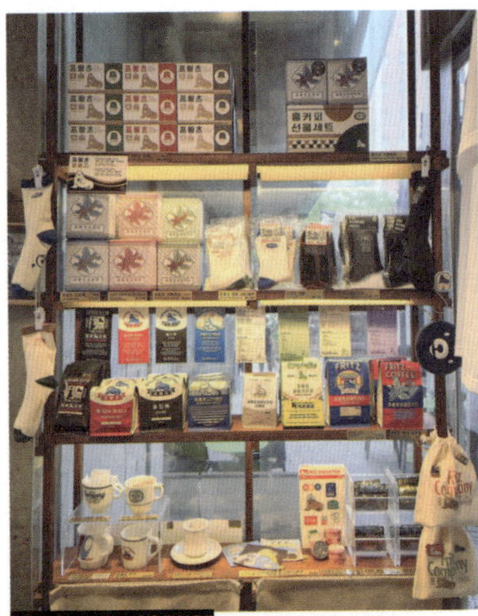

THE MERCH CORNER
Fritz Coffee shops also sell everything from mugs to stickers to sacks to socks, all designed with the same newtro sensibility that shaped their logo

showed off its *jagae*-customized espresso machine for use at events. That was in keeping with its newtro credentials, which had already been solidly established by the design of its merchandise—stickers, mugs, bags of beans— as well as its cafés. Fritz built its reputation in part by repurposing existing, sometimes decrepit commercial, industrial, and residential spaces, most notably *hanok*, the traditional courtyard houses described in chapter 1. This, in part, set off something of a *hanok* café trend, which may be most conspicuous in a Seoul *hat peulleiseu* like Ikseon-dong Hanok Village, but extends all across the country. It involves not just rehabilitating old *hanok*, but also building new ones,

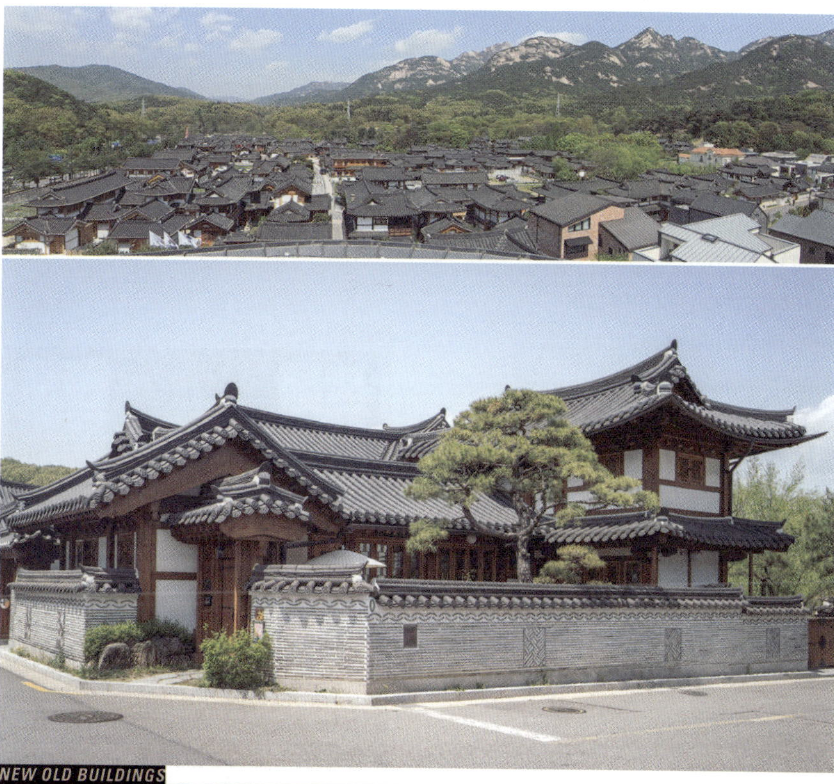

NEW OLD BUILDINGS
Eunpyeong Hanok Village consists almost entirely of traditional Korean courtyard houses— some of which dare to rise to two stories.

as has happened in Eunpyeong
Hanok Village, a quiet residential
development on the outskirts of
the capital.

Different districts are
subject to different building
requirements, but adherence to
tradition can vary even among
individual newly built *hanok*.
Whether they can be designed
with more than one story, for
example, remains a matter of
heated scholarly debate, and the
large expanses of glass seen in
Ikseon-dong certainly can't be
called "period architecture." For
the most part, however, they
do recognizably incorporate
most of the elements that
make a *hanok* a *hanok*, like the
curved *giwa* (roof tiles) and
cheoma (eaves); the *seokkarae*
(rafters), usually exposed and
sometimes rustically uneven; the
dancheong colored detailing; the
geometrical *changho* latticework
and mulberry *hanji* paper on the
windows and doors; the elevated
maru floor, indoors and out; and
the *ondol* underfloor heating
system. Some of these features
have even been adapted to

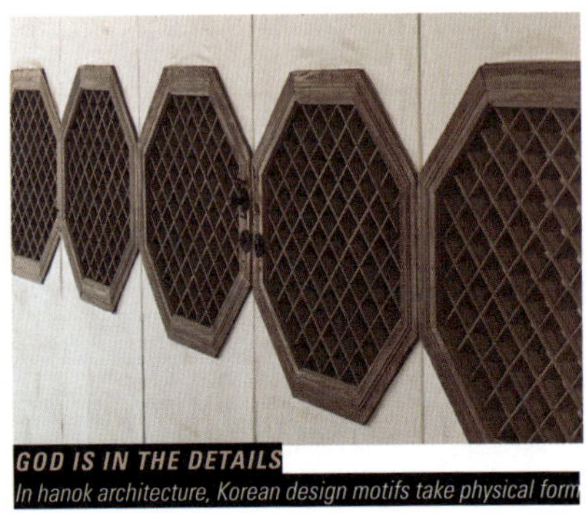

GOD IS IN THE DETAILS
In hanok architecture, Korean design motifs take physical form

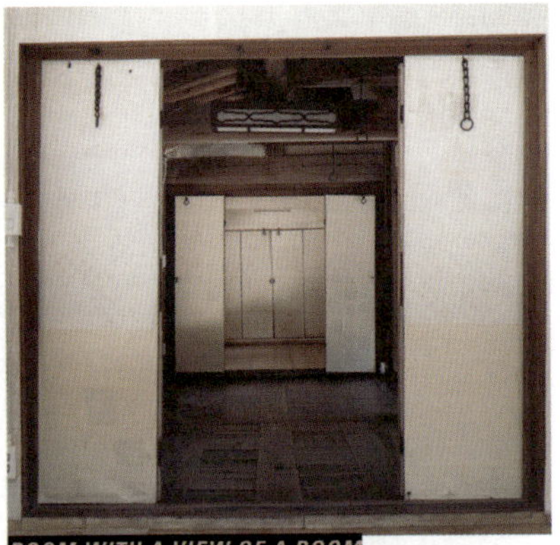

ROOM WITH A VIEW OF A ROOM
*Some of the distinctive ways hanok use space have been
adapted into modern Korean apartments*

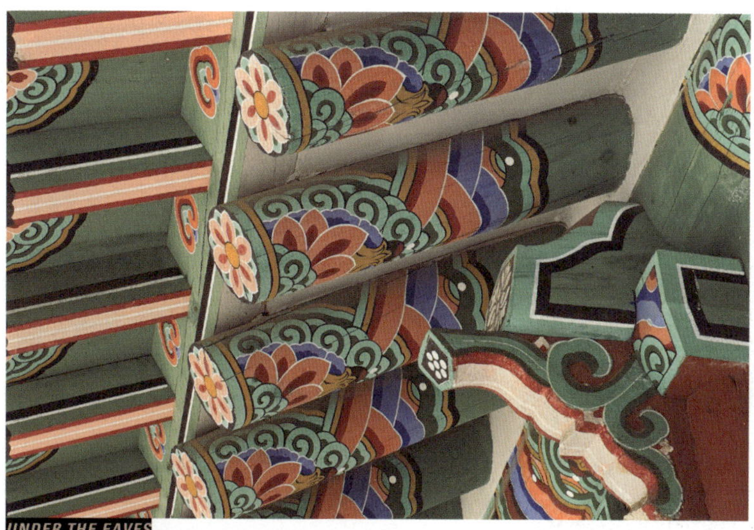

UNDER THE EAVES
In certain hanok, colorful dancheong detailing reaches places
you wouldn't normally look

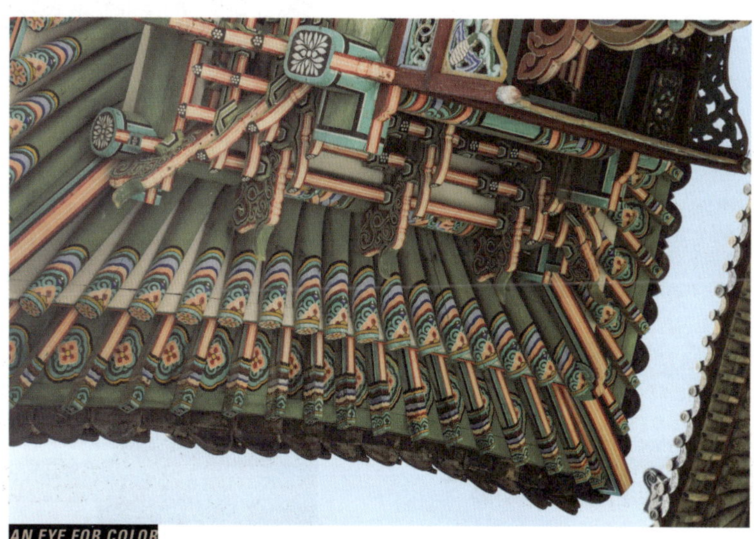

AN EYE FOR COLOR
Hanok aren't hard to appreciate, provided you know
how to look closely at them

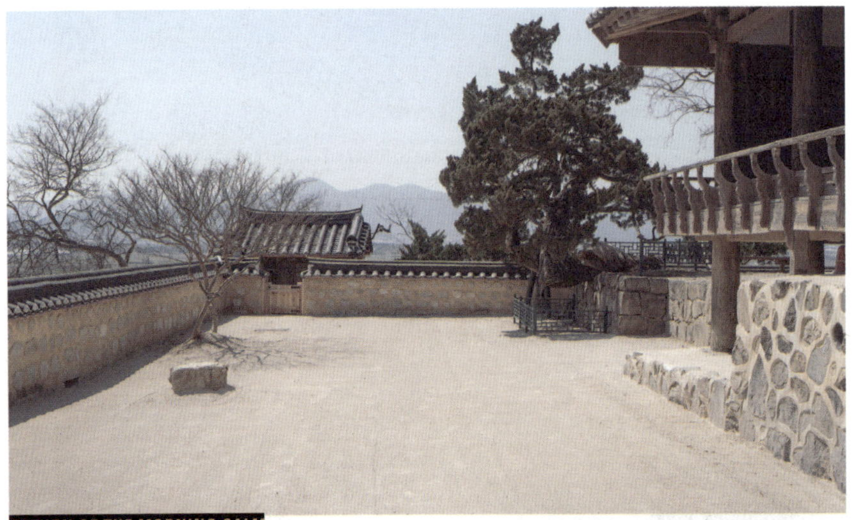

RETURN OF THE MORNING CALM
A visit to a traditional hanok complex can feel like a trip back in time

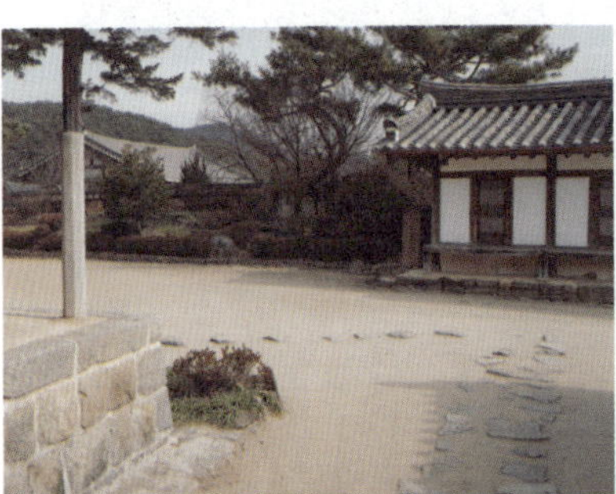

CENTURIES OF INSPIRATION
The use of space in compounds like this one still inspires Korean architects, even those who don't build hanok

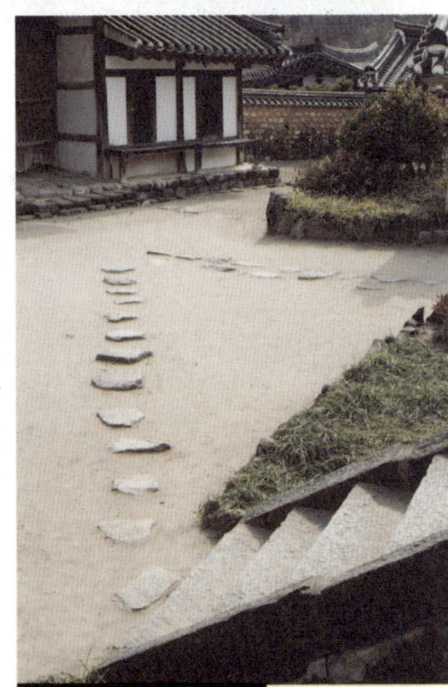

DOWN THE GARDEN PATH
Foreign tourists usually visit the palaces of Seoul, but lesser-known sites can also provide a sense of how the pre-high-rise Korea felt in eras past

imbue, with a classical sense of space, the kind of high-rise apartments in which most modern Koreans live.

Introduced in the 1960s and now the visually dominant feature of Seoul's built environment, those numerous apartment *danji* (or complexes) have grown taller, larger in footprint, and more high-tech with every generation. Although their lack of resemblance to a neighborhood of *hanok*, even urban ones, may be almost comical, there are certain subtle points of continuity. While building individual apartment units with their own courtyards would seem to be architecturally improbable, the designers of Korean apartments in the 20th and 21st centuries have managed to retain some of the important social function of the space defined by the courtyard, called the *madang* (also the word used for one of the narratives of *pansori*, discussed in the previous chapter), in the form of a large central room to which the smaller, private rooms are all connected; Japanese apartments, to single out a contrasting example nearby, often lack such a space.

It may take a little imagination to recognize a *madang* 30 stories above Gangnam. But even in an actual *hanok*, it's possible to stand in a *madang*—a sine qua non of the architectural form—without realizing it. It may have been enclosed and turned into the common area for a guesthouse; it may have been topped with a skylight; it may have been converted into a showroom, as in the *hanbok* design studio's Teterot Salon Ikseon-dong shop, mentioned in chapter 2, or even the indoor-outdoor dining room of a restaurant. Chances are, the food and drink served in such an eatery won't be entirely conventional. The chefs will probably feel a certain reverence for traditional Korean food, whether they grew up with it or not, but they won't be afraid to take it in new directions—and to experiment with newtro flavors.

Food and

Drink

08

By the early 2010s, "K-pop," "K-drama," and "K-beauty" had firmly lodged themselves in the world's English marketing lexicon. (Stephen Epstein, an American professor who specializes in contemporary Korea, has referred to this "letter [K] that acts as a national branding mechanism" as Korea's "Special K.") "K-food" seemed, at that point, to be an inevitable development, especially since the shortest route to enthusiasm for a foreign culture has always run through the stomach. In 2011, the *Michelin Guide* issued its first star to a Korean restaurant, Korean-American chef Hooni Kim's Danji in Manhattan. Five years later, that Bible of fine dining issued its first guide dedicated entirely to Seoul. One could well conclude that the time had come to develop a modern *hansik* (literally "Korean food") geared toward foreign tastes in general and Western tastes in particular, stripped of all but vestigial traces of the native cuisine's rusticity.

Today, in the mid-2020s, it's unclear to what extent modern *hansik* of that kind has taken off. More attention is now paid to a Manhattan "Korean diner" like Kisa, which, though it opened only last year, looks in practically every detail like a *gisa sikdang*—or "driver restaurant," which does most of its business serving humble but hearty meals to cabbies—circa 1980. Kisa's mostly meat-heavy main dishes come surrounded by a varied ring of *banchan* (often, but to my mind unsatisfactorily, translated as "side dishes") including slices of *jeon* (a savory pancake often including green onion); *gyeran-mari* (rolled omelet); and even *so-tteok-so-tteok*, wooden-speared alternating cocktail wieners and pieces of *tteok*, the chewy substance made of glutinous rice flour mentioned in chapter 1. This is a long way from fusion dishes like boiled and sliced *jokbal* (pigs' feet) with soy sauce jelly or avocado *doenjang* (fermented soybean paste) eggplant *bibimbap*.

That would be a long way indeed, both figuratively and literally, since those are just the kind of dishes being served on this side of the world, in those Ikseon-dong restaurants operating out of remodeled *hanok*. Some of those places are serving equally newtro drinks, mixing traditional Korean ingredients—that is to say, traditional Korean spirits—in new forms. Of those spirits, the one most recognized worldwide is, of course, the distilled rice-, potato-, or grain-based *soju*, produced in Korea in one form or another since the Goryeo kingdom, which was founded in the 10th century. Jinro, the dominant *soju* brand, expanded its market

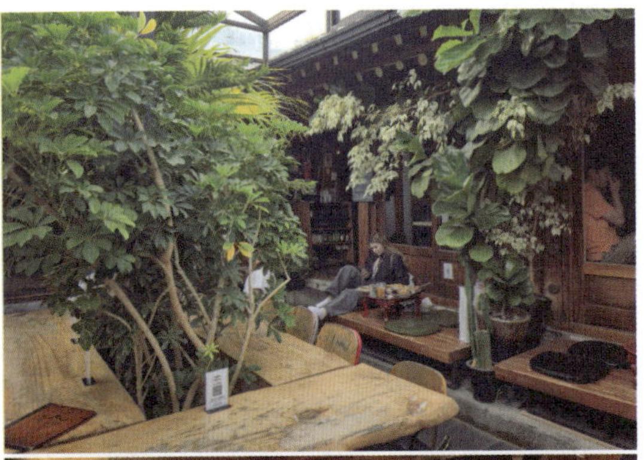

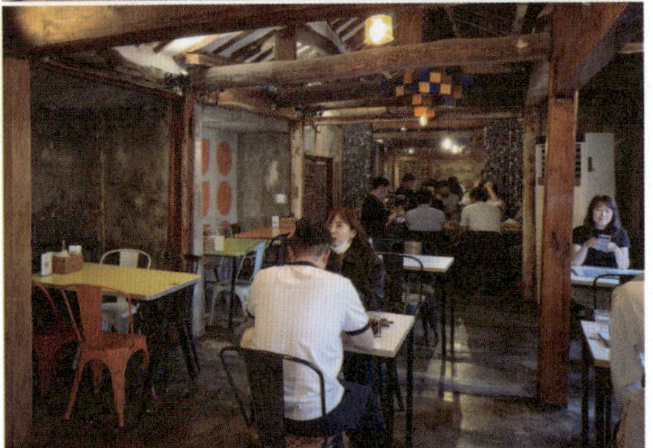

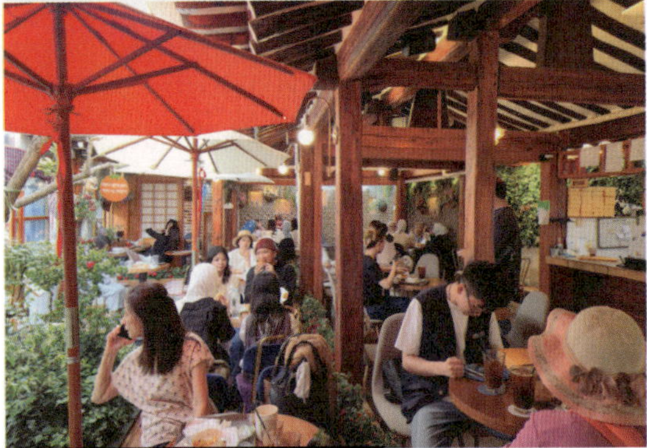

A RESPITE FOR THE MODERN YANGBAN
In neighborhoods like Seoul's Ikseon-dong, hanok have been converted into cafés a world apart from the usual chains—just don't expect to find a table right away on the weekend.

share further still by embracing newtro. In 2019, it launched the "Jinro Is Back" campaign, which involved, among other aesthetic reversions, reintroducing the blue bottles from the mid-1970s through the early '80s (and thus distinguishing itself from the green bottles seen in Korean movies and dramas).

Westerners tend to regard *soju*, Korea's national drink, as strong stuff. Or rather, most Westerners do. I remember a Finnish contestant on *Uri Mal Gyeorugi*, a favorite Korean game show of mine, declaring that, compared to what she drank back home, *soju* was like water. The name of that program translates to "Our Language Battle"; "our language" refers, naturally, to the Korean language, knowledge of which separates the winners from the losers. That particular manner of identifying the non-foreign is common: one hears Korea itself called *uri nara*, "our country"; Korean cuisine called *uri eumsik*, "our food"; and Korean alcohol called *uri sul*, "our alcohol," the many varieties of which have become bases for the latest wave of cocktails.

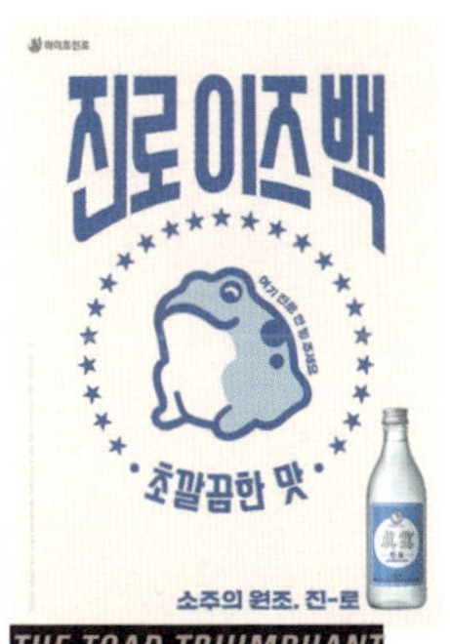

THE TOAD TRIUMPHANT
Jinro soju never went away, but no matter: its newtro-inflected "Jinro Is Back" advertising campaign drew plenty of attention

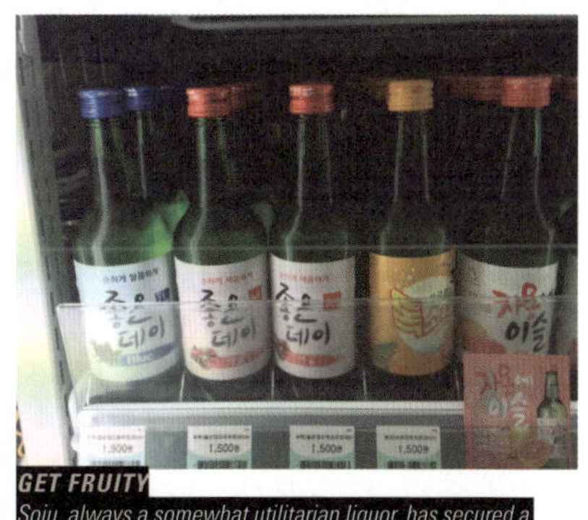

GET FRUITY
Soju, always a somewhat utilitarian liquor, has secured a place in cocktails by now coming in a host of sweet flavors
© Beatlehoon, CC BY-SA 4.0, via Wikimedia Commons

Many types of *uri sul*—or to foreigners, *jeontongju*, "traditional alcohol"—like *cheongju*, a clear rice wine with a long fermentation period that gives it a deep, refined flavor, or the herbal *hongju*, are so flavorful that, to my mind, they're best taken straight. But younger drinkers of *soju*, Korean or otherwise, have shown a tendency to cut it with fruit flavors: *subak soju*, or watermelon *soju* cocktails, and *yuja soju*, made with *yuja* (or, in the widely known Japanese rendering, *yuzu*) citrus tea, have both proven popular, each in its own season. *Soju* has also proven to be an effective agent of Koreanization for a host of classic Western cocktails: in the old fashioned, as a substitute for whiskey; in the mojito, for rum; or replacing tequila to make a *soju* sunrise (which I'd imagine could effectively be branded as a Jeongdongjin sunrise, named for the place on the east coast where some Koreans like to take in the first dawn of the new year).

There's also *bokbunja* (raspberry wine), which makes a rich sangria and has become something of a vogue drink in Korea over the past decade, and *cheongju* clear rice wine, which mixes well with champagne, especially when accented with elderflower syrup. On top of all those drinks, there are even a host of newtro cocktails that have been on Korea's official bartender certification examination for over a decade and which include: the *putsarang*, or "puppy love," made with *soju* from Andong, the most famous city in the country to produce it; the *geumsan*, or "golden mountain," made with *insamju*, or ginseng wine (and supposedly effective at curing whatever hangovers it might cause); and the *hilling* (which takes its name from the "Konglish" version of the English word "healing," as some swear by its ability to bring "relaxation through alcohol," and a term used in countless contexts in Korea), made with *gamhongno*, a powerful, long-fermented, rice-and-millet-based spirit referenced throughout centuries of folktales and literature.

Young women, as previously mentioned, do most of the adventurous cultural consumption by far in 21st-century Korea. When it comes to drinks, they also exhibit a preference for the sweeter and smoother end of the spectrum. Hence the inroads made by cocktails involving *makgeolli*, a milky, low-proof, unpasteurized "rice wine"—as it's often been described in English, if not quite aptly—that has no clear analog in the West. One of the oldest alcoholic beverage in Korea, *makgeolli* first emerged during the Three Kingdoms period, which lasted from the

1st century BCE to the 7th century CE. Also known as *nongju*, or "farmer's wine," it has lately taken forms its early drinkers never could have imagined, being mixed into cocktails with honey, berry syrup, and soda, and marketed internationally in bottled flavors like corn, chestnut, strawberry, peach, and banana.

In the 1960s and '70s, *makgeolli* was South Korea's most popular tipple, a position lost over the subsequent decades due to a government ban on the use of rice for its production due to shortages, a shift to quantity-over-quality mass production, and the importation of more prestigious-seeming foreign alternatives. But despite its rustic image (and its folk reputation for causing headaches), a full-fledged craft *makgeolli* industry began to emerge in the late 2000s, involving

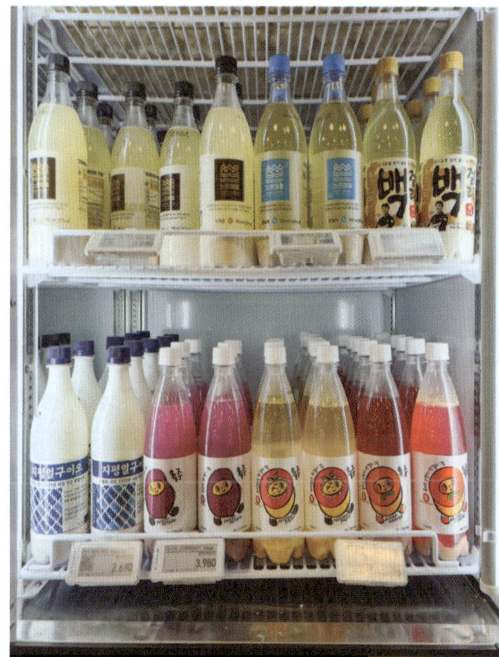

THE FARMER'S TIPPLE GOES COSMOPOLITAN
The market for craft makgeolli has greatly expanded in recent years, to the point that even enthusiasts haven't sampled every variety out there

small brewers in both urban and rural areas of Korea, some of them initially drawing in foreigners due to the drink's sheer distinctiveness. In 2022, The New York Times published an article on the comeback of the "ancient brew." That same year, Untitled Art, an American craft beverage company, announced a hard seltzer-like version of canned *makgeolli*. The product's name? Newtro. (In 2024, even Starbucks Korea got in on the trend by rolling out a *makgeolli*-flavored cream cold brew.)

For much of *makgeolli*'s history, Koreans have made it at home, and at times in secret to avoid the restrictions the state has imposed on the beverage more than once in the nation's history. Both the production and consumption of Korean cuisine itself had long been similarly centered on the home. Hence the enduring public appeal of the term *jipbap*, or "home-cooked meal," which continues to be used even by restaurants and major food companies to this day. In the age of newtro, such advertisements also emphasize *chueokeui mat*, "the flavor of memory," or *eomeoni sonmat*, "the flavor of a mother's hand." The latter phrase has associations similar to "Just like Mom used to make" in English, though for many Koreans of recent generations, some of *eomeoni sonmat* will have come from one product in particular: Miwon, a brand of monosodium glutamate (MSG) seasoning brought onto the Korean market in 1956.

Having never deviated from its original logo, an instantly recognizable *sinseollo* royal hot pot in red-and-white silhouette on its bags, bottles, and packets, Miwon was neatly positioned to ride the newtro wave. In 2020, it published its own cookbook, full of familiar savory dishes reinterpreted, including *doenjang* cream tofu noodles, parmesan cheese *tteokbokki*, and tomato *bingsu*. The following year, it released a line of instant *ramyeon* noodles, a dish associated with the rich umami flavor contributed by its seasoning. Both products make use of their house font, officially released into the canon of newtro graphic design as Miwonche. (Another company also produced a line of newtro-branded cookware, which may remind Koreans of the pots and frying pans they grew up seeing their *eomeoni* use, but which still made me wonder if things hadn't gone a bit too far.)

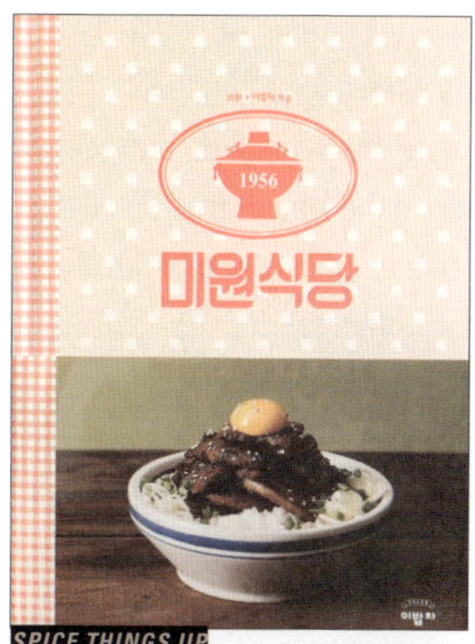

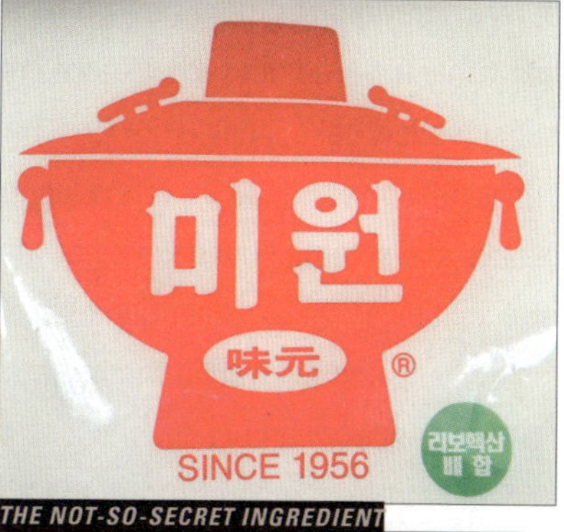

MSG has suffered from image problems in the West, which the makers of products using it have taken pains to correct: the key ingredient in Miwon seasoning, it has been stressed, is nothing more technologically advanced than fermented sugar cane. Also touted are the salutary properties of *uri sul*, from *bokbunja*'s antioxidants to *cheongju*'s amino acids to *gamhongro*'s vitality-enhancing medicinal herbs to *makgeolli*'s abundance of fiber, protein, and lactic acid bacteria, otherwise known as probiotics in the health-conscious parlance of the West. In Korea, where even fried chicken can be sold as a health food, none of this is especially hard to accept. One also hears about the bodily benefits of the so-called "black foods," including black beans, black rice, eggplant, black garlic, and *heukimja*, or black sesame, which appears at the top of the list of 107 grains in the *Dongui Bogam*, the medical manual by the royal physician mentioned in the previous chapter, Heo Jun.

Younger generations haven't shown much interest in the black foods, or at least they didn't before newtro brought them to their attention. Although it has lately flavored desserts like ice cream, macarons, Choco-Pies (a popular marshmallow cake, once a hot item on the North Korean black market), and even drinks like lattes, *heukimja* has a longer history of use in the kind of traditional snacks and sweets now beloved of the *halmennial*, one among a suite of flavors also including *injeolmi* (mentioned in chapter 1) and *ssuk* (mugwort). *Tteok, yakgwa, yanggaeng,* and even such fried treats as the brown-sugar-and-cinnamon-filled *hotteok* pancakes and *gaeseong juak*, rice "doughnuts" soaked in fermented syrup, now benefit from a newtro-granted aura of fascination, as well as from the vague perception of being at least a little bit healthier than their foreign equivalents. As imported holidays have taken their places on the Korean calendar alongside traditional ones, the treats characteristic to both have also mixed flavors and forms. One example of this is the nuts cracked and eaten since time immemorial for *bureom-kkaegi*, a ritual to celebrate the first full moon of the Lunar New Year, and which have lately been packaged and sold like Valentine's Day chocolates.

Of course, there's also a place for foods that don't even pretend to wholesomeness, some of which have enjoyed a newtro-driven resurgence of consumer interest, or even a return to store shelves after a long absence. This includes Star Popeye, for example, a snack that combines fried bits of *ramyeon* noodles and crystallized sugar, or the sweet, mild Baebae cookies enjoyed by young children and adults alike. There has also been a certain amount of speculation about whether the moment of internationalization has come for what Koreans call *hatdogeu* (literally "hot dog"), despite how little they resemble what Westerners think of as hot dogs. The most obvious difference is that they're served on sticks, making them more like corn dogs, though coated with bread-like dough and a layer of sugar, often involving a layer of mozzarella cheese, chopped french fries, or squid ink somewhere in between.

Since the 1980s, the Korean *hatdogeu* has been a typical street food here, and one most enjoyed by students who buy them after a long day at school, which has only been dragged out in recent generations by the all-but-mandatory classes

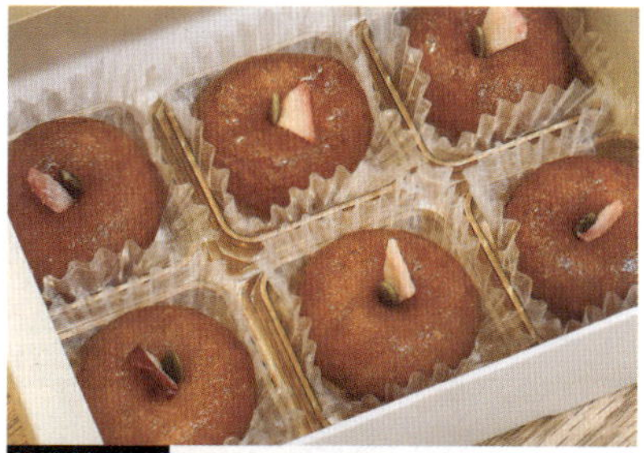

SUGAR HIGH

Everybody appreciates a gift box of gaeseong juak "doughnuts"—at least if they can handle the sweetness

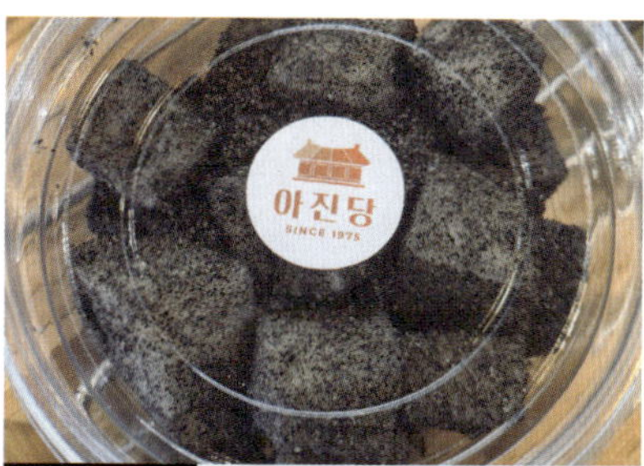

DESSERT STOP

The sweet shop Ajindang has opened a location in Ikseon-dong, the better to satisfy halmennial tastes with heukimja-coated tteok and much else besides

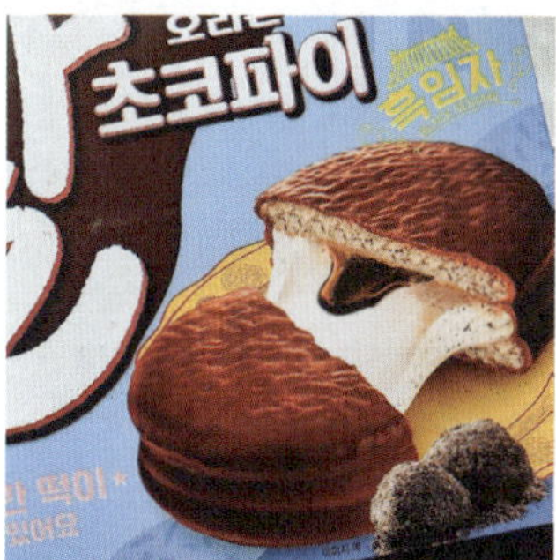

A MODERN SNACK GOES TRAD

Who doesn't enjoy a good old Choco-Pie, especially one whose flavor is punched up with the sesame richness of heukimja?

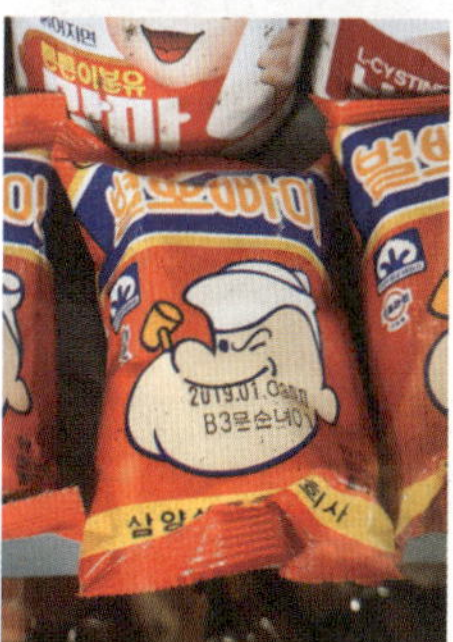

SPINACH SUBSTITUTE

Westerners will recognize Popeye, but they certainly won't recognize Star Popeye, a mixture of fried noodle bits and crystallized sugar (to which they could easily get hooked nevertheless)

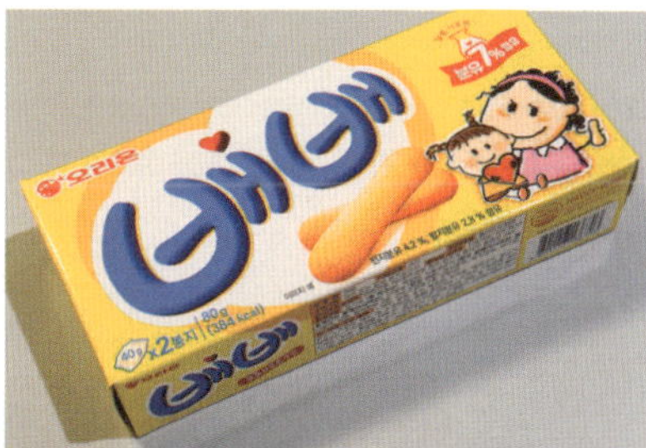

BE MY BAEBAE

Korean parents may buy these mild cookies for their young children, but they'll usually sneak a few for themselves

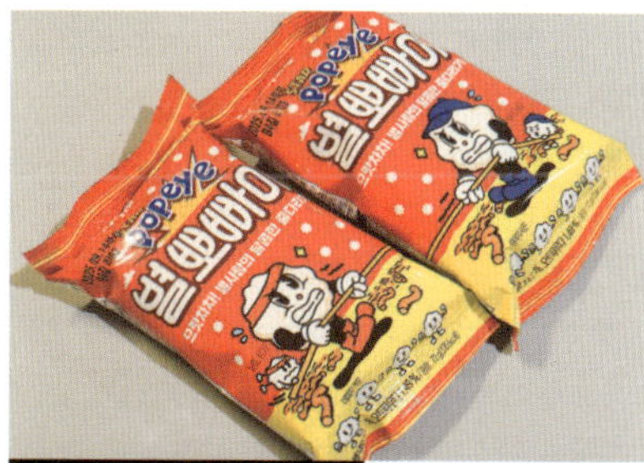

ONE FOR ME, ONE FOR YOU

In its classic bag design or otherwise, Star Popeye can bring even the most disharmonious generations in Korea together

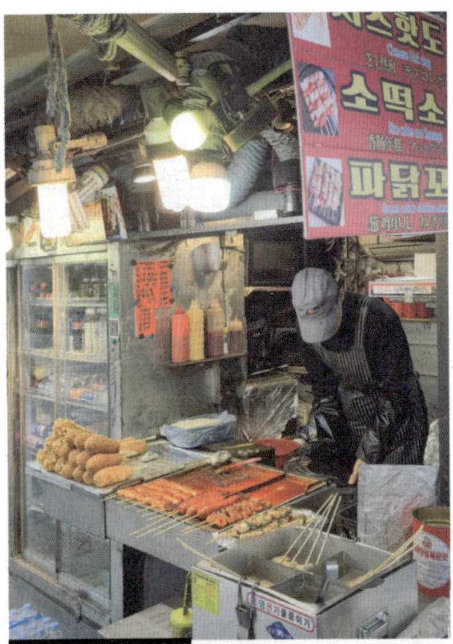

STUDENT'S DELIGHT
This hardworking vendor offers a full complement of speared street food, from hatdogeu (the Korean version of corn dogs) to odeng (fish cake in all-you-can-drink broth).

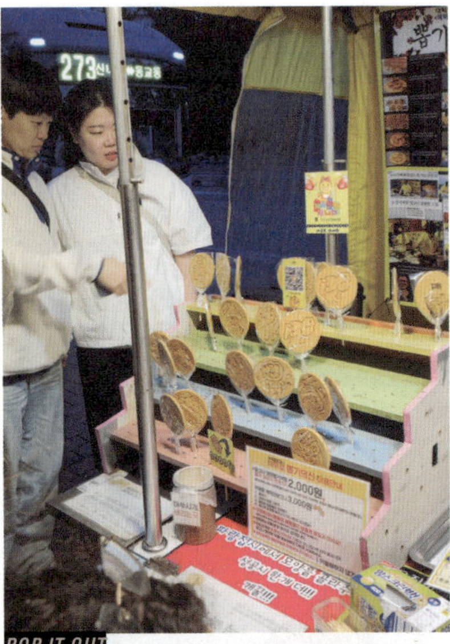

POP IT OUT
Eat cleanly around the shape in the center of a dalgona, or ppopgi, and the next one's free, though these elaborate designs pose a formidable challenge.

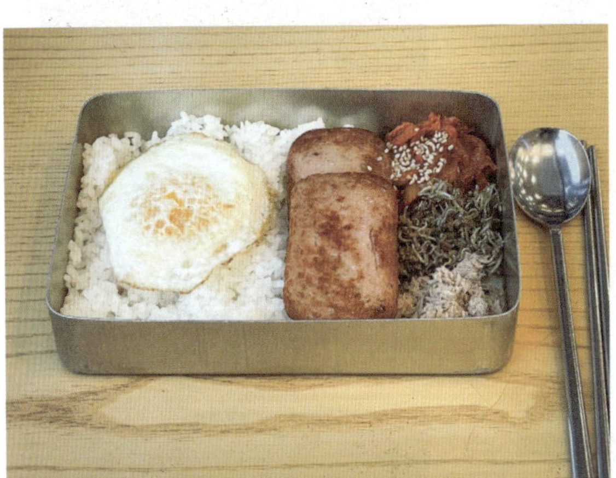

LUNCHBOX MEMORIES
This simple dosirak meal may look ready to eat, but Koreans know that you first have to give it a few good, hard shakes.

at their after-school *hagwon*. A much more venerable kid-oriented treat for sale on the sidewalk is *dalgona*, referenced in chapter 1, to which it would not do injustice to describe as pure sugar. Melted down into a syrup and then hardened in a circular mold, that sugar is embedded with one of a variety of playful shapes, usually stars, umbrellas, automobiles, or rocket ships. Those who can eat away all the candy around the shape without breaking the shape itself customarily get another one for free, a reward unavailable to those who take their *dalgona* in a trendier newtro context, as an ingredient in novelty European-style pastries and ultrasweet coffee drinks.

Eating around the edge of a *dalgona* shape is harder than it seems, especially as dramatized in the Korean Netflix series *Squid Game*, where the stakes are life and death. Given its status as Netflix's most-watched original series (in its first season, at least, by the metric of total hours viewed during the first 28 days after release), it's arguably done more to define the Korean pop culture of the 2020s globally than anything else so far. It's also thoroughly newtro: consider the cheaply vibrant pink-and-green color palette, the metal *dosirak* lunchboxes issued to the characters, and of course, the deadly competitions based on schoolyard games (one of them menacingly presided over by a colossal robotic of Younghee, the design-inspiring old textbook character introduced in chapter 4).

Whether it's *ttakji chigi*, with its goal of using one folded-paper square to flip over another, *jegichagi*, whose players keep a hacky sack-like object in the air with their feet, or the relatively elaborate team-based *ojingeo*, the "squid game" of the Netflix series title, most Koreans over the age of 40 have fond memories of engaging in these childhood pastimes. *Squid Game*'s second season gets a joke out of the younger participants, who would have practically come of age with a smartphone in hand, now knowing how to play them. Such traditional games surely came as just as much of a surprise—albeit not a life-threatening one—to many attendees who learned how to play some of these same games at the first Newtro Festival, discussed in chapter 3. I myself remember first playing them with dozens of other non-Koreans at the Korean Cultural Center, Los Angeles, where I once took Korean language classes.

This was before *Squid Game*, *Parasite*, BTS, or even "Gangnam Style," and

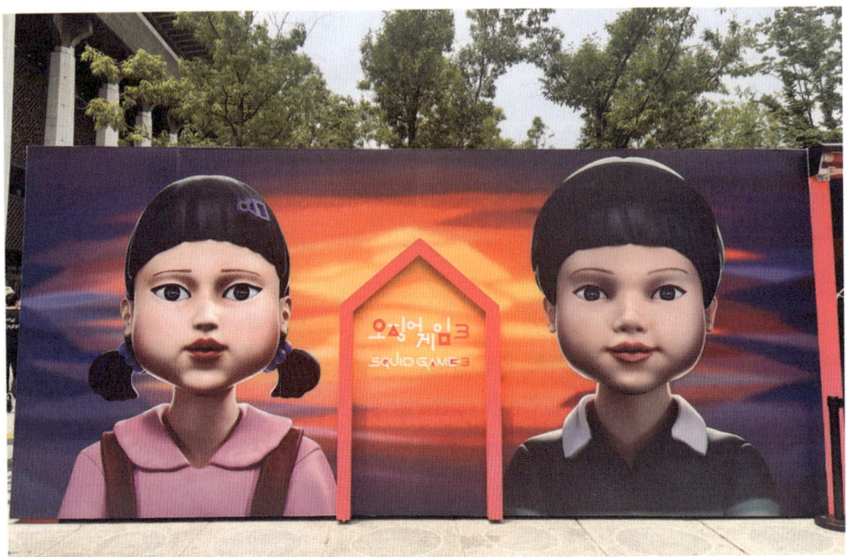

COME PLAY WITH US
Cheolsu and Younghee, those personifications of childhood innocence and curiosity, have much grimmer associations for Squid Game fans

certainly before newtro. But even then, the Korean Cultural Center's introductory language classes swelled with eager students. In all likelihood, some did come mainly for the complimentary foods served before class, be it *jeon*, *japchae* noodles, fried chicken, or simple kimbap (also spelled gimbap), the sliced rolls of seaweed-wrapped rice, vegetables, and fish cake (and often, to the untrained eye, mistaken for Japanese *maki* sushi) without which Korean life would be unimaginable. Yet the majority of people at the Korean Cultural Center seemed to have been drawn there by interest in one aspect of Hallyu or another. They may not have known the words *chonseureopda* or *meotjida*, but they did know that Korean culture was cool, having yet to encounter the grim Western news coverage of Korea, with its disproportionate focus on difficulties like suicide rates, economic and academic pressures, and the belligerence of the country's northern neighbor, or indeed the bitter critiques of Korean society made by the country's own film and literature.

Squid Game's creator, Hwang Dong-hyuk, has spoken about drawing inspiration from what he experienced as South Korea's grindingly competitive economy and sharply class-conscious society. One can imagine what kind of struggles he must have gone through to come up with a scenario in which hundreds of deeply indebted ordinary citizens march toward mass slaughter for the exceedingly slim chance at winning an amount of money that would be trivial to any of the families in charge of Korea's *chaebol*, or large Korean conglomerates. The series' newtro incorporation of the aesthetics and amusements of a simpler time into an ultra-violent "golden age of prestige television drama" streaming series creates an ideal form for this bleak satire. I can only assume that plenty of foreign *Squid Game* fans must surely come away with the impression that many Koreans don't like what their country has become here in the 21st century.

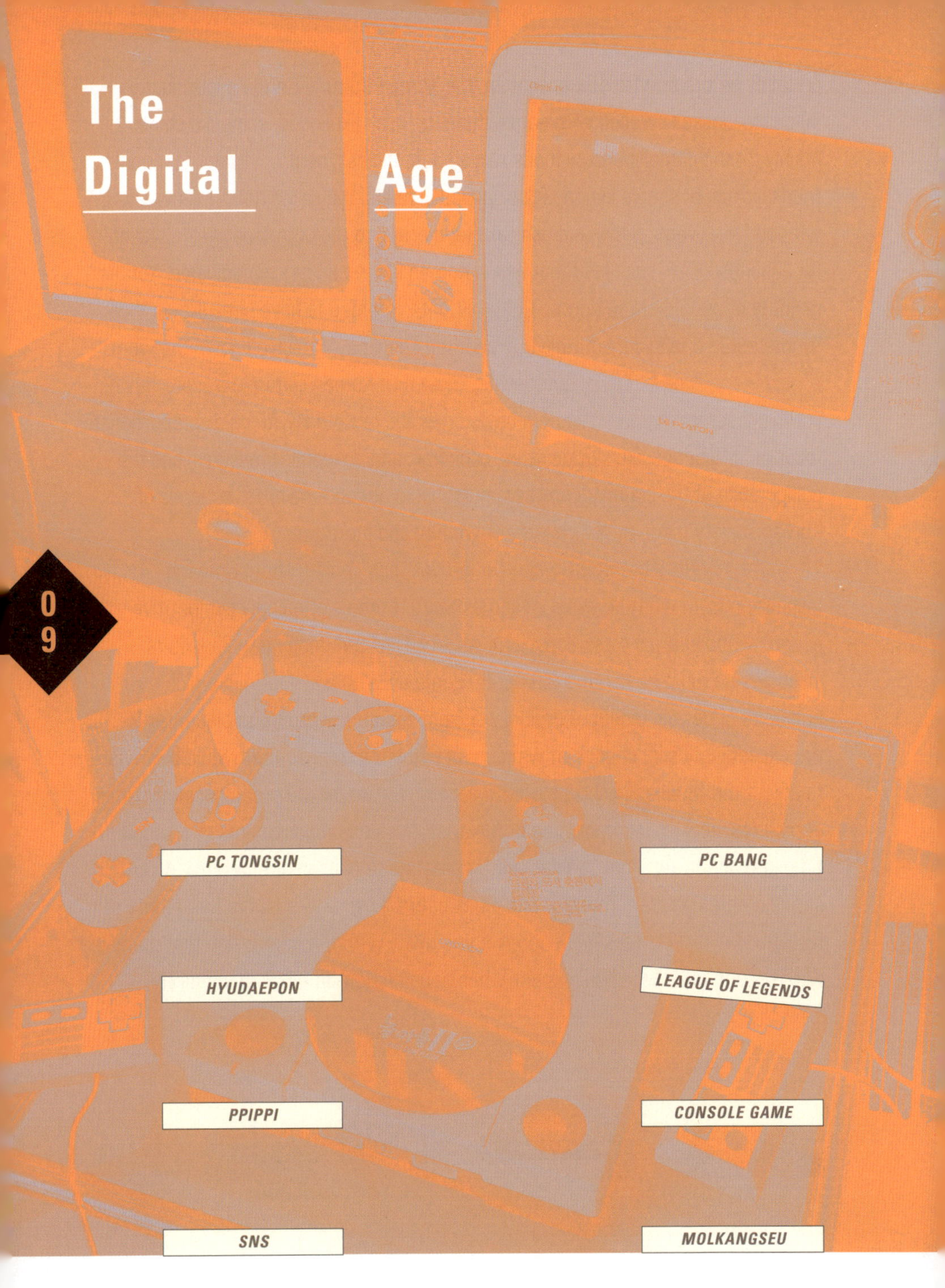

The Digital Age

"The future is here," the American science fiction novelist William Gibson once said. "It's just not evenly distributed." That line has long been taken for an observation about Japan, a country in whose technological and fashion trends he's found a great deal of inspiration. But by the time the quote had become popularly associated with him, in the 1990s, it could have applied just as well, or indeed better, to South Korea. Foreigners familiar with this society at that time understood it to have become an uncommonly "wired" one, in which a great swath of the public enjoyed faster internet connections than in most of the developed world. Having begun with the white-text-on-blue-screen *PC tongsin* (literally "PC communication") bulletin board services available since the mid-'80s, Koreans were living online in an era when many Westerners were still unsure what use they might have for the internet.

Much like the country's fast-forward industrial and economic development after the Korean War, this aggressive push for connectivity had its undesirable side effects. Premature optimization of the online systems Koreans used every day for shopping, banking, and government services resulted in years-, even decades-long dependence on particular technological standards and protocols even after they'd gone obsolete in the West. When I moved to Korea in the mid-2010s, it was only just becoming viable to use an Apple computer here. At the same time, tightly woven into the fabric of everyday life were other technological conveniences it would take the United States years to implement broadly, like fast delivery of food ordered online

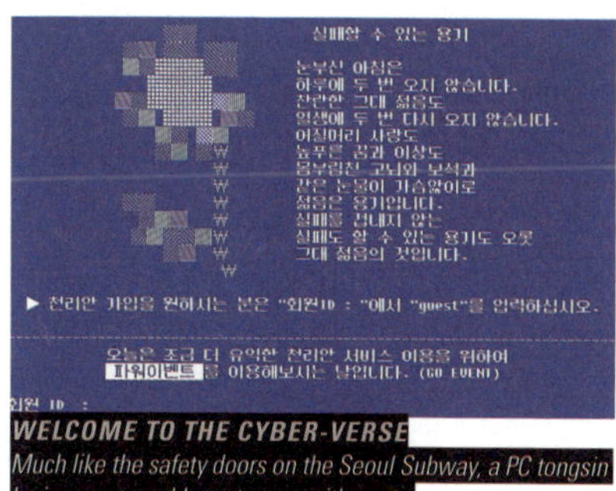

WELCOME TO THE CYBER-VERSE
Much like the safety doors on the Seoul Subway, a PC tongsin login screen could greet users with poetry

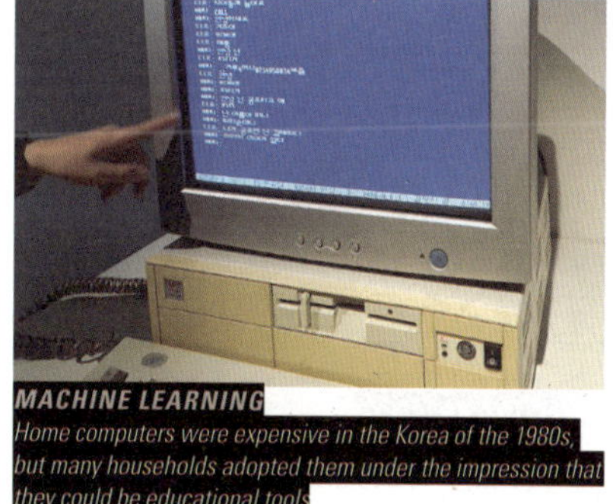

MACHINE LEARNING
Home computers were expensive in the Korea of the 1980s, but many households adopted them under the impression that they could be educational tools

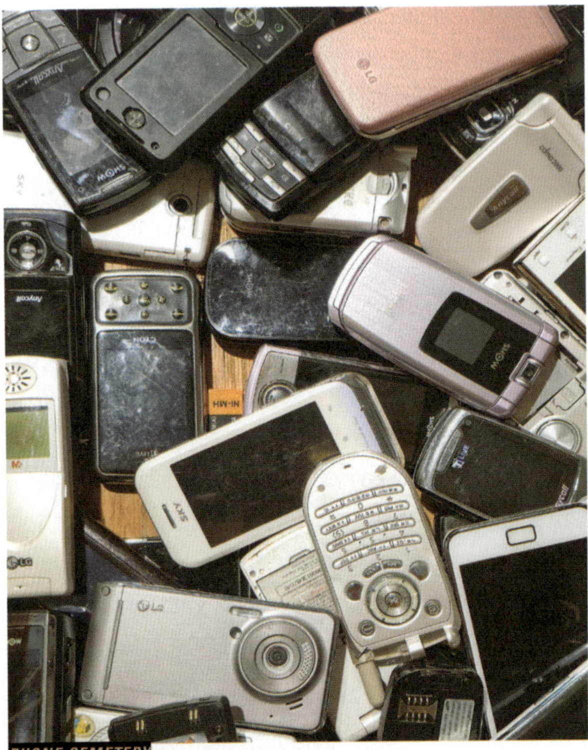

PHONE CEMETERY
Every cellphone, no matter how high-tech and desirable in its heyday, is destined for the junkheap.

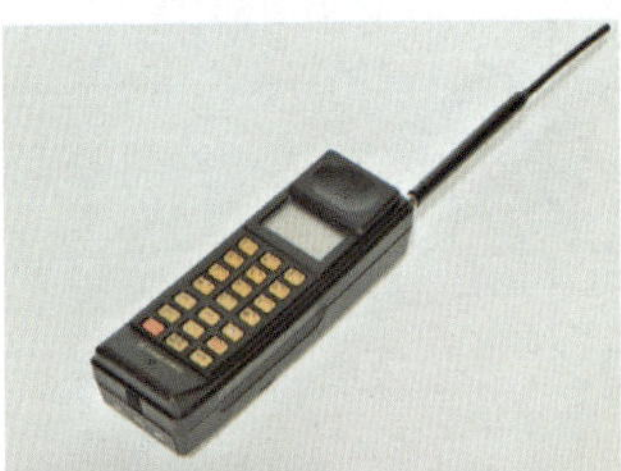

RAISE THE ANTENNA
This early Samsung phone might not look sleek today, but it was a prestige item when it came out.

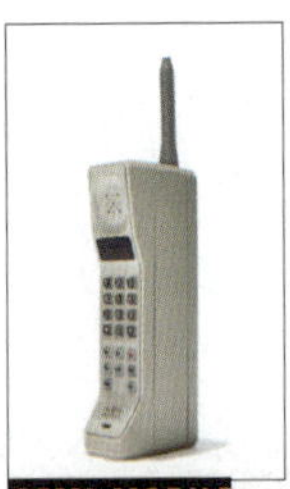

SEMI-MOBILE
Like many countries, Korea looks back with a chuckle on its era of byeokdolpon, or "brick phones."

and seamless transfers of money between accounts at different banks.

That and much else could be done on computers, but as far as I could see, nearly all Koreans preferred to use their phones. As I learned early in my study of the Korean language, they don't refer to these devices as cell phones, as we might say in the West, but *hyudaepon*, a portmanteau of the Korean word for "handheld" and a Koreanization of the English word "phone." Perhaps even more common is the fully Konglish term *haendeupon*, or "hand phone," a fitting description, given how many Koreans always seem to have their phone in hand. A permanent exhibition at the National Museum of Korean Contemporary History in downtown Seoul displays modern cell phones in an evolutionary lineup that stretches all the way back through the first wave of flip phones around the turn of the 21st century to the so-called *byeokdolpon* (literally "brick phones") of the 1980s.

Not that one has to visit a historical institution to behold such artifacts. The owner of the neighborhood coffee shop in which I write these very words has placed a variety of old cellphones along its bookshelves as decorations. Anycall, Ever, mobiBLU, Cyon—these and other now-forgotten brands are represented by battered models that flip or slide open (as well as even older, non-opening "candy bar" varieties), all of which must once have been prized by their original owners.

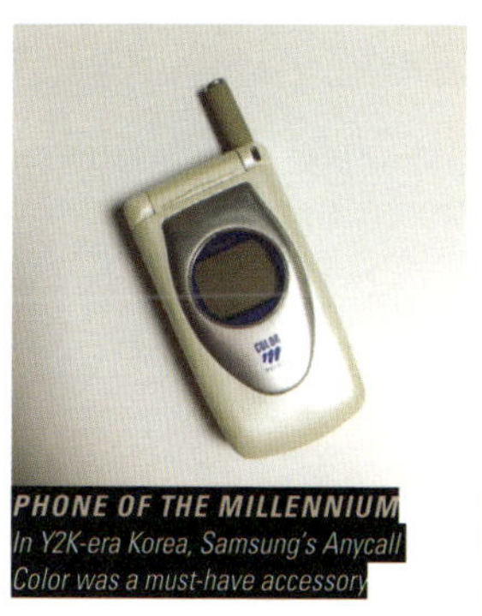

PHONE OF THE MILLENNIUM
In Y2K-era Korea, Samsung's Anycall Color was a must-have accessory

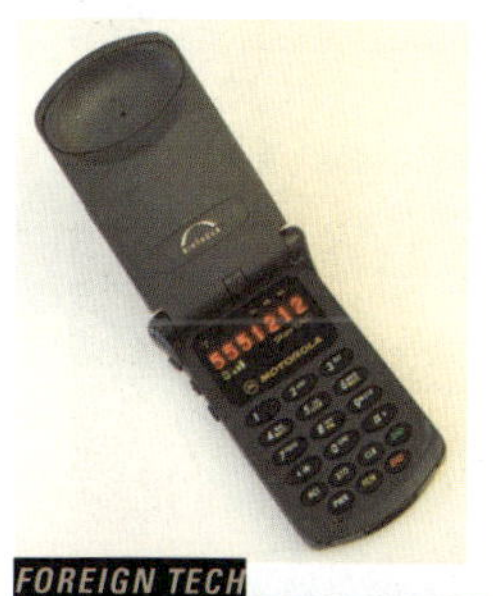

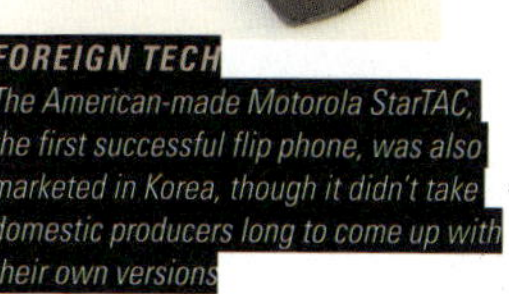

FOREIGN TECH
The American-made Motorola StarTAC, the first successful flip phone, was also marketed in Korea, though it didn't take domestic producers long to come up with their own versions

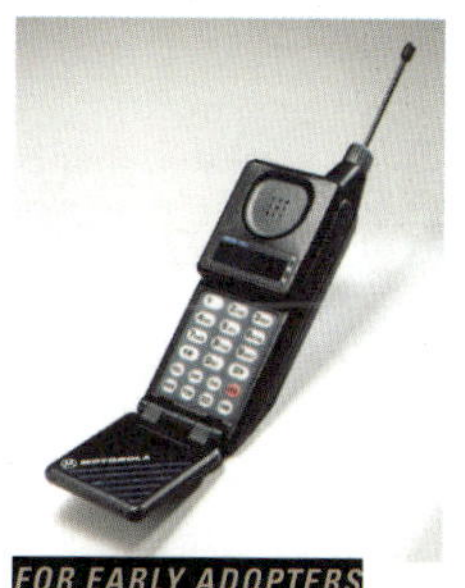

FOR EARLY ADOPTERS
Before the full-fledged flip phone, there was the Motorola MicroTAC, which came to market in 1989

(Incidentally, it's not only their total obsolescence that protects them from theft. One major practical advantage of Korean life is that even brand-new phones and laptops can be left alone on café tables for long periods without fear of their being stolen.)

Scattered among these are devices of another kind, one likely to stir up the nostalgia of Koreans of a certain age while looking practically unrecognizable to the younger generation: *ppippi*. That onomatopoeic word (the Korean language being heavily invested in onomatopoeia in general) refers to what used to be called pagers, or "beepers," in the West. At their height in the mid-'90s, *ppippi* were used by one-third of the South Korean population, among whom an elaborate numeric lexicon developed that was used for a primitive kind of proto-texting. The number 79, for example, is pronounced *chil-gu* in Korean, which is close enough to *chingu*, "friend," while 486 stands for *saranghae*, or "I love you," each of its three digits standing for the number of strokes used to write one of that phrase's three syllables in Hangeul. That number is still today employed in confessions of love, which shows that, though the *ppippi* itself may be gone, the culture it produced hasn't been forgotten.

Pronounced *pal-i-pal-i*, the code 8282 stands for *bballi bballi*, which means something along the lines of "hurry it up." That phrase has also come to stand for the notorious culture of haste among modern Koreans, who have never let

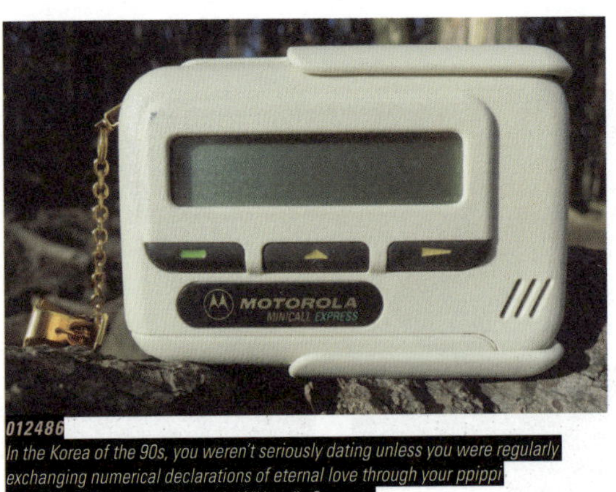

In the Korea of the 90s, you weren't seriously dating unless you were regularly exchanging numerical declarations of eternal love through your ppippi
© R. Henrik Nilsson, CC BY 4.0, via Wikimedia Commons

sentimentality slow them down when it comes time to upgrade to a superior technology. In 1997, when the *ppippi* must have looked like a permanent fixture of Korean society, out came the *sitipon* (literally "city phone"), which wirelessly connected to hardware installed in public phone booths to let its users make calls, if not receive them. Although in theory the perfect complement to the *ppippi*, the *sitipon* was in practice never supported by sufficient infrastructure to make it truly useful in everyday life. But its low price, at least compared to the early models of genuine cellphones then on the market, heralded the coming era when practically everyone could—and would—have a phone in hand. (It would later appear in the hand of the main character's father in *Reply 1994*, symbolizing, if somewhat anachronistically, a bygone era in Korean communication.)

Born in the 2000s and 2010s, members of the current 1020 generation have never lived a day without cellphones, or indeed without perpetually internet-connected *seumateupon* (or "smartphones"). To them, the "dumb phones" of the late '90s and early 2000s have an air of retro novelty, one evocative of technologically simpler times they were born too late to enjoy. That, at least, must be one of the assumptions behind the explicitly "newtro"-branded smartphones brought to the Korean market in the first half of this decade: the stark, almost utilitarian Biner Zero, with its promise of "digital detox," and AGM's "Rugged Phone," with its durable-looking physical keyboard. Even Samsung, Korea's leading smartphone maker (and the resolutely forward-looking Apple's prime competitor), has ridden the newtro wave with its Galaxy Z Flip series, which packages foldable touchscreen technology in a shape reminiscent of the "flip phones" of yore. In 2023, Samsung released the limited-edition Galaxy Flip 5 Retro, whose design pays subtle homage to the company's own SGH-E700, which was very much the phone to have in Korea 20 years before.

However their smartphones look, Koreans tend to use them to do basically the same things. A glance across the screens glowing throughout a crowded rush-hour Seoul subway train will reveal that few activities are as popular as texting and social networking, defining technologies of the early 21st century, and one with which Korea has a longer history than most countries. Cyworld, the first social networking site, was launched as a club project by students at the

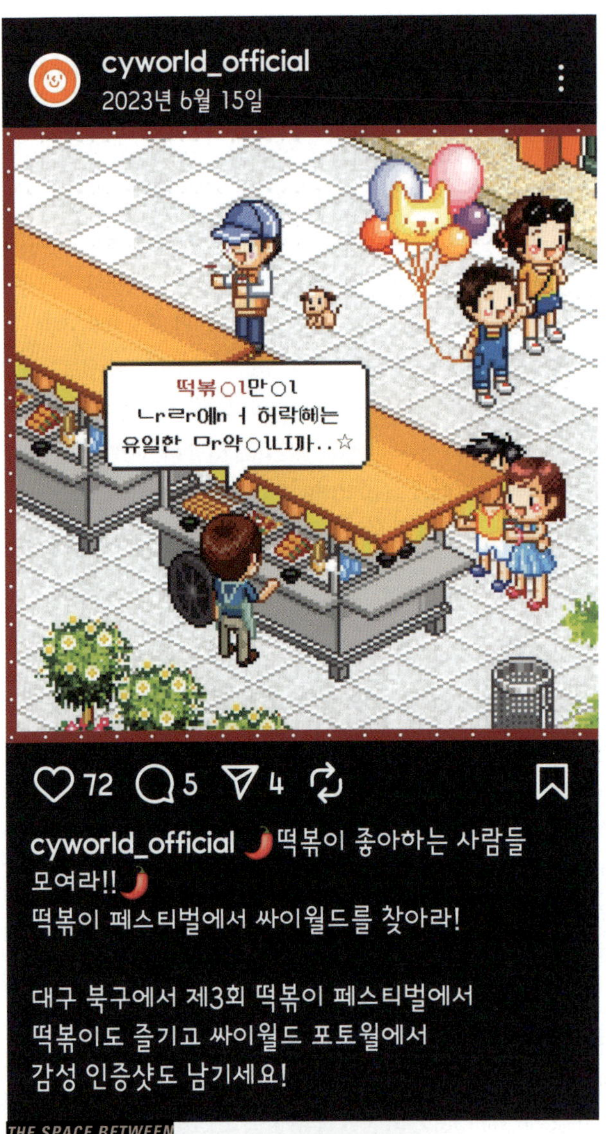

cyworld_official 🌶️떡볶이 좋아하는 사람들
모여라!! 🌶️
떡볶이 페스티벌에서 싸이월드를 찾아라!

대구 북구에서 제3회 떡볶이 페스티벌에서
떡볶이도 즐기고 싸이월드 포토월에서
감성 인증샷도 남기세요!

THE SPACE BETWEEN
Cyworld may no longer be South Korea's dominant social network,
but the brand has kept on adapting to changes in the country's digital life

Korea Advanced Institute of Science and Technology (KAIST) in 1999, well before Facebook, and even before Facebook's own predecessor, Friendster. (The first syllable of its name, Cyworld, stands not for "cyber," as is often assumed, but the Korean word *sai*, or "between," as in the relationships between people.) Its heyday began in 2002, when it introduced tools that let its users make their own mini *hompi*, or "mini-homepages"; by 2010, Cyworld could boast that half the population of the country had signed up for accounts, and that each of its users was no more than four personal connections away, or *sachon* (also a homophone for the word "cousin"), from any other person in Korea.

Factors such as the international spread of Facebook and a large-scale data-theft incident in 2011 (during the brief period of Korea's "real-name" law, which required users of major web sites to register under their real names) put an end to the age of Cyworld. So did the rise of the smartphone, for which it wasn't optimized. The opposite was true for KakaoTalk, a mobile messaging app that, soon after its launch in 2010, seemed to be in use by not just everyone in Korea, but every Korean around the world as well. I happened to move to Los Angeles' Koreatown around that time, and soon started hearing that I'd have no choice but to sign up for it. Since then, KakaoTalk has evolved into a "super app" used in practically every aspect of Korean life, from voice and video calling (especially useful for families with members abroad) to making payments and even ordering taxis. Among Kakao Corporation's many sources of revenue is its vast marketplace for emoticon "stickers." There you can buy one or more of several newtro sticker collections, whose designs express modern Korean sentiments—"I don't have the money and I don't have the time," "No busywork allowed"—with the kind of bold colors, lines, and fonts of the Korean logos discussed in chapter 4.

Koreans may, in the main, use Korean apps, but they're certainly not limited to them. Launched, like KakaoTalk, in 2010, the photo-oriented American social media platform Instagram now stands as not just the most popular app of its kind, but also one of the most popular apps of any kind. The Korean enthusiasm for *Inseuta*, as it's called for short here, has generated an entire vocabulary: *meokseutageuraem*, for example, which refers to posting about food (*meokda* meaning "to eat," a verb now heard even in the West in the form of *meokbang*,

also called mukbang, the video shows whose hosts consume mass quantities
of food on camera), and *inseutagak*, which identifies a thing or place in the real
world especially suitable for photographing and posting. Personally, I've always
left the Instagramming to my wife, who's proven an especially enthusiastic user.
If she weren't, I'd surely have missed out on any number of cultural goings-on in
Seoul that are announced nowhere else. A hashtag search for the word "newtro"
in Korean reveals how widely the concept continues to spread through the public
consciousness, though it must be said that some Instagrammers have a much
keener eye for its manifestations than others.

More than a few of those subway-riding Seoulites pass the time by scrolling
through a seemingly endless stream of videos, which they may be doing on
Instagram, but are even more likely to be doing on TikTok. Having swept most of the
smartphone-owning world over the past decade, it's made a notable cultural impact
in Korea, the synchronized spectacles of whose pop music culture—which inspire
so many eager fans to record their own DIY performances—could hardly be better
suited to that platform. Developed in China, TikTok is the international version of a
popular domestic app called Douyin. Its provenance has inspired no end of security-
related anxieties, especially in the United States, where it was subject to a brief
government ban in early 2025. Although a U.S. ally—and one practically at China's
doorstep—Korea appears to show little concern about TikTok as a vector of Chinese
influence, at least not to the extent of proposing to cut off one of its citizenry's
principal streams of short-form video entertainment. Whether a homegrown app
could now rise to anything with the same prominence is another question.

In Korea as elsewhere, gaming is another popular use of smartphones, though
Koreans characteristically take it to a higher level of seriousness. Here, youngsters
jabbing away on their touchscreens while embroiled in competitive play, whether
against similarly transfixed friends nearby or the entire world online, may not be
wasting their time quite so cavalierly as grown-ups imagine—at least not if they
turn pro. In many countries, professional gaming may still sound like a contradiction
in terms; in Korea, it's been a high-stakes endeavor at least since a critical mass
of Korean gamers embraced the PC game *StarCraft* in the late '90s. Over the past
decade and a half, an even larger sub-industry in Korean esports has grown around

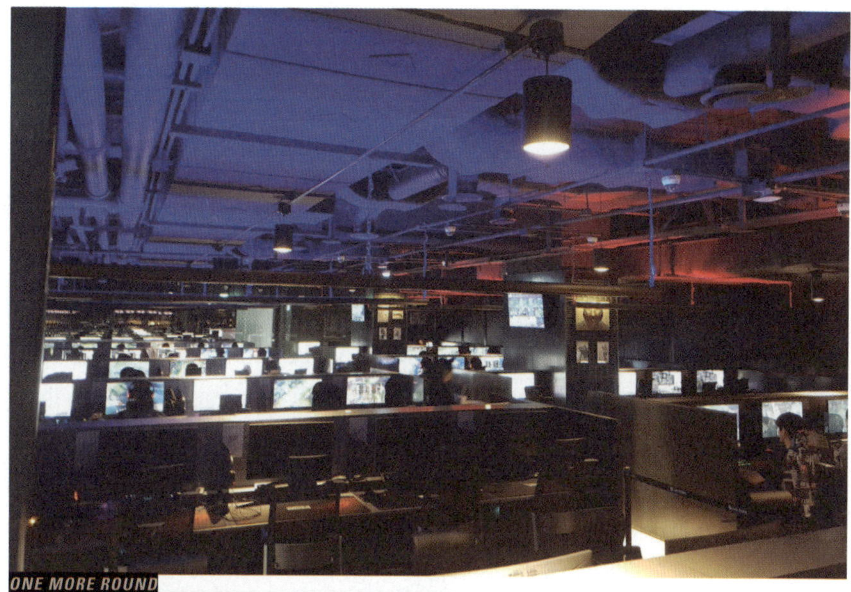

ONE MORE ROUND
Technically, you can do schoolwork or browse the internet at a PC bang, but the vast majority of the customers come to game—and game hard.
© self, CC BY-SA 4.0, via Wikimedia Commons

another American-made real-time strategy game, *League of Legends*. Perhaps unsurprisingly, the greatest *League of Legends* player is universally acknowledged to be a Korean by the name of Lee Sang-hyeok. In this country where computer games are a spectator sport, Lee, better known by his handle Faker, is a hero to hundreds of thousands of gamers.

For the aspiring Fakers of Korea, there is no more common training ground than the *PC bang* (literally a "PC room"), a kind of cross between an internet café and a video arcade that has proliferated across the country since the '90s. In Korean, the word *bang* means "room," and it also appears in the name of a variety of businesses one might pass on a walk down any given Seoul street: the *noraebang*, or "song room," with its private karaoke spaces; the *manhwabang*, or "comics room," with its shelves of illustrated reading material for customers to read day and night; and the *jjimjilbang*, or "steam room," an essential component of any

Korean spa. Filled with computers optimized for gaming, usually dimly lit, and often occupying a basement level of a building, *PC bang* can be dank places, but on the whole, they've smartened up considerably over the decades. One part of the change has to do with increasingly enforced rules against indoor smoking; another is the availability of food, which you can order from and have delivered straight to your computer, with more palatable options than simply instant *ramyeon*. Now you can get not only the *so-tteok-so-tteok* and *hatdogeu* mentioned in the previous chapter but also rice bowls and curry plates.

The *PC bang* would no doubt be a prime candidate for a newtro-era revival, had it ever gone away. In fact, gaming has proven to be one of the few consistent non-academic experiences in the lives of young Koreans over the past couple of generations: kids today frequent *PC bang* as often as or even more often than their parents did (or rather, given the even more male-dominated clientele in the '90s, than their fathers did). But *PC bang* could hardly have become so robust a type of business in the absence of a fairly deep-rooted gaming culture. Many Koreans who grew up in the '80s had plenty of opportunity to familiarize themselves with video games not just at neighborhood arcades but also on personal computers, which Korean society began adopting at a relatively early stage of its economic development. Some will even remember the experience of visiting a friend's house and finding a Zemmix, a sure sign of a wealthy family. First produced by Daewoo Electronics in 1984, the Zemmix can be called the first Korean video game console, despite its hardware having been adapted from the MSX, a popular Japanese computer; its revival in the form of two technologically updated small-scale replica models, the Zemmix Mini in 2019 and the Zemmix Super Mini in 2021, made it the first Korean newtro video game console.

Audiovisually and mechanically simple, the games made for the Zemmix, and indeed any other console of its generation, would have seemed almost unplayably primitive 30 years ago. Today, however, they've regained a charm of their own, and for years now, developers around the world have sought to recreate the look and feel of just such "retro games," which in Korea is evidenced by what's on some Seoul subway riders' phones. In recent years, more than a few of them have been playing revivals of Korean-made games from bygone days. In the late 2010s, the domestic developer NCSoft put out a mobile version of *Lineage*, a fantasy *manhwa*-based massively multiplayer online role-playing game (MMORPG) it first released for personal computers in 1998. (Its fanbase has remained large and loyal enough that many of its players have become *rinjeossi*, a portmanteau of the first syllable of the game's title and *ajeossi*, which means a middle-aged man.) In 2020, Nexon, another major Korean video game developer, launched a mobile revival of its own popular '90s MMORPG, *Nexus: The Kingdom of the Winds*, having already done the same for its *Crazy Arcade*, whose variety of challenges modeled directly on already classic video games had made it a big *PC Bang* hit in the early 2000s. Celebrating its 16th anniversary in 2019, the thoroughly retro-styled, Nexon-distributed MMORPG *MapleStory*—one of the biggest successes in Korean online gaming—opened to its players a set of levels called "Newtro Time," successful passage through which would restore peace to the "Newtro Kingdom."

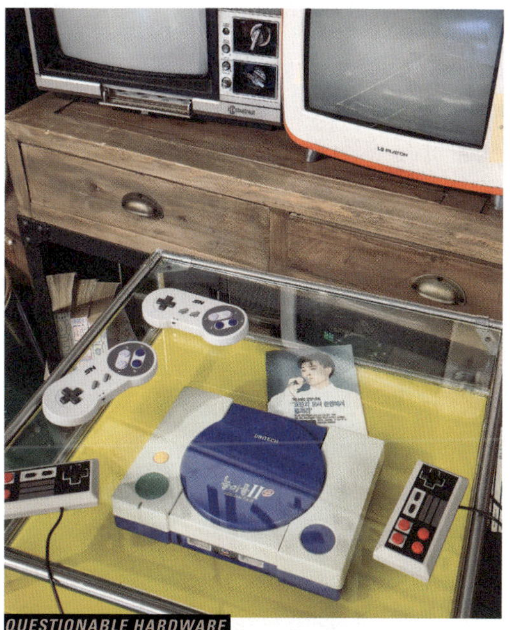

QUESTIONABLE HARDWARE
PC gaming caught on fast in Korea, but Korean clones of popular Japanese consoles appeared only after years of delay

As with many cultural trends, newtro is a phenomenon that young Koreans encounter initially (if not wholly) through their phones. But opportunities to experience its physical reality, or at least replications thereof, continue to arise. In the summer of 2024, for example, the IFC Mall in Seoul put on a Newtro Game Festival, promising "a *molkangseu* with the games you remember." (The trendy word *hokangseu* combines the English word "hotel" and the French word *vacances* to imply something like what English speakers now call a "staycation"; *molkangseu*, by the same token, is a combination of "mall" and *vacances*.) The idea behind the event, a kind of digital version of the Newtro Festival discussed in chapter 3, was that the arcade machines with games from the '80s and '90s brought together for the occasion—some of them played with light guns and rideable motorcycles, artifacts of a more tactile era in gaming—would give visitors a chance not just to escape from the heat outdoors, but also to engage in an entertaining pastime basically familiar to both Koreans in their 30s and 40s as well as their children, the 1020 generation.

One particular type of artifact from the very dawn of Korea's digital age goes unremarked upon by most Koreans, whatever their age, despite the fact that it continues to tick away in shops, offices, and public spaces all over the country— or rather, it doesn't tick, which was one of its original selling points. I speak of the glossy black rectangular digital clocks produced, for the most part, by a company called Pharos. Their displays, sometimes bordered by a wood-grain frame, show not only the time but also, depending on the model, the date (on both the solar and lunar calendar, the latter of which determines such traditional Korean holidays as Chuseok and Seollal), the day of the week, the year, and even the temperature. In their at once homely and elegant severity, they sometimes strike me—more so than *hanbok*, more so than *dakjongi inhyeong*—as the most distinctively Korean objects in existence. Visiting Korea not long ago, an American friend of mine noticed one for sale in a small shop and bought it then and there, no matter the non-trivial luggage space it would occupy on the way back home. This despite his being a virtual reality hardware technician at Meta, the parent company of Instagram and Facebook, and not easily impressed by pieces of technology. The Pharos clock may seem rather unlikely to inspire the next newtro *yuhaeng* (craze), but then, little has been especially predictable in modern Korean life, online or off.

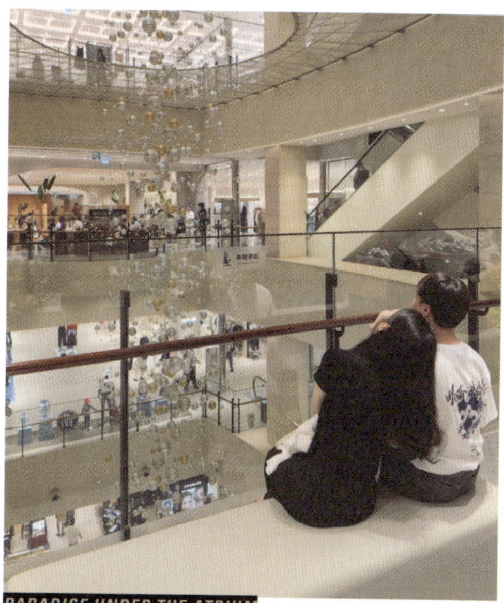

PARADISE UNDER THE ATRIUM
In a sweltering Korean summer, why not take time off to enjoy a molkangseu? There might even be newtro entertainment on offer

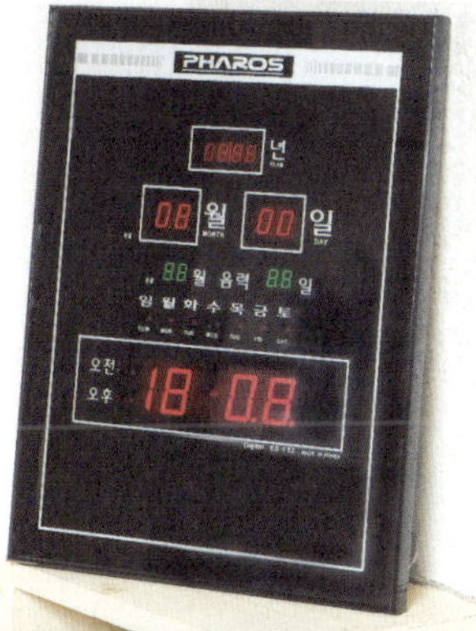

WHY MESS WITH PERFECTION?
Digital wall clocks from Pharos and other brands first appeared in Korea in the early 1980s, and though their internal technology has evolved, their aesthetic has stayed just the same

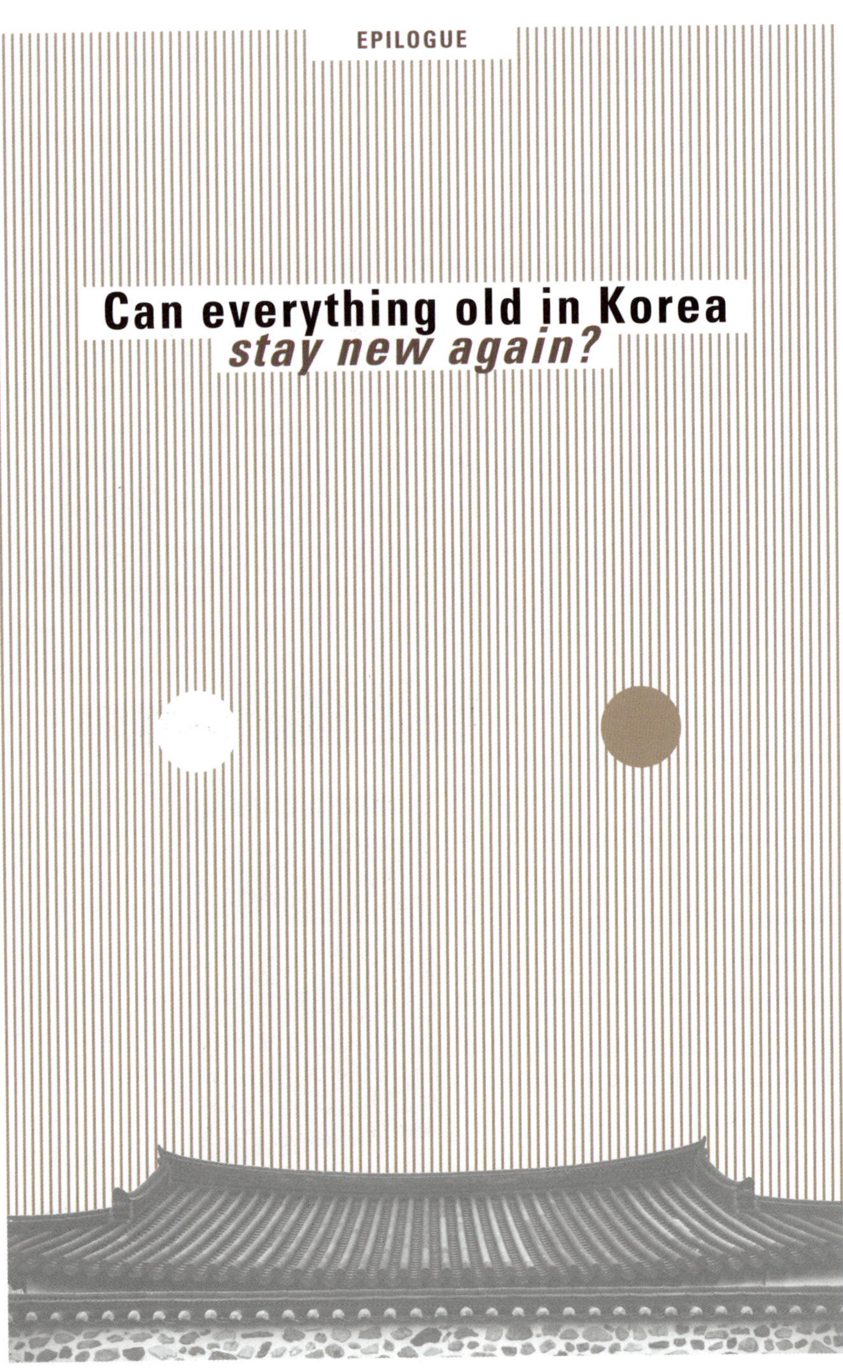

Can everything old in Korea
stay new again?

Whenever I meet foreigners in Korea for the first time, I suggest that they keep two questions in mind during their stay. First, to what extent is this a 5,000-year-old society, and to what extent is it a less than 80-year-old society trying to connect directly to its own distant past? Second, to what extent is this an Asian country, and to what extent is it a country in Asia trying to connect directly to the West? It is, as I see it, all four, in different ways, at different times, and in different places. In truth, Korea has come into the 21st century as something of a *jjamppong*: a seafood noodle stew that's a staple of Korean Chinese cuisine (unknown in China itself), but also a byword for a mixture of diverse and sometimes improbably combined elements. This owes in part to the country's tendency to absorb the influence of larger powers, and not unrelatedly, to the nature of its development over the past century.

The forces that have most clearly shaped the country have been applied since the end of the Korean War—or rather, since the armistice agreement that brought about a ceasefire, if not official peace, between North and South and Korea—during the accelerated development process that amounted to "compressed modernity," in the words of Seoul National University sociologist Chang Kyung-sup. That process is most vividly symbolized by Jeon Min-jo's famous 1978 photograph that captures a farmer working his fields with a traditional ox-drawn plow, a high-rise *apateu danji* (a form of housing described in chapter 2) under construction right behind him. The picture was taken in what's now Apgujeong, a wealthy district of Gangnam, which also happens to be the area in which I stayed during my own first visit to Korea. By that time, the fields were long gone, most of them seemingly replaced by cosmetic surgery clinics.

What made more of an impression on me was the visibility of the *yuhaeng*, or the kind of intense trends that become crazes. Walking around Seoul one day—amid the few *buldak* (literally "fire chicken") restaurants that had proliferated during a recent craze and were still hanging on— I passed more than one young woman wearing a T-shirt emblazoned with an owl made of plastic jewels; for some time thereafter, I saw several of them per day. (At that point, they were presumably being sold in subway station clothing shops, those efficient vectors of many a fashion trend.) But within a few weeks, it seemed, the owl shirts had vanished as suddenly as they'd appeared. I'd seen a few trends in my nearly 30 years of living in the United States at that point, of course, and I'd heard that the cycle was shorter in Korea, which concentrated so much more of its population into so much smaller a space, but never before had I witnessed the entire rise and fall of a single item right there on the streets.

The overwhelming trend-orientation of Korea about which I'd been told—or perhaps warned—struck me as the behavior of a society that had grown used to change per se as a matter of survival, adopting an evolve-or-die mindset on a large scale. Anything new, especially if also foreign, was to be incorporated into the lives of the country's large middle class or those who aspired to join it; anything old, particularly from the past 40 or so years since the war, could inspire the occasional bout of nostalgia, a universal human emotion. Yet if too publicly visible, it could also inspire shame by evoking an only recently escaped inferiority complex to other, supposedly more sophisticated developed countries. When I mentioned the movies from the '70s and '80s like **Night Journey** or **Chilsu and Mansu** that got me fascinated with the Korean language and culture in the first place, people often reacted with surprise, sometimes adding that they'd never heard of those movies themselves.

These days, when interviewed in the Korean media, I'm often asked specifically about my appreciation for films such as those, or for *yetnal* pop music like the songs of Yoo Jae-ha (mentioned in chapter 6). An even more common question—asked, I would guess, on the principle that a fish has no idea of the water in which it swims—is, "What about Korea has changed the most since you first arrived?" While it doesn't feel like quite the same place it did to me a decade ago, I see the change over that time as less in the country itself than in its perception. In a word, Korea has become famous, not just internationally recognized—when, a quarter-century ago, relatively few Westerners knew the difference between North Korea and South Korea—but also respected and even admired, and that changes the way Koreans themselves regard their homeland.

That hardly means they've become complacent or uncritical; as the Republic of Korea has developed, turning from one of the world's poorest nations into one of its richest, its people have become ever more ready to take it to task for what they see as its failures. But having grown up in a Korea that has already "arrived," so to speak, those on the young end of the MZ Generation (and even more so, the current 1020s) react not with embarrassment at the artifacts of the country's humbler past, but with surprise and enthusiasm. I know the feeling: I may, at times, have trouble distinguishing the K-pop girl groups and boy bands that debut each year from one another, or indeed distinguishing Korean blockbusters from the Hollywood spectacles they imitate, but when I go back to cultural works and artifacts from the 20th century or even earlier, I find they still exude the distinctiveness of Korean civilization.

They exude it all the more clearly by contrast when transplanted into more recent cultural contexts. That, at bottom, is the essence of newtro, which draws its appeal from offering a means of not just escaping the overstimulation of the 2010s and 2020s but also of enjoying the resonances between eras that may at first seem to have little in common. Thus, going back to re-evaluate much earlier cultural works and artifacts does its part to close the generation gap, which in Korea resembles a generation chasm: young adults' interaction with their parents here resembles Westerners' interaction with their grandparents or even great-grandparents, so unalike were the Koreas that formed them. Explaining newtro in 2019, one online publication quoted a 28-year-old LP bar DJ as crediting his specialization in spinning "old school" vinyl with giving him something to talk about with his father over *sul*. (Whether it's *uri sul* was not reported.)

Whatever its potential to strengthen familial bonds—always of great importance to Korean civilization—newtro's reinterpretation of the domestic past continues apace. When it was first defined by *Trend Korea 2019*, it would have been easy to dismiss newtro as a buzzword of the moment attached to a phenomenon not meaningfully different from the usual fluctuations of fad and fashion. Now, halfway through the 2020s, it seems to have a kind of staying power not seen in the various *buldak*- and bejeweled-owl-shirt-type Korean pop culture phenomena that have come and gone so far in the 21st century. Some would surely welcome it as a signal of the aggressive trend cycle that has pulled the country—and especially its young people—this way and that for decade after decade finally slowing down to a more psychologically manageable rhythm of life and culturally centered points of reference. It's too early to say whether that's a realistic expectation, but at least one thing is certain: Korea still has plenty of past left to reinterpret.

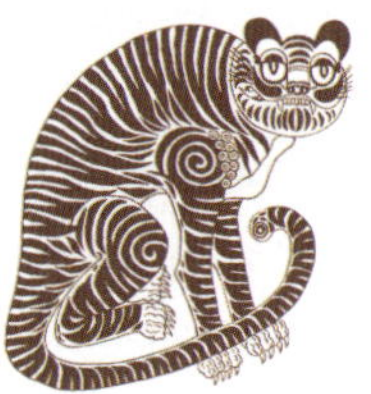